THE 168 DAYS

JOSEPH ALSOP &
TURNER CATLEDGE

THE
168
DAYS

Doubleday, Doran & Co., Inc.

GARDEN CITY, NEW YORK

1938

JK
1561
.A7

PREFACE

A PREFACE IS A FORM of self-indulgence which can only be excused when there is need to explain a book's limitations. Because our book has certain very definite limitations we feel we must indulge ourselves briefly.

Our book is a contemporary history of the famous legislative struggle which began on February 5, 1937, when President Roosevelt disclosed his plan to enlarge the Supreme Court. We have tried to recreate the struggle, to make it live again as a sort of demonstration of the processes of American politics. Our effort has been to make our book as accurate, as complete and as unbiased as any contemporary history can be, but at the same time we are well aware that it has the limitations which every contemporary history must have.

In the first place we have had access to few documents. When the President's private papers, when Senator Robinson's correspondence with Bernard M. Baruch and the day-to-day diary of Attorney General Cummings are made available, they will undoubtedly supplement and probably modify our conclusions. In compensation we have been able to consult the living actors in the political drama. We hope that much that would otherwise have been lost has been thus preserved. Virtually all our information was obtained at first-hand, and we believe that we have questioned every important participant in the court fight except the President himself. But the facts remain that we were not present to observe many of the incidents which we describe and that we have no documentary evidence to support most of our descriptions.

One word more as to the conversations which we quote. They were the subject of some argument between us. Both of us feared that it would give a key-hole air to our story if we quoted words we had not heard. Eventually we recalled that more respectable historians make use of conversations when they chance to be recorded in letters and diaries. On the theory that it was silly to wait for our informants to write down what they told us—some of them indeed had already done so—we ended by including a limited number of conversations which seemed to be authentically reported.

About a quarter of our history, including the main outline, was published some months ago in the *Saturday Evening Post*. It is perhaps pardonable in us to add to our statement of limitations the fact that, since the publication of the *Saturday Evening Post* articles, we have had no objections on the grounds of inaccuracy of a character to make us change any incident. We can only pray that our book will meet with the same happy fate.

JOSEPH ALSOP

TURNER CATLEDGE

Washington, December 6, 1937

CONTENTS

vii

Prologue

THE RESULT of the Democratic national convention in 1932 was anxiously awaited by President Herbert Hoover and his lieutenants of the Republican high command. After three fearful years of depression they suspected that popular enthusiasm for them and their party might have declined from its peak; knowing their opponents, however, they prayerfully trusted that a bungled Democratic choice would make the coming campaign less arduous. Would it be Smith? Would it be Baker? Would it be Ritchie? Would it, perhaps, be Roosevelt? With a breathless uncertainty they followed from Washington the doings in the Chicago auditorium. And then, as someone remarked, William Gibbs McAdoo buried the hatchet—in Al Smith's neck. President Hoover's uncertainty was over, and he and his friends succumbed to a delicious relief. The Democrats, they assured one another, had done it again; they had chosen the weakest available candidate, that amiable member of the Hudson River squirearchy, Franklin Delano Roosevelt.

On March 4, 1933, "the weakest available candidate" was inaugurated President of the United States,

1

while his intoxicated partisans whooped in the streets of the capital and the nation subsided hourly into chaos.

Within a few months he had weathered the first fantastic crisis; he had cheerfully accepted the national authority abdicated by the previous rulers, the large businessmen; he had emerged as the most powerful President in American history. He had also taught the people to know him. His agreeably handsome face, his friendly but imposing presence, his rich, perfect voice with the odd trace of an aboriginal Bostonian flatness —these made his admirable exterior. His great daring, his acute sense of political timing, a taste for power which encouraged him to shoulder the gigantic responsibilities everyone else wished to be rid of—these helped him to sponsor a new kind of national government.

He used the absolute command of Congress acquired in the days of crisis to recognize and treat as national the overpowering complex of economic problems, industrial, agricultural and social, to which his immediate predecessors had sedulously closed their eyes. He made the intellectual liberalism of his circle of able private advisers the dominant new note in national politics; by a series of great measures he extended his own and the federal powers in unprecedented fashion. He educated the people; under his tutelage they learned to expect the federal government to see to their private welfare as well as to the public safety and convenience. And so, after two years of his administration, the voices of opposition seemed to be stilled for good. He was obeyed by a docile Congress. He was adored by many millions of the voters. His enemies, the Republicans, were no better than so many mandrakes; they cried out plaintively, but they had been reduced to a strictly vegetable state. Who was there to say him nay?

The only answer to that question was to be found in the marble and crimson velvet edifice, combining all the worst features of decadent Roman and plutocratic American taste, which houses the Supreme Court of the United States. If they wished to do so, the nine justices could say him nay. By imposing their judicial veto they could block the President's path.

By the winter of 1935 the justices had become the last hope of the conservative interests in the United States. There are historians who assert that the intention of the founders, in establishing the Court as an independent member of the tripartite system, was to set a guardian for property right. In his effort to conquer the economic forces at work in the country, the President had introduced a new conception of property right, and his new conception had been overwhelmingly approved both in Congress and at the polling booths. Therefore the conservative interests resorted to the courts, starting literally thousands of actions to stay the government's hand. In 1935, with great New Deal cases coming before the high bench at last, the businessmen could look to no one but the justices to save them. They looked rather nervously, for none could tell whether the justices would choose to provoke so powerful an antagonist as the President or prefer to recognize the need for a new approach to government.

The court which had to decide between such excruciating alternatives was a court divided against itself. Since the sad time of the Palmer red scare of 1919–20, when the civil liberties were all but written out of the Constitution in spite of the ringing dissents of Oliver Wendell Holmes and Louis Dembitz Brandeis, there had been factions among the justices. The factions were never less united than during the years of the New Deal.

On one side were the four Tories, James Clark McReynolds, Pierce Butler, Willis J. Van Devanter and George Sutherland. McReynolds, a man of granite face and granite convictions, a hater who was unrestrained and furious in his hatreds; Butler, a bludgeon-minded railroad lawyer, pious, hearty, given to interminable anecdote and endlessly persistent with the persistence of a narrow man; Sutherland, gentle, simple, older seeming than his brethren; Van Devanter, genial, kindly, a man whom all men liked—these were the four. As different as they might well be in character, they stood united in their beliefs. Laissez faire, undisturbed property right and the sanctity of contracts were a trinity of doctrines at whose shrine they worshiped daily. Their theory of the best government differed little from the theory which led Lord Melbourne to frown on Lord Shaftesbury, for his notion that children should be prevented from working fourteen hours a day in the dark mines and filthy factories. With the old amateur of patristic learning and London beauty, they believed that the best government would do nothing but keep order and require the carrying out of such agreements as might be duly witnessed and drawn up. The businessmen, nervously counting justices, could rely on them.

Opposed to the quartet of Tories were the three liberals, Louis Dembitz Brandeis, Benjamin Nathan Cardozo and Harlan Fiske Stone. Brandeis, noble minded and prophetic, an Isaiah in an incongruously professorial black silk robe; Cardozo, infinitely learned, delicate, unworldly, a creature of purified intellect; Stone, the big, sensible, healthy man with a taste for humanity so all-embracing that he could be equally close to Brandeis and to Calvin Coolidge—these were the three. To Brandeis, government's mission was to give the citizen the best life possible, not to make itself as small as possible. In the others economic and political predilections were perhaps less marked, but all three joined in refusing to express their predilections in their interpretation of the Constitution. Where the conservatives saw the Constitution as the special, final sanction of their governmental theory, Brandeis and Stone and Cardozo insisted that it was the duty of a justice to leave theory to the other branches, to impose the judicial veto only when the constitutional mandate for it was abundantly clear. On these three the businessmen knew they could never rely.

And in the center were the two moderates, Owen J. Roberts and the Chief Justice, Charles Evans Hughes. Hughes, the Olympian politician, the man whose impersonation of a picture-book Jove is so terrifyingly successful that one expects thunderbolts, the liberal judge whose guiding object was to maintain the prestige of his court; Roberts, the solid, burly, energetic fellow, the Philadelphia lawyer with mild liberal leanings—this was the pair who held the balance of power.

On the face of it one would have expected Hughes and Roberts to hold the Court to a middle road, and so, at first, it seemed they would. They joined the liberals in upholding the New York Milk Control Law in the Nebbia case and, in the gold cases, in allowing the government's right to alter the dollar's content and order the payments of gold bonds on the new basis. Justice McReynolds proclaimed from the bench in his dissent in the gold cases that "the Constitution as we have known it is gone", but his intemperate words were momentarily forgotten. It was the general hope that the Court would follow the election returns and admit the public interest in the economic problems hagriding modern society.

But while the President and his followers congratulated themselves and the astonished businessmen bewailed their fate, a subtle change had taken place behind the curtains of mystery in which the Court is cloaked. Early in 1935 Roberts, the moderate, was already preparing to leave his moderation. The time when the Court would defy the President was almost at hand.

The reasons may only be guessed at; the best guess is that two traits in Roberts, one personal and one of opinion, brought on his spasm of reaction. A man of coarser tastes than Stone, who chose to be Brandeis' disciple, Roberts preferred the company of the Court's conservatives. Butler, with his anecdotes, and McReynolds, with his hard, angular, sardonic mind, appealed to him more than the liberal philosophers. Soon after he ascended the bench Roberts came to be especially close to McReynolds. An affection grew up between them, the strength of which outsiders could only gauge by their intimate, teasing way with one another. And then Roberts, whose training had been the training the financial centers of the East give their lawyers, was completely horrified by the President's unorthodox financial policy. He might have been better able to stomach the social legislation, had he not thought, as he once put it, that the President was taking the whole resources of the nation and "throwing them down the sewer." The same training inclined him to believe what he read in the papers about the President's and his New Deal's purpose to "regiment" the lives of individuals.

Worst of all, his training blinded him to the falseness of the Court's deification in the booming decade of the 1920s, when all America paid tribute to the Court as the ultimate guardian of business and its interests. Roberts himself was an eminent member of just that class of Americans who had erected the doctrine of judicial review into a law of the tables, brought down by John Marshall from a Federalist Sinai and established to protect the United States through the centuries. Thus Roberts, who might have been expected to see more clearly than the four Tories the dangers of an

arbitrary blockade of the President, had no more fear
of it than they. He joined the Tories, and by the
simplest sum in the world the blockade became inevitable.

One is justified in suspecting that the invalidation of
the National Industrial Recovery Act, which took place
on May 27, 1935, was the turning point in the Court's
course. The decision was unanimous, for the grandiose,
unworkable and distinctly oppressive law appealed no
more to the liberals than to McReynolds. The decision's unanimity gave unusual weight to the finding
that the legislative powers had been improperly delegated to the Executive. Moreover, the decision was
popular. Labor disliked it, but the millions who had
had some disagreeable experience of rising prices, irri-
tating code regulations or monopoly newly powerful
under NRA heartily approved it.

Indeed the decision was the President's best piece of
luck during his first term, for it spared him the uncomfortable necessity of lying in the bed he had made. He
did not know his good fortune; he indulged his anger
at the famous "horse-and-buggy" press conference, and
his criticism of the Court was greeted with a storm of
indignation all over the country. Surely the howls of
the editorial pages, the bellows of the politicians and
the milder evidences of popular displeasure suggested
to Roberts and the Tory justices that the performance
of the NRA decision might be repeated with impunity.

It was repeated, over the furious but futile protests
of the liberals. The schism within the Court grew steadily deeper and wider. All the petty dislikes and personal disagreements, which must exist in any group of
nine men gathered at random and forced to work closely
together, were sharpened and deepened until the dislikes became hatreds and the disagreements found expression in semipublic debate. McReynolds, the leader

of the conservatives, was infected with anti-Semitism. He had always detested Brandeis and Cardozo for what they were as well as for what they stood. His fellow conservatives lacked McReynolds' race superstition, but they were shocked by Brandeis' habit of applying a moralist's before a jurist's test to public questions. Cardozo they saw through the eyes of men who had made their names in the rough-and-tumble of the Bar, and they mocked him as one whose cloistered judge's life had never taught him the world's harsh realities. As for Stone, they thought him no better than a traitor to his own practical nature.

The liberals returned the conservatives' dislike and seasoned it with their conviction that the conservatives were leading the Court down the road to destruction. No wonder that as these feelings grew more urgent Washington began to hear of violent words at the justices' weekly conferences on cases. There was an open quarrel in the Court, and sometimes it showed in the Court's opinions, as when Stone scornfully charged his brethren with inconsistency in their Agricultural Adjustment Act opinion and frankly accused them of writing it out of their own economic theories rather than their fair constitutional interpretation. The liberal justices themselves called their conservative colleagues arbitrary and madly unwise. But while the liberals warned, the conservatives laughed, for they cherished the hope that the New Deal was a sort of political nightmare from which the country would awaken on November 3, 1936.

The results of the conservatives' hope are too recent history to be worth rehearsing in detail, but some reference to the conservative decisions after the invalidation of the NRA is necessary to make their effects comprehensible. In the Railway Pension Act case, in the words of the Chief Justice's dissent, the Court "denied to Congress the right to pass any compulsory pension act." In the Frazier-Lemke farm mortgage moratorium and municipal bankruptcy cases the Court placed severe limitations on the federal government's bankruptcy powers. In the Agricultural Adjustment Act decision the Court told the federal government that any effort to treat agricultural problems as national problems was an infringement on the states' prerogatives. The Guffey Coal Act decision set up the doctrine that "the relation between employer and employee is a local relation" and not within the federal government's purview. Thus the Court slammed the door in the federal government's face. While the President and the great majority of the people saw the industrial, agricultural and social problems confronting the nation as national problems, Roberts and the four conservatives had labeled them "Local, do not touch." The businessmen and reactionaries congratulated one another on so sweeping a judicial triumph.

But the justices did not stop there. The New York Women's Minimum Wage Law case brought before the Bench a local treatment of a pressing social-economic problem. Without hesitating an instant the conservatives struck it down, too, at the close of the 1936 spring term. At that even the reactionaries held up their hands in horror. The very stupidest among them realized that the Court could not tell the country, "These may be serious problems, but we're sorry; the Constitution simply does not let either the federal or the state governments handle them."

Actually, of course, the decision in the New York case was merely the culminating symptom of the spasm of political insanity which had attacked the conservative justices in the spring of 1935. Except for the rich and the veterans, the conservatives had raised up against the Court all the great national pressure groups. The workers, deprived of all hope of labor legislation; the farmers, warned that effective farm legislation was not permissible; the millions desirous of a measure of social security, who had seen Congress "denied the right to pass a compulsory pension act"— each of these three huge groups and several minor ones had a specific, bitter grievance against the Court. Worse still, the determined Toryism of the conservative justices had alienated the calmest liberal opinion, and left the Court very few real friends anywhere except at the offices of the American Association of Manufacturers.

Events and situations have their inescapable logic. No appointive body of nine men can fly in the face of public opinion for too long without provoking an answering attack. The fact that the justices were flying in the face of public opinion was pretty completely proved on November 3, 1936, when President Roosevelt was swept back into office on a tidal wave of 27,-000,000 votes. The answering attack on the Court came on February 5, 1937, just three months after the election, when the President presented his court plan to the Congress.

The struggle which followed was the political drama of a generation. Suddenly the shabby comedy of national politics, with its all-pervading motive, self-interest, its dreary dialogue of public oratory and its depressing scenery of patronage and projects, was elevated to a grand, even a tragic plane. Suddenly the old Green Theme of Hubris and Ara, of pride and the fall that comes after, dominated the play. To tell the play's story, to offer a contemporary history of the court fight, is the purpose of this book.

I. BIRTH OF THE BILL

THE ELECTION

March 4, 1933–November 3, 1936

FRANKLIN DELANO ROOSEVELT was the tragic hero of the drama of the court fight. At its start he enjoyed a power like the power of no American president of the past. At its close fortune's wheel had revolved until the President was humiliated and powerless to get his way. What is more, the President's character was the deciding element in the struggle. While the justices themselves were responsible for the court plan, the President was responsible for the plan's nature and the nature of the fight that it provoked. Essentially the fight's course was decided by the fact that the Court had wantonly offended every strongest trait in the President.

Perhaps the most immediate of the Court's offenses was its denial of satisfaction to the President's taste for power. The President regards great powers as his prerogative, and while he is sometimes careless of the prerogatives of others, he is as jealous of his own as was Louis XIV. Since he considered them infringements on his prerogatives, all the conservative decisions angered him; it is significant that those close to him have said that he was most angered by the decision in the comparatively trivial Humphries case. The case arose from

his forcible ejection of William Humphries from a
federal trade commissionership, on the simple ground
that he had no confidence in him. Humphries had been
appointed and confirmed for a definite term; he sued to
regain his place but died while the suit was in progress.
The action was continued by the estate, and when it
came before the high bench the justices directed the
government to pay Humphries' widow the balance of
his salary to his death and sharply forbade future dis-
missals of duly appointed and confirmed officials. The
President saw in the decision the most direct of all possible trespasses on his powers as Chief Executive; he
was completely infuriated.

The Court's conservative decisions not only outraged
his love of power; more important still, they frustrated
his good intentions. Indeed, they virtually denied their
existence, although the most obvious thing about
Franklin Delano Roosevelt is that his intentions are
good. Where his intellectual response to a given situation may be inadequate, where his administrative habits
are often strikingly peculiar, his emotions are generally
deep and true. He is so evidently a man of good will
that the voters, accustomed to politicians of a very different sort, have sometimes been ready to take his wish
for his deed. To him the lot of the underprivileged and
distressed is an ever-present problem. To him the great
dilemmas of modern society are always at hand, calling
for solutions which will usher in an era of greater security and fuller living. To him the whole future is a
challenge, a time to be conquered by forethought in the
present. It was this emotional quality in the President
which gave him his splendid aptness to a troubled moment of 1933.

His excellent intentions are only reinforced by his
unusual awareness of his own historic role—best expressed in his celebrated remark at the time of his first

inauguration, that if he proved a bad president, he was also likely to prove the last president. Such an awareness would oppress most other men to the point of stultification; not so the President. On more than one occasion he has interrupted discussions of the most serious and pressing difficulties with important followers, to tell the worried men to think no more about it, that sooner or later he would get around to clearing the matter up. Once he vouchsafed the explanation that he knew more about psychology, and especially mass psychology, than any expert or professor in the business, and that his knowledge always permitted him to reach his objectives in time. As a former White House intimate has pointed out, he has an almost mystical belief in his own ability to perform his role with perfect adequacy.

No man of such self-confident good will could have knuckled under to the Court forever. Least of all could the President, in whom the Court's reactionary decisions aroused all the vindictiveness and obstinacy which are as strongly his as good intentions or love of power. He wanted to pay off his score with the Court as well as to make his good will effective. The twin desires tempted him to accept the Court's gage of battle, and all his daring, all his carelessness of precedents of the past, all his love for tackling a big job, seconded their motion. Only his sense of political timing restrained him, for he was not disturbed by the prospect of constitutional innovation.

His reverence for the Supreme Court as an institution was of a distinctly limited sort. As early as his 1932 campaign he had interjected into a Baltimore speech the offhand remark that the Court was a mere annex of the Republican administration. At the crucial time of the gold cases he had an answer to an adverse decision already prepared—an address modeled on

Andrew Jackson's celebrated defiance of the justices, in which he planned to tell them, "You have made your law; now enforce it." While the Court fortunately held for the administration in the gold cases, its later decisions provoked him to displays of his talent for private invective which should have made the conservative justices' ears burn. He had, moreover, a rather special conception of the Court's functions, best expressed, perhaps, in an incident of the court fight itself.

Not long after the announcement of his court plan the President was soothing the fears of a doubtful senator. His object was to prove that no road was open to him but the one he had taken. He asked the senator to blame the Court, not him. In proof of the Court's intransigence he recalled an event in the very early history of his first administration. Then, he said, he had been anxious to get along with the Court, and as a first step he had suggested a sort of consultative relationship between them to Chief Justice Charles Evans Hughes. He had intimated that he would like to talk over with the Chief Justice all his important plans concerning the general welfare, to get the Court's slant on them before acting. But instead of accepting the overture in a friendly spirit, the Chief Justice had been Olympianly chilly. He had given the President to understand that the strictest separation between the Court and the White House was not only advisable but necessary. In fact, he turned the President down flat.

"You see," said the President to the senator, "he wouldn't co-operate."

It is hardly surprising, then, that the course of the Court, from the NRA decision to the election in November 1936, produced a feeling of almost personal injustice in the President. At the same time it is interesting that he actually declared war on the Court only four days after the NRA decision, on May 31, 1936.

The decision's limitations on the executive powers had deeply offended him; the four days had given his temper time to reach the boiling point, and Felix Frankfurter and Hugh S. Johnson, who had been summoned to confer with him in his White House office, found him in a fighting mood. He told them that he would not take the Court's action lying down, that he would not stand for it. The country was with him, not with the Court, he said, and he swore angrily to bring the Court into line if he had to "pack it" or "deny it appellate jurisdiction." The wise, disinterested liberal leader and the shrewd, hard-talking ex-cavalry officer heard the President with some astonishment. They tried hard to dissuade him from a public expression of his anger, but they could do nothing, although at that time they were closest to him of all the eager circle playing at palace politics. The press conference at which the President accused the Court of taking the country back to "horse-and-buggy days" took place an hour or so later.

The same answering storm of popular and editorial indignation which encouraged the conservative justices, rather naturally had the opposite effect on the President. He drew the immediate inference from the excitement at his denunciation of the Court that the time was not ripe. Thereafter he made no more public attacks on the Court until the New York Minimum Wage Law decision, when he sarcastically said that the justices seemed determined to create a "no man's land of government." The subject of the Court was often to the fore, however, in his talks with his advisers.

He discussed it most often with Attorney General Homer S. Cummings, whose department's job it was to present government cases to the high bench. He and Cummings reviewed details of strategy in each big case, picked over the available legal personnel and examined the methods of approach. And in the end they always

played the popular game of those days, counting justices. First there were the four extreme conservatives.
They could be written off as opposed. Then there were
the three liberals. They could be counted on to hold for
the government. And in the center were the Chief Justice and his fellow moderate, Roberts. To which side
would they incline? That was the question which the
President and his canny, genial Attorney General asked
themselves before most of the important actions came
before the Court, and when the decisions were handed
down at last Roberts had always made the answer,
"Against the government." In the whole period after
the NRA decision the TVA law was the only major
statute to be approved.

The knowledge that there were at least four men on
the bench who would not hold for the administration
if, as the Attorney General put it, "the Angel Gabriel
himself made the argument" was not altogether soothing to the President. His sense of personal injury increased. He and Cummings felt utterly frustrated, as
though they were confronted with a large blank wall
against which they had perforce to run their heads. It is
scarcely surprising that they began to look for ways
around the blank wall. Soon after the NRA decisions
they agreed that solutions for the court problem ought
to be explored. Cummings promptly initiated studies of
the matter within the Justice Department. Memoranda
were prepared, expedients were tabulated and tested,
and from time to time the President called in Cummings to go over the material as it accumulated.

By the spring of 1936, after the final irritant of the
New York Minimum Wage decision, many of the President's followers were anxious for an immediate assault
on the Court. Among others the beloved liberal
veteran, Senator George W. Norris, of Nebraska, repeatedly urged the President to fight the coming cam-

paign on the court issue. But the superlative Roosevelt sense of political timing still restrained him. He wanted the issue in the election to be himself and not the justices. It may seem difficult to understand why so daring a man as the President should have held back for so long. Yet the clear answer to the puzzle is available in a conversation from the very first year of the New Deal.

Several of the administration's hottest bloods were at the White House one evening, and the President, who enjoys the vaulting talk of his intellectual subordinates, had encouraged freedom of expression. Before long the young men were criticizing the New Deal program. It did not go far enough for them, and they loudly demanded radical additions to it. The President warned them that the time was not ripe for their plans, but they were no more content than George Norris was to be later. To pacify them he told a parable of missionary work among the totem-worshiping Indians of the Northwest.

One man, he said, sought to woo the Indians from their superstitions by main force. He and his fellow zealots marched into the villages and cast down the poles, and he told the tribes to worship totems no longer. Instead they killed the missionary and adhered more fervently to their ancient beliefs. The advocate of force was followed by a wiser fellow, who went to live among the Indians as a friend. Once they had lost their suspicion of him he began going out every night in the darkness, to scrape away a few handfuls of earth from around the bases of the totems. Eventually the poles fell of their own weight, and the Indians complaisantly accepted the wise missionary's substitute for their totem-pole worship. A man who wishes to guide the government in new directions, added the President, must imitate the wise missionary.

When he decided to minimize the court issue in the election the President was merely following the teaching of his parable. He had not abandoned his intention to deal with the Court; far from it. At the very time when, in spite of his opponents' constant challenges, he was maintaining his studious silence, when Democratic speakers who showed inclinations to be firebrands were requested to burn in private only, the President was giving his inner circle of advisers to understand that the Court would be dealt with when the campaign was over and the victory won. A stray reference or so, a prickling in the air around him, an extra firmness in the presidential talk—these warned his intimate counselors that action would not be long deferred.

The inner circle could only guess at what was up, for Cummings, who did not belong to their group, was doing the real work. Until the conclusion of the Court's spring term the exploration of solutions for the court problem had been desultory. One or two men in the Justice Department put in time on it, and Cummings gave to it what spare hours he had. But that summer, while the campaign was at its height, Cummings began an intensive program of research. Secret orders were issued to a larger group of legal experts to join the hunt for a way out. Professor Edward S. Corwin, the Princeton authority on jurisprudence, was consulted; William Draper Lewis, of the American Law Institute, was asked for his opinion, and other friendly luminaries were invited to help. At the Justice Department they were already collating the arguments for and against different amendments and collecting data on the constitutionality of purely legislative measures to bring the Court to heel, while the last Republican challenges were dying unattended on the speech-loud air.

Then came election day. His majority on November 3, 1936, persuaded the President to act at last. He took the 27,000,000 votes cast for him as an endorsement as personal as an appointment to be trustee and guardian of a friend's children. He believed, and he was mightily encouraged in his belief by the Corcorans, the Cohens, the Hopkins and the other members of the inner circle, that the people had given him carte blanche to go forward in whatever direction and by whatever means seemed best to him. The murmured warnings of the politicians on the Hill, that the election must be considered in part as a thanksgiving for improved business conditions, went wholly unregarded. Anything was possible, the President and his friends told themselves. America might be remade on an improved plan the next morning, and none would dare object.

The Historic Muse, that ultimate critic of the public drama of whose poised pencil the President is so conscious, may have some trouble when she has to appraise the character of Franklin Delano Roosevelt. At least, however, she will be able to conclude that all his strongest traits decided him to make his court fight as he made it and when he made it. His shrewd caution had held him back so far. Now the caution was gone. The triumph at the polls had replaced it with such an overconfidence as must come to any man after four years of glittering, uninterrupted success in great matters. The time had come to act; he knew it.

THE PRESIDENT AND CUMMINGS

November 4–December 31, 1936

THE PRESIDENT HEARD the election returns in Hyde Park. Thence he returned at once to Washington, where the Democratic job holders turned out in tens of thousands to receive him as a conquering hero. The gray morning, the odd Washington scene, like a half-finished imitation of the Roman Forum with trolley cars running past the Palatine steps, the cheering mobs, the smiling President in his open car—they made an unforgettable picture. One wondered why the vanquished Republican candidate, accompanied by a selection of Du Ponts and newspaper editors, did not follow the Presidential cortege in chains. One wondered whether the President possessed an inner censor, to take the place of the ribald slave who stood in each triumphing Roman general's chariot, to remind him that, after all, he was no more than mortal. One wondered, above all, what thoughts were in the President's mind as he waved his hat and grinned and nodded gratefully to the shouting people along the way.

There was something symbolic in that welcome to the President, so extraordinary in a city where political heroes are a nickel a dozen and only the sightseers interrupt their business to look at them. The election had transformed the panorama of national politics. By the magic of his victory the President had acquired a super-human stature, and all around him had shrunk. His enemies were proven pygmies; his advisers and the powerful leaders of his party in Congress had lost their importance. The future depended on the President alone; everyone saw that, including the President.

Evidently the problem of the Supreme Court was uppermost in the President's mind, for he was hardly settled at the White House before he summoned Cummings to report on the progress of his labors at the Justice Department. There ensued one of the most singular conversations in the history of the court drama. The setting was admirable—the President's oval, Georgian office, with its pale green walls, its ship pictures, its rather dull view of the White House garden, its big desk between the flags. At the desk was the President, gay, full of an election-born sense of power, but practical withal. Cummings brought a sheaf of papers, and while the President went through them he sat twiddling his pince-nez, as his habit is. A tall, lanky, elderly man, bald, with the alert but self-contained physiognomy of a wise and experienced turtle, he has the knack of never seeming excited. Actually his excitement was intense, but he did not permit it to appear in his demeanor, and the whole talk was on a thoroughly matter-of-fact plane.

The President's mind must have been made up to act, but it is his habit not to reveal his intentions, except by inference, until he has his plan of action chosen. Characteristically, therefore, he treated the interview as though it were just one more of the many progress reports on the Justice Department studies of the court problem which Cummings had made in the past. Months before, the two men had come to a mutual

understanding that the Court would have to be dealt
with sometime. Now the President gave no sign that
he expected to deal with it in the immediate future. The
practical aspects and constitutional implications of a
number of plans for bringing the Court into line were
reviewed in considerable detail. There was some natural speculation on the election's effects on the Court,
and Cummings and the President agreed that such mul-
ish fellows as the conservative justices would never re-
cede from their arbitrary position. The President terminated the discussion by asking Cummings to come
back as soon as he had any new material and command-
ing him to use every precaution to guard the secret of
his work.

That short conversation at the White House was
one of the most important incidents in the history of
the court plan, for it meant that Homer Cummings
would be the President's chief adviser on the great
problem. Nothing could illustrate better how the election had altered the Washington scene. A year earlier,
in planning so momentous a step as an attack on the
Supreme Court, the President would have followed a
well-established program of general consultation. First
his brilliant intellectual advisers, Ben Cohen, Tom Corcoran, Felix Frankfurter, Donald Richberg, Judge
Samuel I. Rosenman, of the New York Supreme Court,
and all the others would have been called in to prepare
the measure. And then, when the measure was ready,
his congressional leaders, Vice-President John N. Garner, Senator Majority Leader Joseph T. Robinson, of
Arkansas, Speaker of the House William B. Bankhead
and their colleagues would have been summoned to advise on its presentation to Congress. Very likely the
members of his Cabinet would have heard nothing of
it until the moment of actual revelation was at hand.

Now, however, the President felt no compulsion to

make his consultation general. He had been talking the problem over with Cummings for some time. He and Cummings could work out a solution together, and even though Cummings was a politician and not a constitutional expert, the solution would certainly be acceptable to a postelection Congress. Thus the President reasoned, and thus he made Cummings his sole helper on the biggest job of the New Deal.

Homer Cummings turned politician and Democrat in the early 1890s, soon after his graduation from Yale. The silvery thunder of Bryan's economic nostrums effected the metamorphosis, which was simultaneous because Cummings was a Connecticut man and in the Connecticut of those days Democrats were so scarce that one who could sign his name, made a habit of blowing his nose and had not murdered his mother automatically became a party leader. Cummings towered above the party average. An extremely canny, pleasant-spoken fellow, with a talent for partisan manipulation, he rose rapidly through the sparse ranks of Connecticut's Democratic hierarchy until he arrived at the summit, the post of national committeeman. There he remained for twenty-five years, and there he was when Jim Farley visited him in the course of his famous shopping trip for Roosevelt delegates to the 1932 convention. At Farley's invitation Cummings promptly climbed on the Roosevelt band wagon, and in Chicago, while Governor Wilbur Cross and the other Connecticut Democrats were sticking out for Al Smith to the end, Cummings was acting as a Roosevelt floor manager. When the pie was sliced after the election Cummings received his just reward—the governor-generalship of the Philippines.

On the way to his post, fortunately, he stopped off in Washington to get his proconsular instructions and say good-by. The attorney-generalship was suddenly left

vacant by the death of Senator Tom Walsh. There was
no time left to cast about for substitutes; Cummings
was hustled into the empty cabinet chair as a temporary
appointee, but from temporary he became permanent.
Although he was the Attorney General of the United
States, however, he was never considered a monument
of legal learning. So far as anyone knew, in fact, his
work in his new job was chiefly notable for an overpowering enthusiasm for the enforcement of the criminal law and for the transformation of the Justice Department into one of the great patronage reservoirs of
the government. Washington accordingly thought him
the kind of legal politico who would be an Elk, a
Mason, an Odd Fellow and an Eagle, and a wise old
fellow who enjoyed his official position and his cheerful life into the bargain.

Actually Cummings was more than that. There were
many things about him which earned him the hearty dislike of the intellectuals around the President, but he
had done an exceedingly hard job and done it fairly
well. More than two thousand lawsuits somehow involving the government were filed in the first four years
of the New Deal. On the passage of the Utilities Holding Company Act alone no less than fifty-six different
actions, all attacking the act's constitutionality, were
immediately begun by the utilities companies. Serious
constitutional questions were also raised in hundreds of
the other suits, covering scores of important laws.
Hearings of cases in which the government had an interest were constantly in progress all over the country.
Injunctions were daily granted to persons seeking to
obstruct the operation of the laws. New suits were
brought before the government lawyers could obtain
settlements in the old. Under such a strain most organizations would have collapsed completely. Cummings'
Justice Department did not. It carried on, haltingly

sometimes, often with difficulty, and always in trouble with the conservatives on the bench, but it carried on.

No doubt the President remembered this when he sent for Cummings that November day after the election. No doubt also the fact that Cummings had been discussing the court problem with the President for so long had something to do with his choice for the big job. At any rate Cummings was chosen.

Elated by the conversation at the White House, excited by his new responsibility, Cummings hurried back to his office to order his research machinery into high gear the same afternoon. The Justice Department experts went to work overtime producing complete surveys of each approach to the court problem and its implications, and reducing the surveys to readable digests suitable for presentation to the President. For two November weeks the messengers hurried back and forth between the department and the White House, carrying the work of Cummings and his experts to the President and returning with the President's "chits", the little slips of paper on which he circulates his suggestions and comments among his subordinates. And for those two weeks Homer Cummings trotted back and forth after the messengers. The President saw him almost daily. Each time he slipped in by the private entrance of the White House offices, for more public arrivals would have started gossip. And each time he slipped out again with the President's order to return at once when he had new data ready.

As Cummings and the President worked on together their excitement rose. The President's mood was a special serious elation, the solemn blitheness which must have invaded Caesar when he had crossed the Rubicon and knew the Imperial City awaited him in the distance. As for Cummings, he was in a high state of delight. He remembered how often he had been passed over in favor of the unofficial advisers of the President's inner circle. He detested these men. He was all the more pleased, therefore, to have superseded them now. He has an awareness of himself as a character in the history books of the future almost as lively as the President's; he was deeply stirred by the importance of his role.

The work proceeded rapidly, although the problem to be solved was sufficiently complicated. Four alternatives confronted the President and Cummings. They could either propose an amendment specifically enlarging the federal powers, or they could humble the Court by statute in three ways: by limiting its jurisdiction, by requiring more than a mere majority of the justices to invalidate an act of Congress, or simply by packing it. Within each class there were numerous variants, and the President and Cummings might have found it formidably difficult to choose one variant from one of the four classes, had they not shared a single point of view on their problem.

Both of them considered the Court the only obstacle in the path of social progress, and both of them blamed the conservative justices for willful obstructionism, for arbitrariness and unfairness. The conservative justices' plea, openly made in at least one opinion, that the Constitution enforced their stand upon them, provoked Cummings and the President to ridicule. Neither was prepared to be sympathetic to the Court, for Cummings, no less than the President, nursed a feeling of personal injury at the Court's hands.

They were agreed that it was the Court, not the Constitution, which had to be got round. Furthermore, the chance of jockeying an amendment through thirty-six out of forty-eight state legislatures in a reasonable time was obviously very slim. An amendment might be proposed, set off a tremendous explosion in Congress and then never do any good at all. Thus the amendment approach was placed well at the bottom of the list of choices. Next above it came the type of bill requiring more than a majority of the justices to invalidate an act of Congress. Senator Norris had already sponsored such a measure, but the President and Cummings suspected that his reading of the Constitution was wrong, that the justices would be able to strike down the act as soon as it was passed.

That left them with the two expedients mentioned by the President in his angry talk with Frankfurter and Johnson: "packing the Court" and "taking away its appellate jurisdiction." There were precedents for removing the Court's appellate jurisdiction of important New Deal measures—Jefferson had exempted his repealer of the Federalist midnight judges law from review by the Court, for example. But the possibility that the lower courts might prove as recalcitrant as the high bench, and the fact that the Constitution specifically gives the Court jurisdiction in certain classes of cases, notably those involving states, both made this approach seem impractical to the President and to Cummings. All their reasoning, therefore, pointed to Court packing as the best way out.

Court packing, as they saw it, went straight to the heart of the trouble, the personnel of the Court. It was simple; it involved no long-term alteration in the governmental structure, and it was clearly constitutional. They realized that it offended against what they privately called a "taboo", but they believed that the taboo had been greatly weakened by the Court's own behavior. Their feeling of injury at the hands of the Court tempted them to the best revenge, and the recent triumph at the polls was always in their minds. What could offended taboos matter when the opposition was dead? Who could oppose them but the same groups so thoroughly trounced only a week or so earlier? Remembering November 3, they could see no trouble ahead.

Such was their state of mind at the end of two weeks work. They had progressed so far without any positive statement by the President that all their talk would come to something. Cummings was on tenterhooks, for he saw perfectly how the wind was blowing, yet he also realized that until the President said in so many words that there would be a court plan, there was always a chance that he might change his mind and decide to wait it out. The President was to leave on his goodwill trip to the Argentine on November 18. A call at the White House just before the President's departure brought Cummings definite assurance at last.

The two men met in the President's office, as they had just after the election, and the meeting had the same calm, practical atmosphere their first meeting had. There was more material to be discussed now, but they discussed it in the same matter-of-fact fashion. Perhaps there was a trace more of assurance in the President's manner and a trace more of excitement in Cummings'. Certainly Cummings had an aching desire to ask the President point-blank what it all meant. Suddenly the President told him. He would present a court bill to the Congress, he said, as soon as one could be got ready, and he hoped that it would be possible to select a specific measure as soon as he returned from the Argentine. Cummings restrained his impulse to jump with joy and agreed that no final action ought to be taken until after the Argentine trip. Two fat bound volumes, one containing proposed amendments and the other proposed bills, had been prepared at the Justice Department at his order. He suggested that the President should take these along to South America and that he should send any new material that his experts prepared to await the President at his ports of call. The

President accepted both suggestions, and Cummings left the White House overjoyed.

The President's South American trip was leisurely. The system suggested by Cummings was followed, and in the intervals between ovations the President gave much time to studying the sheaves of material forwarded to him by the Justice Department. Yet when he returned to Washington on December 15 he was not satisfied with any of the proposed solutions. As soon as he arrived in the capital he saw Cummings and told him that the ideal plan had not been found. Meanwhile he had a fantastic amount of work on his hands. A vitally important measure for the reorganization of the Executive Department was in preparation. The second inauguration was fast approaching, and there had to be an inaugural address. The budget and its attendant message had to be ready for the opening of the congressional session in the first days of January, and so did the President's annual message "on the state of the Union." The natural result was that the President turned over to Cummings the search for a satisfactory court plan.

The task set Cummings by the President was not an easy one, and it had been made more difficult by their joint decision to reform the lower courts and pack the high bench with the same measure. Cummings had long been anxious to improve lower court procedure. Going to law, he felt, was both too expensive and too time-consuming a process. Moreover, the legal road of the New Deal had been so thorny in the lower courts that Cummings was actually convinced of the existence of a "conspiracy" among the leading corporation lawyers to harry the government. Cummings had infected the President with his views, and top-to-bottom reform of the judiciary had come to seem as important to the President as it did to Cummings. Always conscious of

History waiting just around the corner, they both hoped that by effecting a root-and-branch reorganization and providing additional judges on the lower as well as the high bench, they could make their measure as memorable for its improvements in the judicial system as for its subjugation of the Supreme Court. To blend the aims and call the whole simply a judiciary reorganization bill was an obvious expedient.

The difficulty lay in their need of an inclusive principle by which the Supreme Court could be enlarged, new judges in the lower courts provided and the other reforms carried out. They were acutely aware that unless they proposed a definite principle on which to make the increases, their demand for additional lower court judges would start a congressional pork-barrel scramble of dreadful and discreditable violence. And they thought that if they could only find a principle to cover all the increases in the judicial personnel their other improvements could be fitted into it with ease. Yet how to pack a court by principle?

That was the rather appalling puzzle which Homer Cummings was mulling over for the fiftieth time one December morning shortly after the President's return. His desk in the pseudoimperial office among the new Justice Building's frescoes was piled high with papers, all treating the subject. He picked up one after another, glancing at them and putting them down again. There seemed to be no possible answer. And then a thought crossed his mind. Why not make the judge's age the principle? That ought to do it. Cummings is a ruminative man, given to maturing his ideas by a slow process. He put the thought aside, but it came back to him. It kept returning, even after he had knocked off work and gone home. He did not quite see how the scheme would work, but he was certain that it could be made to. He was sure he had seen it mentioned somewhere, but he could not remember where. A couple of days passed before he recalled the history of his department, *Federal Justice,* which he and his special assistant, Carl MacFarland, had just published. That was where he had seen the mention of judges' ages. He was in his office. He sent for a copy of the volume, and when it came he leafed hurriedly through it until he came to a paragraph on page 531, in the midst of a section dealing rather realistically with the circumstances of judicial appointments.

"Others have attacked the problem of old age from another angle," he read. " 'Worn-out judges ought to be respectably provided for, by allowing them to resign on a competent pension,' recommended Attorney General Bates. After a retirement law had been passed, Attorney General McReynolds recommended in 1913 that when any federal judge, except justices of the Supreme Court, failed to avail himself of the privilege of retiring at the age provided by law, the President should appoint another judge to preside over the affairs of the Court and have precedence over the older one. 'This,' said he, 'will insure at all times the presence of a judge sufficiently active to discharge promptly and adequately all the duties of the court.' "

That was it. He knew that the McReynolds memorandum, prepared by the very man who was now the leader of the Court's conservatives, had lain gathering dust in the department files ever since it had been presented to President Wilson. He knew that a bill embodying the McReynolds plan had indeed been passed after McReynolds' elevation to the high bench. But why limit it to the lower courts? The question leaped to the eye. Why not appoint an extra justice of the Supreme Court for every one who had passed the retirement age and failed to retire? A hasty calculation of the sitting justices' ages showed him that putting the retirement age at seventy and extending the Mc-Reynolds plan to include the Supreme Court would allow the appointment of six additional justices. A great joy invaded him; he had conceived the court plan.

During the next day or so Cummings busied himself roughing in the details of the plan and preparing a careful study of it for the President's inspection. Each of his groups of experts had a special assignment, and each brought in a favorable report. The historical researchers turned up the fact that in 1869, when the Supreme Court had held the whole financing of the Civil War unconstitutional in the greenback cases, a bill almost precisely similar to the one conceived by Cummings had passed the House of Representatives. Then radical Republicans had sponsored it and had clothed their purpose to pack the Court in talk of the "incapacity" of its members. What was more, said the historical researchers, two such leading figures as Garfield and George Frisbie Hoare had voted for it. The statistical men gathered figures to show that the plan would supply an adequate number of new judges on the lower as well as on the high bench. The constitutionalists approved its legal aspects. As the reports came in Cummings' confidence in his scheme grew into an almost religious conviction of its efficacy.

He had a long-standing appointment with the President for a day or so after Christmas, and he resolved to offer his plan then. When he went to the White House he carried the drafts of a number of alternative plans, and he handed the President the whole packet with his own favorite at the bottom. Although he still twiddled his pince-nez and pretended unconcern, he watched the President going through the papers with the liveliest agitation. Cummings has his own peculiar quixotries, and while he longed to have his special plan approved he did not feel he should impose his judgment on the President. That was why he had put his plan at the bottom of the packet. That was why, when the President commented on the plans above it, he returned noncommittal answers. The President's fancy might have been taken by any one of them; they were the carefully sifted pick of all the Justice Department material. Cummings waited breathlessly until the President had gone over the last of the other plans. Some objection had been found to each.

Now it was the turn of the Cummings plan. The President glanced over the sheets on which it was outlined, then asked Cummings a couple of questions. The answers appeared to be acceptable, for he returned to the outline and read it through with care. A discussion of the plan followed, in which the President betrayed such delight that Cummings left the White House pretty sure his favorite would be chosen in the end.

His half assurance became certainty during his next call at the White House, which occurred almost immediately. At the same time the plan's minor features were also sketched in. The chief of these was the notion of "roving" judges to clear up lower court congestion, under the management of the Chief Justice and a proctor of the Supreme Court. It had been embodied in a memorandum presented to the President a year or so before by William Denman, an intimate of Tom Corcoran's and now judge of the Ninth Federal Circuit Court of Appeals. It was tacked onto the general plan pretty well as Denman had outlined it and tied into the whole by making the extra judges' appointments dependent on the ages of the sitting judges. With this addition and one or two others the court plan was finished.

The President had been enchanted with the plan from the start. Its half origin in the mind of McReynolds, most die-hard of the justices, captivated him. All his puckish, slightly malicious pleasure in turning the tables on his enemies was brought into play. All his desire to surmount the Court's blockade of his program promised to be satisfied. Even a secret wish to break the power of his party's conservatives, which had grown strong in him since the election, promised to be fulfilled—the Democratic conservatives could never stomach such a plan; they would oppose it and be beaten. Altogether the President felt that the plan was better than he could have hoped. Later he was to describe it to an intimate as "the answer to a maiden's prayer." And thus it was that the President made the first of the three great decisions which affected the whole course of the court fight; made it alone except for Cummings, in secret and without the advice of the men on whom he had most relied in the past.

No one, not even among those closest to the President, was aware of the step that had been taken when it was taken. Solicitor General Stanley Reed helped Cummings with his research before and after the selection of the plan, but he had no hand in the decisive action. Assistant Attorney General Robert H. Jackson first learned of the plan's existence when he read of it in the newspapers. The Cabinet was in a state of happy ignorance, and Tom Corcoran, Ben Cohen, Felix Frankfurter and the other members of the brain trust knew nothing of the great event.

Benjamin V. Cohen and Thomas G. Corcoran, the brilliant pair who were on top at the time in White House palace politics, were often credited with having a hand in originating the court plan. Actually they had less than none. They came closest to the discussion at Thanksgiving time, when Solicitor General Reed asked them to prepare a memorandum on approaches to the court problem. Unaware of the imminence of action, they worked at their paper all through December and submitted it early in January, after the Cummings scheme had already been chosen. Such was their ignorance of the true state of affairs that they rather dismissed the idea of extra judges and placed most weight on a proposal for a constitutional amendment not unlike that later advocated by Senator Burton K. Wheeler, of Montana. The Cohen-Corcoran amendment would have permitted Congress to override court decisions on the specific point of law concerned, by a two-thirds majority at once and by a simple majority after an intervening election. It would also have allowed Congress to validate state acts thrown out by the United States Supreme Court.

Cohen and Corcoran had, to be sure, toyed with the idea of packing the Court. Entirely on his own initiative Corcoran had suggested it to Senator Wheeler a year or so earlier, and he and Cohen had even got to the point of writing Wheeler a speech on the subject, which the senator had refused to deliver. But in the interval so many people had called packing the Court the only wholly inadmissible solution to the puzzle that Cohen and Corcoran had abandoned their first position. Unlike the President, they noticed the weather signs indicating that a great storm would blow up out of such a scheme, and Senator Wheeler was quite misled by Corcoran's early suggestion when he later laid responsibility for the plan at the Cohen-Corcoran door. Indeed it is one of the notes of tragedy which repeat themselves through the history of the court fight that Wheeler was so wrong. Had the President consulted these advisers of his, he might have ended by deciding to pack the Court, but he would have made his decision in a different fashion, and he would have chosen a different plan.

THE WHITE HOUSE SECRET

January 1–February 3, 1937

THE OLD YEAR DIED wearily in Washington. Tremendous preparations were afoot for the President's second inaugural, and the city was much preoccupied with the appalling but profitable prospect of an immense influx of victorious Democrats. Members of Congress were trickling back to town, announcing their plans for the coming session. Republican leaders had begun to wonder aloud whether the voters would think their party smelled the sweeter by another name. Only at the Justice Department, where Cummings was already drafting and redrafting the court bill behind locked doors, and at the White House, which regularly hummed with activity, was anything really happening. With the court bill chosen, the President was hard at work on his message to Congress on the state of the Union, which had to be delivered on January 6.

Cohen and Corcoran were contributors to the message, which was full of muted thunders against the Court as the chief obstacle in the path of social progress, and big with a muffled warning to the justices that unless they could fall into step their powers would be curbed. Some of these passages were supplied by Cummings. Corcoran, the member of the team who maintains contact with the President, must have wondered what it all meant when he discussed it with his "Boss", but the President offered no explanations. Nor did he offer any explanations to the Cabinet when he read the message at the meeting of January 5. The message contained the statement that "the vital need is not an alteration of our fundamental law." A couple of the cabinet officers asked whether that did not foreclose the amendment approach to the court problem, to which the President replied that it did not; that it merely indicated that no amendment was needed, although one could be resorted to. The men at the cabinet table, on tenterhooks with curiosity, waited for more, but the President stopped there.

Indeed it was a time when it hardly seemed that the President needed to offer explanations to anyone in the world. The glories of the election had not yet faded, and when January 6 came, hero-worshiping crowds stood patiently in the rain outside the White House and at the Capitol to see the President on his way to the chamber of the House, where the Congress awaited him in joint session. The senators and representatives cheered him to the echo when he arrived, oddly attired in the high Tory church clothes of a prewar English squire. The slight, vainglorious touch of assertive ego in that dark gray cutaway coat and matching trousers suited the President as he stood at the rostrum, accepting the cheers and then reading the paper in his rich, perfect voice. Everyone was wondering whether there would be references to the Court, and when they came they, too, were applauded.

"The statute of NRA has been outlawed. The problems have not. They are still with us. . . . The vital need is not an alteration of our fundamental law, but an increasingly enlightened view with reference to it.

. . . Means must be found to adapt our legal forms and our judicial interpretation to the actual present national needs of the largest progressive democracy in the modern world. . . . The judicial branch also is asked by the people to do its part in making democracy successful. . . . The process of our democracy must not be imperiled by the denial of essential powers of free government."

The sentences were scattered through the speech. For each of them the President used an extra emphasis, as though he meant to intimate that they were more than a mere discussion of a serious problem in rather general terms. Yet his words did not let the cat out of the bag. They merely allowed those with sharp ears to hear the animal meow, and of all the five-hundred-odd members of Congress who applauded so lustily, only Representative Hatton W. Sumners, of Texas, the upright, learned chairman of the House Judiciary Committee, really believed what his ears told him. He saw at once that something like the court bill must be coming, and in an effort to avert it he promptly revived his judiciary retirement bill.

That measure, whose story is one of the oddest little sideshows in the history of the court fight, had first been offered at the previous session. Already Sumners had foreseen that the Court's conservatives would run the Court into real trouble. He had sounded out the situation, and he had learned that two members of the right wing, Justices Van Devanter and Sutherland, were anxious to resign. He had been told that nothing but the lack of adequate retirement provisions for justices was holding them back. This may seem hard to believe, for a law committing Congress to pay resigning justices their full salary until their death was already in effect. But in the first place, as it was explained to Sumners, Van Devanter and Sutherland feared that a hostile Congress might impose on them such salary cuts as Justice Holmes had suffered, after his resignation, from the economy bill of 1933. In the second, they did not wish to become subject to the income tax, as they would have with the loss of their judicial status.

Sumners had received definite assurance that after the passage of a measure meeting these human fears of the two justices, they would both leave the Court. Therefore he had cooked up a bill preserving their judicial character for them by establishing a new position of retired justice and giving it some minor judicial functions. He had successfully steered the measure through his committee and onto the floor, only to have his delicately conceived plan upset by a filibuster by his fellow Texan, bull-mouthed Tom Blanton, who thought no man deserved more than his own annual honorarium of $10,000. Now Sumners revived the bill again, in the hope that it could be got through and the retirements over and done with before the President made his move.

While Sumners lobbied for his measure through the Capitol corridors, the rest of Washington worried about the court problem. After the election the scene of the political drama had narrowed, until the President's study at the White House was its chief setting. Now, with Congress in town again, it seemed to broaden, and much was heard from the Hill.

Senate Majority Leader Joseph T. Robinson and Speaker of the House William B. Bankhead both announced for a constitutional amendment as the session opened, and Senator Henry F. Ashurst, of Arizona, chairman of the Senate Judiciary Committee, started to push a very broad one of his own. A number of liberals headed by Senator George Norris announced plans for a sort of amateur constitutional convention, and the dilemma of the high bench was much agitated

by the farm and labor groups. Back in November the
farm leaders had transformed Secretary of Agriculture
Henry A. Wallace's crop insurance conference into a
pep meeting for the re-enactment of the AAA, and they
had not forgotten what they wanted. John L. Lewis,
chairman of the Committee for Industrial Organization, loudly demanded that something be done about
the Court, and other, less powerful spokesmen of the
workers chimed in after him. The talk went on, but
without a word of command from the White House it
was just talk, and only Hatton Sumners realized that
word of command would come.

The President was in a serene mood, clandestinely
preparing his word and foretasting his pleasure in the
fireworks of the future. His inauguration was drenched
in torrents of rain, but he moved through it with his
smile; taking the oath from the Chief Justice, whose
damp whiskers waved in the biting wind; riding down
the long avenues in a cloudburst; sitting alone at lunch
in the White House Red Room while an invited mob
stared at him across a low barrier in the door; watching the endless parade from his dripping reviewing
stand. All through the other stands they murmured
that when he took his oath he stared straight at Hughes
and repeated his promise to abide by the Constitution
as if it had been an accusation. There were little jokes
about how he had failed to give the justices apoplexy
with his message on the state of the Union and was
trying pneumonia on them now.

The decorations for the inaugural ceremonies had
not been removed when the Democratic congressional
leaders learned that their hopes for a quiet session and
an early adjournment were to be disappointed. The
President had ceased to consult them; when he was
ready he simply let the troubled group know that the
session would be anything but quiet. A farm bill, a

wages and hours bill, a bill to establish new water and conservation authorities like the TVA all over America, an executive reorganization bill so sweeping that it required Congress to resign to the presidency forever virtually all its powers over the executive branch except that of appropriation—these were the major items on his staggering program. They would have given ample work to two ordinarily docile Congresses even without a court bill, and there can be no better proof of the fact that the President was suffering from an attack of political folies de grandeur than his expectation that they could all be passed.

The work on the court plan was going forward apace. At the White House the President nursed his delightful secret, while Homer Cummings and the serious, hard-working Solicitor General, Stanley Reed, labored over their papers and law books at the Justice Department. Only one man was allowed to help them—Cummings' personal assistant, Alexander Holtzoff, a squat, thickly bespectacled little man with a passion for legal hairsplitting, whose talents naturally fitted him for the post of private Doppelgänger to an important official. Cummings and Reed and Holtzoff took the most extraordinary precautions to conceal what they were up to. If opinions were desired from the department legal experts they were requested without explanation, and only on the specific point concerned. If data were wanted they were asked for out of the blue, and puzzled Justice Department men found themselves compiling statistics on the ages of federal judges, studying the congestion in the federal courts and collecting figures on the number of petitions of certiorari refused by the high bench without in the least knowing how all the material was to be used.

Three documents were being prepared—the bill itself, the President's accompanying message and a

letter from the Attorney General to the President to
support the message's arguments. In a series of conferences at the beginning of January, Cummings and
the President had invented the expedient of the letter
and settled the approach to the court problem to be
expressed in it and the message. Seduced by the neat
perfection with which their plan embraced court packing in a general principle, influenced by the importance
they gave the reform of the lower courts, they resolved
to make the "reorganization of the judiciary" their
main topic. They would ignore their purpose to pack
the Court; they would omit all mention of the pressing
reasons which had started them on their hunt for a
court plan; they would scarcely mention the Supreme
Court's reactionary blockade of the New Deal. Instead
they would rest their argument on the incapacities of
aged judges, on the courts' delays and on supposed
indications that the justices of the high bench could
not get through their work.

That was the second profoundly important decision
of this period before the presentation of the court plan.
Like the first, when the plan itself was chosen, it was
made in haste and a sublime overconfidence. Cummings'
Yankee cunning, the President's passion for a good,
smart political trick, overpowered them both. As they
plotted it out together they would avoid the incon-
veniences of offending the "taboo" against court packing by raising a tremendous hullabaloo about something
quite different: the need for judiciary reform. They
would confuse their unhappy enemies, give their nervous
adherents an excuse for forgetting the real nature of
their bill and maintain the argument on a purely
factitious ground until the obedient Congress could
perform its servile function. Once more Cummings, the
proud author of the court plan, acted as the idea's
salesman; once more the President bought the idea

blindly, perfectly willing to believe that he had the power to pack the Court unnoticed.

Bill, message and Attorney General's letter were simultaneously drafted in the opulent privacy of Cummings' office. The bill's provisions had been pretty well settled on, and a first draft of it had been got ready by Cummings and Reed before the New Year. But the phrasing was difficult; the utmost exactitude was required. Cummings and Reed redrafted it again and again, twelve times in full and many more than that if revisions of clauses and sections are to be counted. Holtzoff was a large contributor to the Attorney General's letter, which was intended to give additional statistical support to the indirect arguments of the President's message, and he offered some suggestions in regard to the message itself. With his assistance Cummings and Reed redrafted the message and the letter almost as many times as they did the bill. At length the three documents were got into shape Cummings was ready to consider final.

He had been in frequent touch with the President while the drafting was in progress, and now he took all three documents to the White House. The President passed the bill almost as it stood. He criticized the letter rather elaborately, but it was passed also, after Cummings had made a final revision of it along the suggested lines. Only the message remained. Conscious that it would be one of the most important state papers to carry his signature, the President insisted that it must be perfect, and to insure perfection he called in Donald Richberg and, later, Judge Rosenman to help on it. Richberg had left a Chicago law practice to serve in the NRA; thence he had risen to be a confidential White House adviser, a sort of minor-league Frankfurter. Rosenman was an old and close friend of the President's. Both owed their selection to the fact that, like Cummings, they had been discussing the court problem with the President from the very first.

Considerably more than half of January had passed when Cummings took the bill, the letter and the message to the President. With the first two out of the way intensive work on the message began at once at the White House. Usually Cummings and the others came in after dinner, at the moment when the presidential ménage leaves the dining room and goes to the living quarters upstairs. Ordinarily everyone dining at the White House sees a film in the upstairs hall; when there is business afoot, however, the President leaves his family and guests and retires to his cozy oval study-living room. In those late January days the President saw few films, for the discussions of the message went on almost every evening in the study, among the ship models and bits of sentimental bric-a-brac which fill the room with the atmosphere of a pleasant, traditional family life.

The President and Cummings, Richberg, Reed and, at the end, Judge Rosenman all made themselves comfortable in the study's big chintz-covered chairs. Copies of the message in its latest form were handed round, and all the members of the group criticized them. The President, with his peculiar sense of stylistic fitness, is no slipshod critic, and he inspired the others with his own regard for the rightness of every detail. The continuity, the length, the use of evidence to support the points, the phraseology—all were discussed. Every conceivable problem connected with the message, except the most important, was before the meeting; the wisdom of the message's indirection was not questioned, either because the President and Cummings convinced the others that their smart trick would work or because the others did not care to object after the President had made up his mind. On strictly stylistic questions the

freest speech prevailed. Sometimes there were long
arguments; occasionally there was a general agreement.
The President stimulated the talk, listened to the suggestions, offered some himself and made the final decisions.

Meanwhile the strategies of the bill's presentation
and the subsequent struggle were also settled on. For
the fight itself a simple plan of campaign was chosen.
The Court had bitterly offended labor, the farmers and
the liberals. The President believed he could count on
the most energetic support from each of the three great
groups, but just to make sure he intended to use the old
device of the carrot held before the donkey's nose to
make the donkey go. The wages and hours bill for
labor, the farm bill for agriculture, such measures as
the little TVA bill for the liberals had already been
publicly announced or privately promised. Each group
was hankering for its own legislation. What could be
simpler, then, than to set Congress to work on the court
bill and keep it at work until the bill was passed? Thus
the three groups would have great inducements to get
the bill passed and out of the way; their anxiety for its
passage would be increased by the doubtfulness of the
Court's reaction to their promised special legislation;
their resentment against the Court would be reinforced
by their own self-interest. Thus the President and
Cummings reasoned, never doubting for an instant that
the three groups could be counted on to fight for the
bill with a prodigal fury.

The President was so sure of the three groups' support that he saw no need to consult their leaders before
the bill's presentation. He and Cummings were both
anxious to give the maximum surprise with their plan,
and they feared the premature disclosure which consultation might cause. Therefore advance commitments
were not to be sought from such men as Lewis, George

Norris and the leaders of the farm organizations. They were not to be partners in the big enterprise of the court bill; they were to be the President's docile followers. And thus the preparation period's third momentous decision was made, once more in haste, once more in overconfidence and for the sake of one of those coups de théâtre, those grand political transformation scenes, for which the President had a strong if slightly childish partiality.

The decision to consult no one naturally included the congressional grandees. If anything, there was even less concern about the important men on the Hill than there was about the prospective nonpartisan allies in the fight. The election had settled the opposition's hash in Congress, and there were huge Democratic majorities in both houses. The men who managed the majorities had an all but unblemished record of perfect subservience to the White House; they also had the inconvenient habit of offering advice when their advice was asked. The court plan had been worked out to the last detail; advice could only be embarrassing, and here again there was the possibility of a leak. Therefore neither Garner nor Robinson, neither Bankhead nor the House majority leader, Sam Rayburn, nor the chairman of the two judiciary committees nor anyone else was to be admitted to the secret. The carelessness of congressional feelings was carried so far that the President and Cummings determined to attach a copy of the bill to the message, as though to suggest that congressional erasure of the merest comma would not be allowed. No one was to be warned. No one was to be permitted even to seem to have participated in the great scheme. Message, bill and letter, the whole thing was to be flung at Congress and the country without advance notice, to be left or taken. There was not the slightest doubt in the President's mind that they would be taken.

At last all was in readiness. The President was jubilant, and in the final days he broke down and showed what he had ready to Tom Corcoran, to his chief congressional lobbyist, Undersecretary of the Interior Charles West, and to several other members of the inner circle. With them he was like a proud father exhibiting a favorite son to an old friend. The unhappy members of the inner circle felt precisely as though they had been confronted with a child in whom any but fond parental eyes could see the symptoms of incipient disease. All of them were astonished; all of them saw more trouble ahead than the President looked for; some of them, like Tom Corcoran, were completely horrified by the indirections of the message, its highly sophistic reasoning and its implied condemnation of old age. But the time for radical changes had passed. There was no purpose to be served by arguing with the President, and they muted their expostulations. The President was in no mood to heed minor danger signals, and as the great hour approached his confidence grew yet more serene, yet more unthinking.

Foreground and Background

IN THE LAST DAYS of January 1937 the political situation rather resembled a painting whose background is so superb, so rich with light and glorious with color, that the figures of the foreground go all but unnoticed. The background was the election and, stretching away behind the election's blaze of triumph, the long vista of success down which the President had walked from his first inauguration. At first glance the foreground seemed equally bright. The President was in full possession of all his immense power. His majority in Congress was the largest any President had ever enjoyed. His party was outwardly unified. He was surrounded by a circle of brilliant and faithful private advisers. He was served by legislative lieutenants who hardly knew the meaning of the word "disobedience", yet commanded his troops ably and forcefully. Every circumstance seemed to promise him a future as opulent with victory as the past.

The splendid panorama of political prosperity did not, however, bear too close an inspection. Among the crowding, formally submissive figures the knowing eye discerned many with dark looks and discontented, even rebellious expressions.

The official opposition, to be sure, had all the plaintive ineffectualness of an irritable but moribund invalid. There were but sixteen Republicans in the Senate, but eighty-nine in the House, and in both chambers they had been so demoralized by the election that they were scarcely worthy of notice. It was within the Democratic party itself that trouble was to be looked for. Strangely enough the election had diminished the President's control of his followers. The senators and representatives had that second-term feeling of independence which comes with the knowledge that another name will head the ticket at the next voting, and the very hugeness of the Democratic majorities destroyed their partisan cohesiveness.

The ever-docile House, with its rigid system of rules, could still be positively counted on, but in the Senate there was a clear off-chance of misfortune in the future. There were, in the first place, fully a score of the seventy-six Democratic senators whose conservatism had already openly disaffected them to the New Deal. The pre-election impulse to party regularity had made them sing small in the past; they were still somewhat muted by the recollection of the November triumph's completeness, but they could be expected to leave the party reservation on the first major issue. The President was not much concerned with them, for they belonged to the wing of the Democracy which he hoped to cast off, in the interests of a unified and untrammeled progressivism, by 1940. Moreover, they were balanced by a rather larger number of convinced New Dealers, composed in the ratio of about one to two of serious members of the left wing and legislators whose trip into office on the President's coattails had taught them the value of subservience. Nevertheless, the disaffected conservatives had twenty senatorial votes.

Besides the conservatives and the official New

Dealers there was a third large group who may be described as the orthodox Democrats. These men, most of them Southern politicians for whom officeholding was a lifelong profession, had always uncomplainingly accepted any proposal on which the President stamped the party label. From their ranks had risen the party's leaders in Congress, Garner and Robinson, Harrison and Byrnes, Bankhead, Rayburn and the other members of the powerful Southern oligarchy. The oligarchs had ruled Congress for the President with a perfect faithfulness; they had accepted his peremptory orders; they had submitted with good grace to an absolute and distinctly humiliating exclusion from the administration's councils on policy; in their enthusiasm for the President's success as a party leader they appeared to have forgotten the natural conservatism of their Southern background.

Now, however, they had begun to suffer severe pangs of inner doubt. All of them were convinced that the President's spending policies, which had worried them from the start, had become definitely dangerous at last. All of them were disturbed by the President's laissez-aller attitude towards the labor movement, for in their constituencies semifeudal labor relations were still the rule. The independent-minded among them were preparing an insurrection on these issues, and the threat was all the more serious because the President had depended so entirely on them that he had allowed them to organize the congressional machine, to fill the important committee chairmanships and key positions with their men. They had, moreover, an immense influence with the fourth important class of senators, the moderate New Dealers, those representatives of the great American middle class who approved the President's objectives but longed for a more deliberate approach to them.

In this subterraneously confused congressional situation three vigorous pressure groups had to be reckoned with. The first, and perhaps the most important, were the liberals, whose strength was chiefly derived from the pressure of public opinion. By his policies the President had made intellectual liberalism the new dominant note in national politics, and senators had learned to listen with respect to liberalism's representatives on and off the Senate floor. The independents, Norris and Robert M. La Follette, of Wisconsin, and such Democrats as Burton K. Wheeler, of Montana, had a larger national stature than all but two or three of the official Democratic leaders, not only because they represented liberal opinion, but also because the President had singled them out as the ideal New Dealers. They could be taken as advance samples of the kind of Democratic party the President hoped to shape, and their unity and the unity of like-thinking publicists and leaders in the country at large was tremendously important to the President.

Besides the liberals there were the farmers and labor, the two pressure groups whose strength lay in the mere force of their voting backing. On the surface it seemed that the President could depend on them as unquestioningly as it seemed he could depend on the liberals, but here again there were factors in the situation not apparent to the casual observer. The farmers cherished a considerable remnant of agricultural conservatism, and their persecution complex made them the least grateful and the most greedy of all the lobbies which infest the capital. Their organizations could never be trusted to repay their obligations, for they regarded whatever they received as an inadequate part payment on the national debt to an unhappy agriculture.

As for labor, its ranks were torn asunder by the

bitter strife between John L. Lewis' Committee for
Industrial Organization and the American Federation
of Labor, headed by William Green. The brief and
delusive truce to which the two factions submitted during the presidential campaign had ended the moment
the voting was over. The fighting had begun again with
a redoubled fury, and by the end of January it was
clear that the President would find it appallingly difficult to maintain a neutral attitude without offending
one faction or the other. Already the dynamic Lewis
was growing angry with him, while there were many
leaders of the A. F. of L. who held him responsible
for the rise of the CIO. Obviously, then, the reactions
of the labor groups were not entirely predictable.

Such was the general situation in the late January
days when the President was putting the finishing
touches to his court bill. He had made his three great
decisions. He had chosen his measure, determined to
present it not on its own merits but as a general reform
of the judiciary, and resolved to consult no one before
its presentation. When the time for presentation of the
bill came at last each of the decisions was bound to have
its repercussions in the general situation. Each of them
was a potential irritant, a potential detonator of some
of the explosive forces the situation contained. Therefore it is now worth examining the nature of the three
decisions in some detail.

To begin at the beginning, the bill itself was simple
and straightforward enough. It provided:

First, that when any judge of any federal court who
had been on the bench ten years waited more than six
months after his seventieth birthday to resign or retire
the President might appoint a sort of coadjutor for
him in the same court.

Second, that the number of judges in any court
should be permanently increased by the appointment

of additional judges, but that the membership of the Supreme Court should not be increased by more than six, nor the membership of any of the lower courts by more than two, nor the general total of the judiciary by more than fifty.

Third, that the Chief Justice might assign extra circuit judges to any circuit court of appeals where a press of business occurred, and that extra district judges might be similarly assigned to district courts with crowded dockets; that the senior judges of the circuits to which the extra judges were assigned might object to the assignment; but that the Chief Justice might make the final decision in the matter.

Fourth, that the Supreme Court might appoint a proctor, to watch over the status of litigation, investigate the need for assigning extra judges to congested courts and recommend their assignment to the Chief Justice.

So much for the bill. Its primary purpose was obviously to solve the problem created by the Supreme Court's arbitrary and reactionary course. Yet in accordance with the President's second great decision, this real purpose of the court bill was not once referred to in the President's accompanying message or the Attorney General's letter. Not once in either document were the very aims which the President had emphasized in his message on the state of the Union so much as recalled; since the writing of that message the President and Cummings had been seduced by the fascination of a smart trick, and the whole emphasis of this later message was placed on judicial delay and inefficiency, on the incapacity of aged judges to deal with modern matters and on the supposed injustices worked against poor litigants by a clogged judicial system. In the message more than five hundred words were exhausted before the first oblique intimation that the bill was intended to apply to the Supreme Court at all. In the Attorney General's letter the Supreme Court was scarcely mentioned.

At the outset of his message the President announced that his sole desire was for a "reorganization" of the judiciary, which he cheerfully compared to the reorganization of the executive branch then before Congress. He pointed out that the Congress had clear constitutional authority to "reorganize" the judiciary and in this connection gave his first hint of what was up by recounting the various historic changes in the size of the Supreme Court. He rehearsed at some length "the complexities, the delays and the expense of litigation in the United States", which, he said, were causing the courts to become "chiefly a haven for the well-to-do." And then he got down to the meat of his argument, the attack on the Supreme Court's numerous refusals of petitions of certiorari. Petitions of certiorari are litigants' first applications to be heard by the Court. The President sought to prove that by declining to hear many cases the Court showed inability to transact its business.

"Even at the present time," wrote the President in his message, "the Supreme Court is laboring under a heavy burden. Its difficulties in this respect were superficially lightened some years ago by authorizing the Court, in its discretion, to refuse to hear appeals in many classes of cases. This discretion was so freely exercised that in the last fiscal year, although 867 petitions for review were presented to the Supreme Court, it declined to hear 717 cases.

"If petitions in behalf of the government are excluded, it appears that the Court permitted private litigants to prosecute appeals in 108 cases out of 803 applications. Many of the refusals were doubtless warranted. But can it be said that full justice is achieved when a court is forced by the sheer necessity of keeping up with its business to decline, without even an explanation, to hear eighty-seven per cent of the cases presented to it by private litigants?"

It was directly after this argument, so ingenious, so pat to the occasion but so specious that no single member of the White House inner circle failed to be horrified by it, that the President made his first open statement of intention. And even that was so curiously, so nonchalantly phrased that its meaning was all but soothed away by its very mildness. It was simply that the Supreme Court's refusal to hear so many cases made it "seem clear" that "the necessity of relieving present congestion extends to the enlargement of the capacity of all the federal courts." Even here the President failed to mention in so many words his plan to pack the high bench, nor did he do so before he passed on to that "subject of delicacy, yet one which requires frank discussion"—the age of the judges.

The subject was indeed discussed with considerable frankness. The President's whole point was that the judges were too senile to know what they were doing, and he made his point without more ado, declaring suavely that "little by little new facts become blurred through old glasses fitted, as it were, for the needs of another generation; older men, assuming that the scene is the same as it was in the past, cease to explore into the present or inquire into the future." Thereupon the President made his recommendation that "younger blood to vitalize the courts" be supplied by "additional judges in all federal courts, without exceptions", and wound up on the minor subject of reform of the lower bench. Nor did the Attorney General's letter differ in any important respect from the President's message.

Thus the second great decision. By the third, the bill, swaddled in these singular explanations, was to be

lightly tossed to a perfectly unprepared Congress and
an unwarned country.

In the light of the general political situation already
described these decisions seem strange now, but they
seemed no less strange at the time to the worried
members of the White House inner circle whom the
President admitted to his great secret at the end of
January. For the positive step of court packing, it
could be argued that it was the only way to his end
open to the President. Although the moral argument
for the amendment method was strong, court packing
was still the only proven and immediate expedient by
which to meet a situation that all but the extreme
reactionaries conceded must somehow be met. To be
sure, it meant the inevitable loss of every one of the
score of disaffected conservative Democratic votes in
the Senate. To be sure, it was certain to arouse the most
intense opposition of all the proposed legislative approaches. To be sure, it was bound to make the all-
important liberals nervous, for the lesson of Fascism
abroad had taught them to cherish the institutions of
democracy at home with an extra fervor. Grant the
need for a court bill, however, and the first great decision seems reasonable enough. It was wildly reckless
to ask for so many additional justices on the Supreme
Court, but a request for some additional justices was
naturally suggested by the logic of events.

It was the second decision, not the first, which
horrified the members of the inner circle. They knew
that no one, in Congress or out, would be deceived by
the fantastically disingenuous cloak of argument in
which the President and Cummings had wrapped their
bill. They rightly thought that an open statement of
the necessity of curbing the Court, accompanied by a
straightforward exposition of the strong points in
favor of the court packing method, would have been

more acceptable. They half foresaw how the disingenuousness of the presentation would make the liberals still more nervous, how a split would develop in the liberal ranks just when liberal unity was vital. They realized the other dangers to which his indirections would lay the President open—the bitter attacks on his motives, the possibility that he would be forced to abandon his first line of argument, the embarrassing strategic consequences of so cumbersome an apparatus of offense.

As for the third decision, its perils were not immediately apprehended, although they should have been apparent enough. Had the President obtained commitments from the labor and farm leaders, had he made the leading congressional liberals his partners in the court bill enterprise, he would have been absolutely sure of their unquestioning support. Instead he decided not to consult them, because he believed they would support him anyway, without advance commitments. Considering the nerves of the liberals, the conservatism of the farmers and the angry disunion in labor's ranks, he ran a frightful risk of finding himself deserted by the allies on whom he relied with such carefree confidence.

These dangers in the general political situation were not so great that careful management could not overcome them; the real danger lay in the fact that the election had made the President's management anything but careful. In the past four years he had become accustomed to personal government. Brilliant as many of them were, his advisers were almost without exception unofficial. They had their political existence as mere extensions of his personality, and even among the members of his Cabinet there were only two, Henry Wallace and Secretary of State Cordell Hull, who would not have returned to immediate obscurity with

the loss of their posts. His past relations with Congress
had led him to expect a servile acquiescence in any
measure he matured in the privacy of White House
council, and the large pressure groups had demanded
and received so much from him that he had ceased to
question their co-operation. But before the election he
had always been cautious. He had consulted his congressional leaders; he had helped them to plan their
campaigns by warning them of his intentions; he had
allowed them to pretend to some responsibility for the
formation of policy. And he had dealt with the pressure
groups in the same fashion.

Now the election had caused him to throw caution
to the winds. How he no longer troubled to consult
anyone, how he withdrew into his private circle of
advisers, how he believed that compliance with his
wishes had become automatic—all this may be seen in
the story of the birth of the court bill. The governing
factor in the whole queer business was his election-born
overconfidence. As it was to prove the governing factor
in the whole long struggle over the Court, it may be
well to close this digression with the best available
measure of the pitch to which the President's overconfidence was carried:

"There is hereby authorized to be appropriated,
out of any money in the Treasury not otherwise appropriated, the sum of $100,000 for the salaries of
additional judges and the other purposes of this act
during the fiscal year 1937."

That clause from the bill was a candid announcement that the President expected his portentous measure to be passed, signed and embodied in the law long
before July 1, when the fiscal year 1937 came to its
close.

II. ATTACK

REVELATION AND REACTION

February 3–February 19, 1937

ON THE EVENING of February 3 the President and
Mrs Roosevelt gave their last big dinner of the winter
season—for the judiciary. As a party it was about on a
par with most other such official entertainments, being
too stiff to be amusing and too little pompous to be
impressive.

The company was cheerfully mixed, as the company
generally is when the presidential household submits to
its corvée of official hospitality. The guests of honor,
of course, were the Chief Justice and his associates. All
the members of the Court but Brandeis, who never
goes out in the evening, and Stone, who was just
recovering from an attack of amoebic dysentery, were
in attendance. Then Attorney General Cummings and
Solicitor General Reed headed a delegation from the
Justice Department, and Senator Ashurst and Representative Sumners led selected groups from the two
judiciary committees of Congress. Donald Richberg
and Judge Rosenman represented the President's unofficial advisers; there were a couple of the auld
acquaintances who must not be forgot, and the President's cousin, Mrs Warren Delano Robbins, who has

deep mauve hair and looks like all the women in all the stories about the diplomatic set rolled into one, added an effective note of worldliness. Judge and Mrs Irving Lehman, a large contributor to the Democratic campaign fund, the Gene Tunneys, several newspapermen, someone from the navy and someone from the army, George Harrison, president of the New York Federal Reserve Bank—these were all there, with enough more to make up the dinner list to eighty.

After dinner there was music and a reception, at which the President showed himself in more than ordinarily good spirits. And well he might have, for he was enjoying one of those ironical little moments which he dearly loves. At his table he had assembled all but two of the justices of the court he was preparing to subjugate, and all the men who had worked with him to prepare its subjugation. It was as good as the Duchess of Richmond's ball before Waterloo; better, for while the party lacked the advantages of champagne, the military figure, gaiety and bright uniforms, it topped the duchess's celebrated rout by being given on the eve of a great battle by the commander of one side for the members of the other. The only fly in the President's ointment was that no one except himself and Cummings, Richberg and Reed and Rosenman knew enough to extract its full savor from the occasion.

The following afternoon the President communicated with Joe Robinson and Speaker Bankhead. He told them rather mysteriously that there would be an important announcement at the cabinet meeting the next morning, and he asked them to bring Sam Rayburn and Ashurst and Sumners along with them. He also ordered the secretarial staff of the White House to report for work the next morning at the highly unusual hour of six-thirty. Accordingly at 6:30 A.M. on Feb-

ruary 5 the puzzled stenographers and mimeographers
trooped into the White House offices, rubbing their
eyes and wondering what was up. They found the
President's message on the judiciary, the Attorney
General's accompanying letter and the court bill all
waiting to be mimeographed in hundreds of copies.
They set to work energetically, and in less than four
hours they had the required number of copies prepared.
By that time the members of the Cabinet and the congressional leaders had begun to assemble.

Some little while before the President was ready for
them they were all in the long, low-ceilinged cabinet
room, some of them seated at the big cabinet table
waiting and chatting, some of them walking listlessly
up and down or gazing out the windows into the wintry
White House garden, wondering what was in store.
Only Secretary of the Treasury Henry Morgenthau,
Jr, was absent. Of all those present, from Vice-President
Garner down to Senator Ashurst, who had recently
described court packing as the "prelude to tyranny", no
one but Homer Cummings knew what was going to
happen. Cummings sat a little apart, twirling his pince-
nez in his fingers, wearing a slightly self-important air.
Shortly before the President came in from his office the
wanderers and window-gazers joined the others at the
table. The whole leadership of the Democratic party,
the whole official directorate of the nation's business
was there, waiting for marching orders from the President.

He came in hurriedly, followed by a secretary with
a sheaf of papers—the same mimeographed copies of
the President's message, the Attorney General's letter
and the court bill which the stenographers had started
work on so early. The secretary strewed the papers up
and down the cabinet table. The President gave every
one a genial good morning. The others at the table

picked up the documents, but their rapid glances at the first page or so of the message told them nothing. The President opened the meeting at once.

He had very little time, he said, because he was due at his press conference in less than half an hour. He announced his purpose to humble the Court and explained what the papers were. Then he read a few snatches from the message, briefly amplifying on the printed words. No one spoke. Joe Robinson, obviously disturbed, flushed mahogany and stared down at the table top, as though his fate had been written in the wood for him to decipher. Of the cabinet members only Homer Cummings, still twiddling his eyeglasses, seemed unconcerned. The others did their best to keep their astonishment out of their faces, but it was a poor best. Hatton Sumners watched the President alertly from under his bushy eyebrows. He was making a momentous decision. Henry Ashurst, who was cast for a part in the play like Malvolio's and Mercutio's rolled into one, sat straight up in his seat with his head tilted back, staring up at the ceiling. The President did not ask for comments.

It was all over in a very few minutes. The President broke off as hastily as he had begun, saying that he was sorry he had to leave, but the press was waiting. He told them they would know all about it, anyway, in a couple of hours, since he was sending the message to Capitol Hill at noon. He evidently feared that some newspaperman would get wind of what was up before he personally announced it, for his final injunction to those present was to say no more about the matter and to leave the papers on the table. Then he left the room for the most jubilant press conference he ever had.

It was an extraordinary occasion, that press conference. At his desk sat the President, holding one of the mimeographed copies of his message, the letter and the bill. Before him in a crowded semicircle stood the representatives of the press of America, some of them delighted, some of them deeply disturbed, all of them astonished at what the President was revealing. He began by reading his message, explaining it as he went along far more fully than he had taken the trouble to do for his Cabinet and the congressional leaders. His air was positively sprightly, and especially so when he came to the passages concerning the fate of the Court. He smiled constantly, and once he threw back his head and laughed aloud. He seemed to be asking the assembled newspapermen to applaud the perfections of his scheme, to note its nicely calculated indirections and praise its effectiveness. When he was done reading and explaining he said he would answer questions. They came, enough of them to keep the conference going almost until noon. Finally the last query had been answered, and the "Thank you, Mr President" which breaks up press conferences was uttered by someone in the front row. He asked that no word of what he had disclosed be written until his message had actually been received in the Senate or the House; and the conference was over.

The meeting in the cabinet room had broken up wordlessly shortly before the press conference began. The cabinet members and congressional leaders went out to their cars, pushing their way through the crowd of newspapermen in the front hall. The congressional leaders set off for the Hill together in two motors. After they had left the White House, after they had turned down past the Treasury, Hatton Sumners spoke to the men with him.

"Boys," he said, "here's where I cash in my chips."

It was the first announcement of opposition to the plan, and it was to prove a major factor in the actual struggle. Sumners' decision, so quickly arrived at, so stubbornly held to, bulked largest in the final White House determination to let the Senate deal with the plan before the House. That came a little later, however, after days in which all Washington seemed to be running around in circles, bellowing incomprehensively to itself.

The message and its attachments fell like an explosive shell upon the Congress shortly after midday. The confusion and puzzlement to which so many of the President's abrupt moves have reduced his followers were never more publicly apparent. In the House a broadcasting apparatus had been hurriedly installed, and the nation heard the message read simultaneously with the representatives. The quickest reaction was that of Representative Maury Maverick, the forceful Texan left-winger, who caught onto the message's meaning at once, scribbled his name on one of the mimeographed copies of the bill and dropped it in the House bill hopper a couple of minutes after the reading clerk was done. But the great majority of the unhappy legislators did not grasp the import of the message; they settled down to glance through the mimeographed copies which had been put around on their desks. Meanwhile the news spread like wildfire, and before long the floor of the House was seething with excited members, all asking one another just one question: "What do you think of it?" in tones expressing anything from horror to jubilation.

In the Senate the public spectacle was less remarkable, for a senator's first reaction to an extraordinary event is to retire to the cloakrooms or the lobbies to talk it over there. Joseph B. Keenan, the chunky, shrewd assistant to the Attorney General who was to have a leading part in the fight as one of the President's chief representatives on the Hill, arrived at the Capitol just in time to witness the spectacle in the big lobby behind

the Senate chamber, the senators' main private forum.
Poor man, he was completely dumfounded, for although
his position should have made him privy to any contemplated legislation, he had not heard a whisper of what
the President and Homer Cummings were cooking up
together. Keenan was only on the Hill because he had
an influential friend for whose benefit he wanted to trot
out a few senators at lunch, and he could not have been
more astonished when Henry Ashurst dragged him out
of the public reception room into the closed Senate
lobby to get his opinion on the court plan.

It was while the message was still being read, and
the first sight that met his eyes was Vice-President
Garner, who had left the rostrum, expressing his reaction to a group of senators by holding his nose with
one hand and energetically making the Roman gesture
of the arena, thumbs down, with the other. Then poor
Keenan himself was engulfed by the men around
Garner, all demanding explanations, all wanting to
know the background of the bill. Since he had no idea
of what was in the bill or in the message he could only
look wise, say nothing and watch those around him.

Of all the men in the lobby Garner showed the most
positive disapproval, although as it turned out he was
to support the plan for a while. The courtly Ashurst,
usually so conspicuously clothed in a slightly awry statesman's toga, usually so promptly loquacious on any subject, was silent and withdrawn for once. Within a fort-
night before he had made his "prelude to tyranny"
speech, denouncing court packing, giving the name of
"libelers" to those who imputed such an intention of the
President, and calling for his omnium-gatherum amendment. It took Ashurst a whole day to make up his mind,
and it was late that afternoon when he issued his one-
line statement that he was in "favor of the President's
proposal", through the office of the secretary of the

Senate. Among the others Senator Nathan L. Bachman, the witty, sensible Tennessee Democrat who was Keenan's closest friend, showed some misgivings; he was destined to become an opponent of the bill, and his death would later be greeted with delight by the administration as a chance to put an adherent in his place. The rest showed, first, amazement and, second, admiration of the President's daring in pulling so large and startling a rabbit so suddenly out of his hat.

On that first day, taking it by and large, there was every evidence that the President's brutal take-it-or-leave-it strategy had succeeded. In a statement dictated huggermugger in the hour between the cabinet meeting and the convening of the Senate, Joe Robinson approved the bill and predicted that it would pass. Speaker Bankhead echoed Robinson, and other eminent administration Democrats followed along. Sumners immediately informed White House emissaries of his decision to oppose the plan, but he agreed to keep silent for a while. Ashurst reversed himself. Although the Republicans foamed expectedly at their mouths and one or two of the firmest Democratic conservatives, like Senators Edward R. Burke, of Nebraska, and Harry F. Byrd, of Virginia, joined them in announced opposition, the reports that trickled into the White House were handsomely reassuring.

The President congratulated himself on having done it again, and gossiping, goggling Washington was strongly inclined to agree with the President. The general view of the situation was best summed up that evening by Senator Carter Glass, whom the President well named the "unreconstructed rebel." Almost eighty, the old Virginian was the last representative of an earlier American conservatism, for which sound money, states rights and economical government had not become less important than the freedom of industry to do what it pleased and the ultimate authority of big business. He had known a Civil War childhood; as a self-made editor he had taken a principal part in the politics of his state; he had served Wilson as Secretary of the Treasury and declined to serve Franklin Roosevelt; he had been elected to the House nine times and to the Senate four, without ever once promising the voters anything except to act as his conscience dictated. He hated the court plan with every fiber of his body, and when a reporter telephoned him at his home in Lynchburg to ask him how he stood he proclaimed it openly. The reply to the reporter's question came back over the wire so clogged with the old man's bitter scorn for the spinelessness of a Congress which did not share his hatred that each sibilant was a sharp, separate hiss.

"Of course I shall oppose it," Glass said. "I shall oppose it with all the strength which remains to me, but I don't imagine for a minute that it 'll do any good. Why, if the President asked Congress to commit suicide tomorrow they'd do it."

Thus Washington on February 5. The President has the habit of reading the papers while he breakfasts in bed, so it was over his breakfast tray that the first wave of national reaction broke noisily the next morning. He scanned the editorial pages with more than a trace of ruefulness and some anger, for prophecies of ruin and warnings of dictatorship to come were editorial writers' small change that day. The reactionary newspapers, which is to say the large majority, sounded like a swampful of banshees on a bad night. The great old-fashioned liberal journals, the middle-of-the-roaders which had been coldly friendly to the New Deal, gave excellent imitations of Mr Gladstone hearing that one of his reformed harlots had hit the primrose path again. Even that small group of highly influential papers, the much valued supporters of the President during the election campaign, behaved like hens which had hatched out, not a swan, but a cockatrice. The only abstainers from the general chorus were Joseph M. Patterson's powerful New York *News,* J. David Stern's Philadelphia and New York papers, the *Record* and the *Post,* the labor and left-wing press, and a number of papers in the South.

But the hollow ineffectiveness of the press had been pretty completely demonstrated by the election, and the President had made up his mind in advance that the press would oppose him. It was far more disconcerting, therefore, when letters and telegrams, nine to one against the plan, began to pour in on a frightened Congress and when the shrieks of the editorial pages deepened to a roar of protest from all over the country.

The atmosphere of the time immediately after the plan's announcement is impossible to reproduce in full. It was too strange, too uncertain, too charged with variable forces to be fully apprehended, even then. All over the country the most singular persons began to strike attitudes and declare their readiness to "save America." A township of prosperous Connecticut commuters, ex-Landonites to the last man, solemnly went through the ancient ritual of a New England town meeting and wound up with a carefully antiqued "memorial" against the court bill. Richmond Pearson Hobson, the elderly prohibitionist hero of Manila Bay, flew to the Court's defense. Almost overnight highly bogus "Committees to Preserve Our Liberties", "Associates for America" and dozens more of the same sprang up like mushrooms on the compost heap of idiocy which is the political thinking of a huge class of the American rich.

But the hullabaloo was not all nonsense by any means. There were plenty of indications of how deep the issue went, of how determined the opposition to the President would be. Bar associations met and condemned the bill furiously. The churches, and especially the Roman Catholic Church, always nervous over religious liberties and grateful to the Court for strong decisions protecting them, showed signs of acute uneasiness. The senates or assemblies in several states, including Texas and Nebraska, prepared to pass resolutions against the court bill. No day passed without a statement from some more or less eminent citizen, often one who had favored the President for re-election, bitterly denouncing his court plan. Worst of all, there were signs that Middle Class America, the plain people who had voted for the President in droves, was stirring uneasily and questioning the plan's wisdom.

The President was taken completely by surprise by the strength of the national reaction. His criterion for judging it had been the pitifully ineffectual Republican campaign. He had foreseen the same sort of shambling, apologetic, shamefaced appeal. Instead the roar of protest was unified, reverberant and clearly meant business. By and large, in those first weeks, the major voices in it were the same voices which had cried out against the President during the campaign—the press betrayed this rather clearly in the excited prominence it gave any protests coming from persons or groups who had supported the President. But where they had been on the defensive during the campaign, they were on the offensive now. It was this and the new uneasiness of the middle class which the President failed to recognize. After the first shock he told his advisers that the reaction was precisely what might have been expected; that the protests were tainted at the source and that they should not be taken as indicating anything but the gathering of the "economic royalist" cohorts for a last stand.

"The people are with me. I know it."

That was the President's theme, repeated over and over again, to his advisers, his lieutenants, his wavering supporters, anyone who would listen. Yet some things happened which he strangely failed to take into his account when he mocked the opposition. Men like Oswald Garrison Villard and John T. Flynn, men who certainly could not be called economic royalists, publicly castigated the plan. Morris L. Ernst and other like-minded liberals set desperately to work behind the scenes to get a substitute accepted. Such defections thoroughly astonished the President. He could scarcely believe it when old friends, men who had always been counted fervent New Dealers, joined the opposition's ranks, as many did in the very first days after the plan's disclosure. And one of the defections hurt the President deeply. It was that of Felix Frankfurter.

American public life has produced no more curious phenomenon than Frankfurter. A perfect specimen of that daring but disinterested intellectual type which is the splendid flower of the Jewish people, he had in him a strain of practicality which enabled him to do what so many intellectuals cannot—make himself and his ideas felt. Born in Austria, brought to this country in 1894 at the age of twelve, he made his mark early as an immensely brilliant student of the law. Only eight years, chiefly occupied in such public offices as that of assistant federal district attorney, elapsed between his graduation from Harvard Law School and his appointment in 1914 to be one of its professors. In that post he came to be the intimate and cherished friend of Justices Holmes and Brandeis; he made himself known as a great legal scholar; he fought nobly for the lives of Sacco and Vanzetti; above all he became an influence on the thought of his most promising pupils. Each year the best of the students left the law school inspired with Frankfurter's humane, realistic, rather left-wing liberalism.

When the New Deal began he acted not only as a one-man employment agency but also as the most intimate and potent of the President's private advisers. He knew the young liberals of America as no other man did, and he supplied literally scores of them, men whom he had taught to believe that government is the servant of all the people, to fill key positions in the new administration. For this reason, and also because of his closeness to the President, Frankfurter had more responsibility for the liberal intellectual cast of the New Deal than any other single individual.

With the President his relationship had been so intimate that during his first administration "telephoning Felix" was an almost daily habit of the President's when Frankfurter was not in Washington. They had drifted apart somewhat before the court plan was hatched—Frankfurter knew nothing of the plan until its disclosure—but nevertheless the President would probably have preferred Frankfurter's good opinion to any other. And Frankfurter heartily disapproved of the court bill for two reasons. While he disliked court packing, he was willing to let that pass, but he could not stomach the silly, misleading indirection of the approach or the cruel injury which the age pretext did to the first New Dealer of them all, eighty-year-old Justice Brandeis.

During the course of the fight he showed his hand only once, when an anonymous article on American politics appeared in the British magazine, the *Round Table*. The article, which was written by a Washington newspaperman, suggested Tom Corcoran and Ben Cohen as the probable authors of the court bill. Corcoran and Cohen are two of Frankfurter's boys. Both are close to him; he admires both of them warmly.

Therefore the article annoyed him deeply and he wrote
off a letter of protest to an American friend whom he
wrongly imagined to be the writer of the *Round Table*
article. His letter was forwarded to the editor of the
British journal, and from England excerpts trickled
back to Washington. Otherwise Frankfurter disclosed
his feelings only to his intimates. Thus his attitude
towards the court plan was chiefly important as a symptom, but merely as a symptom its importance was tremendous.

Other men with Frankfurter's sympathies were even
more upset than he by the indirections of the plan, but
the plan's indirections were not the only thing about it
that upset the liberals. The precedent it set, the pre-
scriptive right to tamper with the judiciary it gave the
executive and legislative branches, frightened many
liberals who feared its use in the future by conservative or semi-Fascist administrations. The fact that it
failed to provide a permanent remedy for the Court's
right of review annoyed many others who held the left-
wing opinion that the Court's right is no right but a
wrongly assumed power.

These doubts from the natural supporters of the
court plan might have been forgotten had not the President's substitution of sophistries for real arguments
weakened the whole favorable response. Instead of dis-
guising court packing in a "reorganization of the
judiciary" the President had succeeded in making the
court packing the only thing anyone thought about for
an instant, whereas by another presentation he might
have kept the behavior of the conservative justices uppermost in every mind. The disguise was obviously the
most flimsy sham, and the President had let himself
appear ashamed of his best appeal, that the Court had
to be packed because certain things had to be done which
the Court had wrongfully and arbitrarily forbidden.

The President's three momentous preparatory decisions, to pack the Court, to pretend not to and to consult no one on his plan, were already bearing fruit to set his teeth on edge, but the President appeared blandly unaware of it. The opposition of the conservatives proved far stronger and more aggressive than he had expected, and he only repeated, "The people are with me." The liberal united front so vital to his welfare in the coming fight had strikingly failed to materialize, and he had a tag for that too. He and his circle use a contemptuous name for any man who chooses to oppose them, whose liberal record is too good to let him be lumped in with the Tories, self-interested economic royalists, Lord Macauleys and the like. They call such men "perfectionist liberals", and it was as "perfectionists" that the President dismissed the liberal opponents of the court plan.

Precisely the same forces were at work in the New Deal's congressional following as in the country at large. Among all but a dozen or so of the most rabidly enthusiastic there was a gnawing uneasiness, and the congressional leaders themselves, Robinson and Garner, Bankhead and Rayburn and the others, privately regarded the President's demand for a round half-dozen additional justices as "pretty raw", as Robinson put it. The "raw" flavor in the plan made them as uncomfortable as cockchafers impaled on a particularly large pin, and they cast eagerly about for ways to get off. First they had hopes of Hatton Sumners' judicial retirement bill. They thought that perhaps the right-wing justices would leave the Court in spite of the court plan, and so the measure was rushed to passage in the House on February 10 and hurried over to the Senate. The odds were ten to one it was too late, for the justices would have to leave the Court under fire, but there was just the off-chance that if the bill became law Congress might be spared the disagreeable necessity of acting on the court plan at all.

Then they hoped that the President might be willing to accept a smaller quota of new men on the high bench. All the leaders thought that in asking for so many extra justices the President was simply showing his good horse-trading training. In the face of the violent reaction in the country and the uneasiness in Congress they considered it wisest to begin arranging a compromise at once. A group of them, led by Garner, went to the President to put their case before him. They told him that they thought he should have some sort of law to meet the court problem, and they promised to get it for him. They asked to be empowered to fix the thing up, probably on the basis of two or three instead of six additional justices, and they warned him that the issue was tearing at the vitals of the Democratic party in Congress. The President laughed in their faces, so loudly that a number of them were exceedingly annoyed and resolved there and then to offer no more advice unless it should be requested of them. Indeed the President was in a laughing mood in those days, when suggestions of compromise were made. An individual senator, who was frankly opposed to the bill, also pressed him to ask for a smaller number of justices. He answered with a broad smile:

"Why, Senator, would you *pack* the Court?"

It is hardly surprising that a few of his harder-headed advisers thought the President was living almost in a dream world. His insistence that the "people were with him", the calm carelessness with which he accepted the news of serious defections in his own ranks as well as the roars of a united opposition, his constant references to the election and the use he made of it as the text for a sermon on optimism, his firm refusal to listen to his leaders in Congress—all these were alarming symptoms.

It was not that his fight was lost. The fight was anything but lost, for the court problem remained to be solved, the country wanted it solved, and he could enforce his plan as the solution. It was his strange failure to recognize the difficulties of his fight that troubled his advisers. When he cheerfully announced to them that he would make no speech on the plan in February, that he would not mention it in his scheduled address to the Democratic victory dinners on March 4, and that he would maintain his silence until after his return from Warm Springs several weeks after that, they were all but frenzied. They pled for an immediately aggressive policy. He replied that there was no need to bother, predicted that if he deferred speaking the opposition would weaken so fast that he could knock it out with only one or two strong oratorical punches, and once more repeated his theme:

"The people are with me. I know it."

RECRUITING

February 5–February 19, 1937

POLITICAL CONFLICT is different from ordinary warfare: the armies are largely recruited after the war begins. This was especially true of the court fight, in which the attack had been so secretly prepared. While the reactions to the plan, from the press, the politicians and the country, supercharged the Washington air with a tense excitement, the really important events of the first two weeks after the plan's disclosure took place quietly in the lobbies and corridors, restaurants and offices at the Capitol. A word given over a luncheon table in one of the dingy restaurants where the legislators feed themselves, a half sentence dropped between puffs at a senatorial cigar in the Democratic cloakroom, a vehement promise to a little group in someone's office —these were what tipped the balance one way or another, for or against the President. Both sides were recruiting as though their lives depended on it.

On the administration side, the President was in active command of his forces. His usual procedure in great legislative engagements had been to let his congressional leaders provide the generalship, while he merely received their reports and accepted or rejected their suggestions. But this fight was different. As rulers will when they feel a campaign calls for real ability, he had superseded his generals and taken the field in person. His habit of consulting his congressional leaders had been broken by the election, and something of his new carelessness of their opinions may be seen in his reception of their compromise demand. Now it was a rare occasion when he conferred with them at all.

Only Joe Robinson, the big, brutal, forceful man who served the President as leader of the Senate, could not be dispensed with. He was a bashaw too powerful and too useful to be thrust aside, and while his advice was anything but eagerly sought, his help in herding his fellow senators into line was calmly called for. For the rest the President chose his chief lieutenants from the White House inner circle. Corcoran, Cohen, Charles West, Keenan, Bob Jackson, James Roosevelt, Charles Michelson—these were the President's principal advisers and the officers of his troops. They made a sort of general staff at the White House.

Of the group Corcoran was perhaps the most important, because he was able to speak most often and most authoritatively in the President's ear. Comparatively young—about thirty-five—his rather cherubic appearance and his keen, springing, unhampered mind combined to make him the perfect infant prodigy of politics. He first signalized himself at the Harvard Law School, where his brilliance is still recalled; thence Felix Frankfurter sent him to serve a term as secretary to Justice Oliver Wendell Holmes, whose favorite protégé he was; from the great Holmes's chambers he went to a New York law office, but, bored with the prosperous intricacies of corporation law, he seized the opportunity offered by an opening in the counsel's office of the Reconstruction Finance Corporation and returned to Washington again towards the close of the

Hoover administration. Thus he was already on the ground when the President was inaugurated. As one of the brightest of Frankfurter's bright young men, he found the New Deal just his dish, and soon after the first inauguration he began the rapid rise through the crowding ranks of competitors which ended when he found himself closer to the throne than any other. He was a sort of Ivan Petrovsky Skivar among the New Dealers.

He could imitate Irving,
Tell fortunes at cards and play on the Russian guitar;
In fact quite the cream of the Muscovite team
Was Ivan Petrovsky Skivar.

He could play the accordion, sing any song you cared to mention, read Aeschylus in the original, quote Dante and Montaigne by the yard, tell an excellent story, write a great bill like the Securities Exchange Act, prepare a presidential speech, tread the labyrinthine maze of palace politics or chart the future course of a democracy with equal ease. He was volatile in his ideas and rather Jesuitical in his methods, a good friend and a venomous enemy. His talents made him a great favorite with the President, who bestowed on him the accolade of a nickname, "Tommy the Cork", otherwise reserved for Secretary of the Treasury "Henry the Morgue" Morgenthau and Judge "Sammy the Rose" Rosenman. Extremely ambitious but also sincere, with all his versatility he was a public servant of a caliber seldom found in the government. Unfortunately he had marked defects for the job he had to do.

He and Joe Keenan were jointly assigned to handle the Senate—a heavy responsibility and a very difficult one. Corcoran went into it handicapped from the start by his faint contempt for the legislative process, which he regarded as a messy business, to be got over

as quickly as possible, like an attack of the mumps, and
by the fact that being infinitely more intelligent and
better informed than most senators, it was very hard
for him to get along with all but the most sympathetic
and the most venal. Keenan, on the other hand, was
an ideal choice. A short, red-faced man, with a flavor of
the race track and the political clubhouse about him, he
reassured the legislators by his mere appearance. And
while he did not pretend to share Corcoran's intellectualism he had plenty of shrewdness, plenty of hard
practical ability and an honest devotion to the President and his objectives.

His debut in the New Deal occurred in 1933, when
he left a Cleveland law practice for a post in the Justice Department's criminal division. There he caught
the eye of Cummings, who appointed him his assistant,
with special powers over judicial patronage. The large
senatorial acquaintance which he made while dealing
out the judgeships and the fact that the Justice Department had to be represented in the management of
a judiciary bill procured his admission to the arcana of
the White House. A new man, he was at something of
a disadvantage in the inner circle, whose members hold
cheaply the practical politicians they do not disdain to
use.

The assignment of Corcoran and Keenan to manage
the Senate was an innovation, for Joe Robinson had
always before been allowed a free hand. The assignment of Charles West to dragoon the House into
obedience merely continued an established custom. By
title Undersecretary of the Interior, West had been
the White House's extremely effective lobbyist among
the representatives ever since 1936. He started his
career as a political economist at Harvard and elsewhere, and it was from the chair of political economy
at Denison University that he had come to Washing-

ton in 1931 as one of Ohio's Democratic congressmen. After two terms he made the mistake of trying to get the party's senatorial nomination in Ohio away from the champion baby kisser of the United States, Senator Vic Donahey. He was defeated, and the President, who recognized a useful man when he saw one, soon gave him the Interior Department place, with the understanding that his real work would be on the Hill. Tall, gangling, pleasant mannered and wisely shrewd, with bat-wing ears into which unhappy lawmakers loved to pour their troubles, West made himself indispensable among the representatives and at the White House. He stood a little apart from the other members of the inner circle, however, not only because his duties were more specialized, but also because his habit of mind was more independent.

The fourth important personage in the little group was the President's son, James Roosevelt. Amiable, handsome, politically ambitious, he owed his position to his father's desire for someone about him whom he could trust completely, someone whose interests were inseparable from his own. He had been brought to Washington to serve his father as secretary only a few months before, and Washington was already making little jokes about "the crown prince." In manner and, as much as possible, in thought he patterned himself on the President, and the relationship between the father and son was very close. A good many in the White House circle disliked him, for they regarded him as an interloper, and they saw him superseding them in the cherished privilege of the President's ear. Once before the President had planned to install him in the White House offices, but his competitors for presidential favor had succeeded in persuading the President to revoke the order. Now he had become a fixture, and the rest of the inner circle accepted the situation with what good grace they could muster.

Corcoran, Keenan, West and James Roosevelt were the principal officers of the new general staff. Another presidential secretary, Stephen Early, was a minor member, and old Charlie Michelson, publicity man for the Democratic National Committee, whose industrious ghost-writing had long made Democratic orators suspiciously literate and intelligible, also sat in on the staff meetings with his assistant, Edward L. Roddan. Robert H. Jackson, the agreeable, mild-mannered upstate New Yorker who brought to the assistant-attorney-generalship a remarkable intelligence in a very hard head, was an occasional adviser, while Ben Cohen, Corcoran's equally brilliant but somewhat less excitable partner, spoke in the council chiefly through his friend. Both Corcoran and Cohen worked closely with Jackson; the trio formed a sort of intellectual bloc. Each of the other staff officers operated alone, although there were the friendships and enmities which naturally grow up in any small, closed corporation. Equally naturally, they all played the game of palace politics; except for Jimmy Roosevelt, whose position put him hors concours, and Michelson, who was too world-weary to bother, they all competed for the President's ear.

They were informed of their new preferment above the congressional leaders almost immediately after the court bill was announced, and they promptly took over the leadership in the fight under the President. To coordinate their efforts they formed the habit of holding daily general staff councils in the White House offices. Sometimes they gathered early in the morning, before the senators and representatives had reached the Hill; sometimes the meetings took place in the late afternoon when the legislators had dispersed again to their homes;

occasionally there was a staff lunch. Reports were made,
new strategy was suggested and criticized, expedients
were adopted and plans for the future laid at the daily
councils. The members of the staff also reported indi-
vidually to the President, but James Roosevelt acted
as his father's eyes and ears on ordinary occasions. If
there was an argument he related the opinions of both
sides to the President, and the President decided between the two; if there was no disagreement on a proposed plan he put it before the President, received his
approval and brought the approval back to the council
of the next day. There was ample work to do from the
start, for there were immediate signs that the President had seriously underestimated the opposition's
probable strength in Congress.

One of the most disquieting came the very morning
after the court plan's disclosure, while Homer Cummings and Keenan, who had just learned he was to be
detached from the Justice Department to serve on the
general staff, were going over the Senate list together.
Cummings exhibited a supreme confidence, learned
from the President. Of the Senate's membership at that
time, seventy-five were Democrats; sixteen were Republicans; one, Bob La Follette, was a Progressive;
one more, George Norris, was an independent; the two
Minnesota senators, Shipstead and Lundeen, were
Farmer-Laborites; and one of South Dakota's seats
was vacant. The President was counting on all but a
few of the most confirmed Tory Democrats as well as
all four of the minor party left-wingers, and he even
had hopes of two of the Republicans, Nye and Frazier,
of North Dakota. Cummings made the presidential
estimate his own and outlined it to Keenan. Keenan
disagreed with him flatly.

He warned Cummings that the administration would
have to expect defections in the ranks of its most de-

pendable supporters, and he named Senator Joseph C. O'Mahoney, of Wyoming, and Senator Tom Connally, of Texas, as likely to oppose the President. The small, eloquent O'Mahoney had received his first big political boost as Postmaster General James A. Farley's assistant, had landed in the Senate from that springboard and had made a name for himself as a serious, energetic and convinced New Dealer. The representative of a beet-sugar state, he was also heavily obligated to the administration for help on sugar bills and would need more help in the future. As for the japish, clever Connally, he had a long record of Democratic orthodoxy, and he owed the President much for a personal interference on his behalf in the last Texas primary. Cummings remembered all these things and laughed in Keenan's face.

Somewhat irritated, Keenan made an immediate effort to prove his point. O'Mahoney, he knew, was sick in bed at the Wardman Park Hotel. He did not wish to disturb a sick man himself, but he thought that Jim Farley was close enough to the Wyoming senator to call him at any time. Keenan promptly telephoned Farley. As it happened, the Postmaster General was in New York, but his Washington staff put Keenan through to him on a roundabout telephone hookup. Keenan made his request that Farley check up on O'Mahoney. A full week passed before Keenan heard from Farley, but he knew that Farley must have reached O'Mahoney an hour or so later, when O'Mahoney himself called the Justice Department. He had learned, he told Keenan, that there was some question about how he stood on the court bill. Well, he would be glad to say how he stood. He considered the court bill "obnoxious", "undemocratic" and an "insult to the Senate", and he would never be able to "stand for" it. And not so very long thereafter Keenan's pre-

diction as to Connally was confirmed, when Connally
publicly committed himself against the court bill—
thereby enraging the President, who accused him of the
blackest ingratitude.

Meanwhile the conservative Democrats, whose beliefs and inclinations only differ from those of the Republicans in that few of them are dominated by large
industry, proceeded to join the opposition en bloc.
Glass and Byrd, of Virginia, Smith, of South Carolina,
George, of Georgia, Copeland, of New York, Gerry,
of Rhode Island, Edward R. Burke, of Nebraska, and
nearly a dozen more went over in the first few days.
The same process was at work in Congress as in the
country. The groups which had been disunited, chick-
enhearted and on the defensive during the campaign
were now united, determined and full of a new courage.
The President actually almost enjoyed the reports of
these defections, however, for his desire for a remade
Democratic party was always present in his mind.

The really upsetting disappointment of the first days
was West's discovery that Hatton Sumner's strong
stand had produced a majority of five against the bill
in the House Judiciary Committee. Such a state of
affairs in the usually servile House was a severe blow.
In the first place the committee hearings could not be
controlled by the administration. And in the second,
an unfavorable majority in the committee meant that
the House could only take up the bill after a public
display of administration strong-arming. A petition of
218 members to discharge the committee or a suspension of the House rules by a two-thirds vote were the
necessary preliminaries to action, and under these circumstances the rules required that action be deferred
for a while. The House leaders, Speaker Bankhead and
Sam Rayburn, strongly opposed both moves. They
could, they argued, dragoon the bill through the House,

but they judged that they would leave the House sore and angry and all the more ready to rebel once the bill came back from the Senate.

Bankhead and Rayburn converted West, and the three of them tackled the White House. They had up-hill work, for the President was used to making a grand public showing of his almost dictatorial power in the House before sending controversial measures to the Senate. The general staff was split wide open on the question. James Roosevelt alone remained on the fence. Keenan and Tom Corcoran were both extremely anxious to follow the usual procedure, and the other minor members of the group ranged themselves on one side or the other. Keenan and Corcoran maintained that, in the first place, the House could be handled much more easily than the Senate, since the fact that all the representatives must go before the voters every two years makes them unusually responsive to admin-istration pressure. And in the second place they pointed out that, even though strong-arming might be neces-sary, if the House could be successfully put through its smooth and servile paces the psychological effect in the Senate would be excellent. The discussions in the White House were protracted. In the end the President sided with Bankhead, Rayburn and West. It was agreed that the Senate should take the bill up first.

The general staff promptly concentrated every re-source on the Senate; all the administration's various allies in the chamber and out were called on for help, and the tempo of recruiting among the senators was tremendously speeded up. It was a piecework job, like all legislative recruiting. There was Senator James H. Hughes, of Delaware, a new member, but important because he had been assigned to the Judiciary Commit-tee. The Democratic Senatorial Campaign Committee, run by the redoubtable Joseph F. Guffey, of Pennsyl-

vania, had lavished help on Hughes in his struggle to
be elected. Senator Guffey was therefore told off to
handle him. Senator Robert J. Bulkley, of Ohio, was
talked round by his fellow Ohioan, Charles West, and
one or two other particular friends.

Chicago's Kelly-Nash machine was mobilized to deal
with Senator William H. Dieterich, of Illinois, another member of the Judiciary Committee. A strange,
sour, heavy man with the mentality and appearance of
the old-fashioned politicians whom Davenport used to
cartoon, Dieterich was strongly inclined against the
court plan, yet the Chicago bosses had little trouble
converting him. As he put it delicately to a member of
the opposition, he couldn't "kick the President in the
pants and get renominated." A third Judiciary Committee member, Senator Marvel M. Logan, of Kentucky, was also wavering. Kentucky wanted flood-
control legislation, and the state's ebullient governor,
A. B. "Happy" Chandler suddenly popped up in Washington, called at the White House and emerged to
reveal that Kentucky would have its flood control and
that Senator Logan would support the President's bill.
He even foretold that the senator would make two
speeches for the measure. Senator Logan later confirmed Governor Chandler's predictions as to himself
in full, although the manner of their making distinctly
irritated him.

The Kelly-Nash organization in Chicago was not
the only powerful political organization to contribute
a senatorial mite. With the possible exceptions of patronage and public money, nothing impresses political
bosses so much as the votes which bring these blessings,
and the feudal barons of local politics had been mightily impressed by the President's November victory.
Frank Hague in Jersey City; the aboriginal Pender-

gasts in Kansas City; the Louisiana ring, that incredible junta of Huey Long's ex-lieutenants who had made their peace with the New Deal after the timely withdrawal of tax suits against them known as "the second Louisiana Purchase"—they all did their duty like little soldiers, and Smathers, of New Jersey, Truman, of Missouri, and Ellender, of Louisiana, became sure administration votes. And where there were no bosses, no administration bigwigs to whom senators were obligated, no convincing friends, other persuaders were used.

So it is that the government has worked since the time of George Washington. What was unusual in the early days of the court fight was the supersession of the congressional leaders by the White House general staff and the energetic personal part publicly taken by the President. The President had an idea that the Senate was like a nervous horse, needing only a little gentling to make it obedient, and so his first step was to start interviewing the doubtful. The system, as he and the general staff planned it, was to call one or two waverers down to the White House with an administration supporter or so, to talk the bill over and to lead the waverers gently to the light. The idea was that if you put a gray sheep with a white and treated them both kindly, the gray one might turn white by contagion.

In view of his state of overconfidence, it is easy to understand why the President hoped for so much from the interviews, but they were distinctly disheartening. He asked for no commitments, but he rather expected to get some. He did not get any, and in lieu of a commitment he received, from one senator at least, a very solemn warning. The senator was a close White House friend, and he knew of the President's awareness of himself as a prominent personage in the history books

of the future. The senator began by criticizing the
court plan and predicting trouble for it in Congress.
The President pooh-poohed his criticisms, laughed at
his fears and reminded him of the vote on November 3.
After such a victory he could not be beaten, argued the
President. The senator rose and walked to the door.
At the doorway he turned.

"I'm not only thinking of the court plan and its effect
on the fundamentals of our government," he said rather
grandiloquently. "I'm thinking of Franklin D. Roosevelt. I don't want history to record that at the height
of his career Franklin D. Roosevelt suffered a bitter
defeat at the hands of Congress."

Usually when a friend gets to the home-truth stage
the President has a way of laughing the matter off. He
did so time and again during the court bill fight, but on
this occasion he neither tossed his head back with a
smile nor looked out the window as though uninterested
nor used any of his other mannerisms indicating disagreement and displeasure. Instead he flushed—
whether from annoyance or an inner doubt the senator
never knew—and looked straight ahead of him with a
fixed gaze.

Even so the President was still supremely confident
on February 19, the day on which the decision to open
the ball in the Senate was officially disclosed. His confidence was not without foundation. In the House an
informal poll conducted by West and Representative
Fred Vinson, of Kentucky, revealed a majority of one
hundred for the bill, and there were indications that
the majority could be brought up to two thirds of the
membership by the more extreme forms of administration pressure. In the Senate things were more ticklish.
The unanimity of the conservative Democrats, the defection of such regulars as O'Mahoney and Connally,
the painfully evident lack of enthusiasm among the

rank and file, all suggested that the situation there was doubtful.

Nevertheless, the President had the New Deal bitter-enders, like Sherman Minton, of Indiana, the future justice, Hugo L. Black, of Alabama, and the Wisconsin Progressive, Bob La Follette. He had such recruits as Dieterich and Bulkley and Ellender and Hughes. And he had the leadership and their immediate followers, who had finally accepted the fait accompli presented to them. On February 19 the men definitely committed to the court plan numbered about thirty. The number of those definitely committed to the opposition was roughly the same, leaving the power to decide to a great group of the center in which all but two, Shipstead and Lundeen, were Democrats.

Among these Democrats of the center doubt and dismay were all but universal, yet there were two immensely strong forces tending to hold them in line. The first, of course, was the party tie, greatly reinforced by the senators' desire to remain faithful to a President so loaded down with political laurels. And the second was their belief that something must be done about the Court's reactionary blockade of the New Deal. As has been remarked already, a solution to the court problem was wanted; the President had the power to enforce his bill as the only solution, and so long as the problem did not solve itself his power gave him an immense tactical advantage.

Once more roughly speaking, the Democrats of the center numbered thirty-three. To give the President a majority for his bill only eighteen had to resolve their inner conflict, between their doubts and their twin desires to see the court problem solved and to stay regular, in the President's favor. After testing the situation Joe Robinson reported that there would be better than a bare majority, that the President could count on fifty-four and perhaps fifty-five approving voices. Keenan, who had conducted an independent check for the general staff, was only one or two votes less optimistic.

Such was the foundation of the President's serene confidence. During the whole two weeks of frenzy after the announcement of his plan his confidence had wavered only once—during an interview with George Norris. The interview was the climax of an incident which, more than any other in the court fight, demonstrated how bad the President's judgment had been in laying his plan of campaign, how optimistic his assumptions. As in the cases of most of the others, there was, to be sure, some justification for the President's cheerful assumption that Norris, although too old to bear the brunt of hand-to-hand fighting, would take the intellectual leadership of the court plan's proponents the moment the plan was disclosed. No one had felt more strongly the need for action against the Court than the great old man of liberalism, the wise veteran of a lifetime's struggle for the poor and the oppressed, the politician who has been named the exception proving the rule: "The Almighty never made an absolutely honest politician." He had urged the President to fight the election on the court issue. He had spoken bitterly against the Court while the President was preparing his bill. He had a very strong bill of his own, requiring a seven-to-two vote of the Court to invalidate a congressional act.

Yet the President's assumption was dead wrong. Had he guessed right, so great was Norris' prestige, it is more than likely that there would have been no trouble from the doubting liberal element which eventually destroyed the President. Instead Norris disliked the court plan so heartily that he was on the point of going into active opposition to the President for the first time in the history of the New Deal. His reasons

were the same reasons which moved a number of liberals outside Congress to oppose the court plan. He
feared the precedent, asking himself how he would
have stood if "Harding had offered this bill." He was
distressed by the plan's failure to limit the Supreme
Court's power of review. And he not only disliked the
sophistries of the plan's presentation; he missed the
call to his warrior spirit which another presentation
might have made. His reasons seemed so fundamental
to Norris that on the very day of the plan's disclosure
he said flatly:

"I am not in sympathy with the plan to enlarge the
Supreme Court."

At the White House that statement caused not only
consternation but, among the men around the President
at least, downright anger as well. That the end justifies
the means has always been a great point of belief with
the more intellectual members of the President's inner
circle. Convinced as they are of the vital necessity and
wisdom of their schemes, these men have rarely boggled
at expedients promising to bring them closer to their
goals, and Norris' stand irritated them profoundly.
They murmured against him (and still do) as just one
more "perfectionist liberal", a man who could not work
with others, a man whose vision had been distorted by
pride of authorship of another plan. Nevertheless they
recognized that they could not do without him. The
President, who may well not have shared his close advisers' feelings, hurriedly summoned him to the White
House for a chat.

Norris obeyed the summons, and the President em-
ployed all his great persuasive arts to drive home his
powerful point—that no amendment could be got
through and that no other approach but court packing
was clearly constitutional. Norris was only partly convinced; he still hoped to procure the substitution of

another plan for the President's, but he left the White House willing to go along for the sake of getting some sort of action. Even so, his first distaste had been too public; his subsequent lack of enthusiasm was too marked. A deal of damage was already done.

It may well be asked just why Norris' failure to be enthusiastic was so damaging, why the nature of his doubts was so important, why his complete defection would have been such a deadly blow to the President. The answer was inherent in the situation. The President's bill had produced a united front among the conservatives. Every Republican, from Hiram Johnson, of California, to Warren R. Austin, of Vermont, was against it, and the Republicans had already been joined by every conservative Democrat, from George, of Georgia, to Walsh, of Massachusetts. But the conservatives were too few and too discredited by their complete rout in November to carry on the fight alone. Although they had picked up a few such moderates as O'Mahoney they could not hope to recruit a majority unless enough liberals joined them to take the curse of reaction off their cause. And even so the fight was all but hopeless so long as the President's bill remained the only solution to the court problem.

Those were two of the great questions confronting the opposition: Could some other satisfactory solution to the court problem be found? And: Would enough recognized liberals be impressed with the reasons which had made Norris doubt? There was still a third. Even if the liberals did join the opposition, would the conservatives be sensible enough to let them fight in the front lines, reserving for themselves a less conspicuous role? In an effort to answer the first and most pressing of the three questions virtually every senator who joined the opposition rather futilely offered his own patented constitutional amendment to curb the Court.

The other two had already been answered during those frenzied first weeks.

Only a day or so after February 5 the three most powerful Republicans in the Senate, Minority Leader Charles L. McNary, of Oregon, Senator William E. Borah, of Idaho, and Senator Arthur H. Vandenberg, of Michigan, met quietly at the Capitol. The wise, urbane, cynical McNary put a momentous suggestion before the meeting. He argued that if the Republicans lay low, if they avoided partisan expression like the plague, the Democrats would be greatly encouraged to fight among themselves. Borah and Vandenberg agreed, and each member of the trio promised to shut up his own Senate following.

Their troubles by no means ended there, however. If any of the small group of naturally loquacious statesmen recognized as entitled to speak for the Republican party should speak on the court bill, the senators knew that the jig would be up. First to be tackled was John D. M. Hamilton, chairman of the national committee. He was reached in New York immediately after the senators' conference, and he agreed willingly enough to keep quiet, for the time being at least.

Next on the list was Governor Alfred M. Landon. The vanquished presidential candidate was scheduled to address a Lincoln Day dinner of the National Republican Club in New York on February 9. The junta of senators shuddered when they heard that he planned to dedicate his whole speech to a sort of combined I-told-you-so and call to arms against the court bill. House Republican Leader Bertrand H. Snell was hurriedly dispatched to the city to catch him and quiet him. Unfortunately Landon got word of Snell's mission in advance and flew into the kind of temper any politician will fly into if you tell him that his utterances are likely to do anything but good. Consequently Republican

Vice-Chairman William Castle and Chairman Hamilton had to be mobilized. They met Landon at the train,
soothed him, as it were, in the taxicab and talked him
round in a long conversation at the Murray Hill Hotel.
His speech was rewritten that afternoon. As it was delivered that evening it passed over the court plan with
a solemn generality.

As though the arrival-of-the-marines in-the-nick-of-
time, *Perils of Pauline* flavor was not already strong
enough in the whole business, the hardest job of all was
still ahead. Immediately on the disclosure of the plan
ex-President Herbert Hoover had issued a bitter statement, and Borah, Vandenberg and McNary knew that
he was preparing a much longer and louder blast for
the radio. Over their cigars, in the late Pullman com-
fort of a Capitol office, the trio discussed the best approach to Hoover. As McNary and Borah had a lively
awareness that the ex-President detested them both,
Vandenberg was deputed to tackle him. Vandenberg
did not dare to beard him unprepared. He called in
Mark Sullivan, the columnist, a fishing crony of
Hoover's. One afternoon by prearrangement Sullivan
telephoned Hoover in New York and warned him
vaguely of what was coming. A few minutes after Sullivan had hung up Vandenberg put through a call.
Rather nervously he revealed the decision of the senators' meeting and asked Hoover to join in the conspiracy of silence. Hoover was deeply suspicious.

"Who was at that meeting?" he asked. "Who's trying to muzzle me?"

Vandenberg told him. At the mere mention of Borah
and McNary the ex-President exploded. For a good
many minutes the long-distance wire sizzled with a denunciation as strongly phrased and as strongly felt as
any to which Mr Hoover could have been provoked
by the court plan. Then Vandenberg returned to the

attack. His arguments were good, and Hoover was emotionally anxious to do everything he could to defeat the bill. Vandenberg won in the end, but his victory was only temporary. Hoover broke his silence briefly in a short speech at Chicago a few days later, and then word came from Palo Alto that he was once more at work on a full-dress excoriation of the bill for radio delivery. The senators were at their wits' ends. There seemed to be nothing to do but threaten to disclaim the ex-President, which Borah promptly did. As a last chance Hoover's friend, Henry P. Fletcher, general counsel and former chairman of the Republican National Committee, was sent to the West Coast to see what he could do. After a very *mauvais quart d'heure* he succeeded in his mission, although Hoover never abandoned his opinion that the Republicans were fools to stay silent.

Then Hamilton began to be a danger point. There was heavy pressure on the national committee to fling itself aggressively into the fight; the argument was made that the court plan would pass anyway, that if it did it would become a great issue, and that the Republicans ought to make the issue their own by abandoning their hole-and-corner policy. Along in March Hamilton was getting ready to succumb to the rich temptations of oratory—always so difficult for politicians to resist—and, what was worse, Vandenberg was inclined to join him. Borah and McNary managed to calm them, only to be confronted, a month or so later, with an announcement that Hamilton planned to hold a radio symposium of four nationwide broadcasts, to discuss the issues of the day. That time the senators really grew angry. Every kind of heat was applied to the over-eager chairman. He was told in rather frank terms what the senators thought of him; he was threatened with reprisals and soothed with kind words; Governor

Landon was called on to help sit on his head. Finally he abandoned, or rather, modified, his scheme, and so the Republican conspiracy of silence was successfully maintained until the very end of the court fight.

Probably no single thing so much annoyed the administration strategists as the Republican self-restraint McNary, Borah and Vandenberg schemed for that day so early in the struggle. Confronted for once by silent Republicans and a quiescent Liberty League—it, too, had been taken care of—the Democratic leaders were deprived of the irritant they had most relied on to give fervor and cohesion to their forces.

The conspiracy of silence was the opposition's negative gain, answering as it did the most pressing form of the question: Would the conservatives be sensible enough to let others fight in the front lines? A very positive gain took place at a lunch at the Dodge Hotel, about a week after the first meeting of McNary, Borah and Vandenberg. In the Dodges' rather dark dining room near the Capitol Tom Corcoran and Senator Wheeler, of Montana, the old allies of the Utilities Holding Company Bill battle, took refuge one midday from prying eyes. Corcoran opened the conversation, and Wheeler's understanding of his opening, vague as it had to be in such a delicate matter, was that Corcoran promised him he might nominate two or three of the new justices if he would go along on the court plan. Wheeler declined the honor. They argued about the bill for a while. Then Corcoran pounded the table.

"It's going to pass," he said.

"I tell you it isn't going to pass," Wheeler answered. "And what's more I'm going to fight it with everything I've got."

The discussion prolonged itself briefly. Corcoran warned Wheeler that he would regret his decision and pleaded with him at least not to take a leading part.

Finally he did get him to promise not to announce his position for a while. The lunch broke up with a certain coldness between the two men. Wheeler waited a day or so, then issued his statement on February 13. Before it was known downtown that the statement was in the hands of the reporters Charlie Michelson telephoned Wheeler. The President wanted his old friend Burt to dine at the White House that night, said Michelson. Would Wheeler come? Wheeler told Michelson that the President had better "save the plate for someone who persuaded more easily", and the invitation was not pressed. Thus it was that the opposition acquired its leader.

The opposition was very fortunate, for Wheeler had behind him a record of angry, often unrepaid but always unrelenting fighting on the liberal side which could be matched by few men in American politics. He had begun as an obscure young lawyer in Butte, Mont.; he had continued in his state legislature, and, once arrived in the United States Senate, he kept right on. His bloodthirsty investigations of the larger squalors of the Harding era, his energetic advocacy of public ownership of power and his warfare against the smug prosperities on other fronts, his vice-presidential candidacy on old Bob La Follette's Progressive ticket in 1924—these had made a sufficient name for him.

Before the 1932 convention he had had a deciding influence in lining up the Northwest delegates for Roosevelt, and at Chicago he had taken the lead in portraying the issue between Roosevelt and his competitors as the issue between liberalism and reaction. When the President was elected, therefore, he had had reason to expect some show of gratitude. He got none. His advice was not asked. His help was not called for, except in the single great instance of the Utilities Holding Company Bill, for passage of which in unsoftened form he was largely responsible. And his wishes were not consulted. His bitterest enemy in Montana was the powerful lawyer-lobbyist, J. Bruce Kremer, state national committeeman until the talk of his prosperous Washington doings grew too loud. Kremer stood for everything Wheeler most loathes—for bossism, for a friendly alliance with the financial interests, for tempering the governmental wind to the fat lamb. Wheeler thought he had a right to expect that Kremer would get no help from the administration in state politics; he deceived himself. Kremer's intimate friend, Homer Cummings, moved into the Department of Justice, and Justice Department patronage was lavished on the Kremer machine until Wheeler grew ragingly angry.

So when the court plan was proposed Wheeler was already in a rebellious mood. The dominant trait in his character is, moreover, suspicion, and while he was quite as anxious as the President to find some solution for the problem of the Supreme Court's arbitrary conservatism, he was deeply suspicious of the solution offered by the President. Essentially his liberalism is based on a sincere passion for good government. He had always disliked the strong personal flavor of the President's administration, which seemed wrong to him. Confronted with the court plan, he instantly saw what it implied—a heavy alteration of the whole governmental balance of power in favor of the White House—and, being suspicious, he feared there might be more to it than that. His rebelliousness, his vision of the plan's meaning, his suspicious fears, such a sharp distaste for court packing in general as George Norris had had—these influences all combined to make his opposition to the bill a prompt response to its proposal.

It was inevitable that he should have become the opposition's leader as soon as he joined it. He had all the necessary qualifications. A Democrat, he made the

fight nonpartisan. A liberal of unblemished record, he
was a counterspell for the curse of reaction. A veteran
in the Senate, he had reputation and experience to
clothe him with authority. Nor were his qualifications
confined to these outward suitabilities. His great forte
was legislative fighting. His suspicions gave him a peculiar prevision of the enemy's next moves. He was
energetic and tireless. He knew every twist and turn of
the legislative game, and he was not above using its
more brutal expedients if they promised to be helpful.
Although he had his good share of vanity he knew how
to soothe the vanities of others, and he worked well
with his team.

The effect of Wheeler's decision was felt at once.
The White House had relied on young Bob La Follette
to round up the independent left-wing votes of the
Northwest. Wheeler beat him to it. Senators Nye and
Frazier, of North Dakota, joined Wheeler as soon as
he had talked with them, and Senator Henrik Shipstead, the Minnesota Farmer-Laborite, was to be another, later Wheeler recruit. The opposition well
understood the tremendous gain they had made in
Wheeler. At a dinner for anti-court plan Democrats
given by Senator Millard E. Tydings, of Maryland,
Wheeler was officially recognized as leader.

Wheeler marked the occasion with a little speech.
Looking up and down Tydings' well-appointed table,
he saw most of the conservatives in the Democratic
party, men with whom he had disagreed on almost
every issue. He told them that he knew he was in
strange company, and he permitted himself a sardonic
calculation of all the improbabilities in one rather
fawning diner's promise to make him President. He
declared that he was delighted to be able to act with
them, but he warned them in strong terms that they
would have to let him and others like him do the lead-

ing for which he had been chosen. The senators present may not have liked being lectured by Wheeler; senators rarely enjoy being told what is what by someone else. But they fully understood the good sense of what he had to say.

A rough organization was also put together at the Tydings dinner. Its central element was a steering committee, whose outstanding members were Senators Frederick C. Van Nuys, of Indiana, Burke, of Nebraska, Peter G. Gerry, of Rhode Island, Byrd, of Virginia, Walter F. George, of Georgia, Josiah W. Bailey, of North Carolina, Bennett Champ Clark, of Missouri, Connally, of Texas, Tydings and Wheeler. The pale, precise, efficient Gerry was chosen to act as whip, and a remarkable system of intramural lobbying was set in motion. Day after day the active Democrats of the opposition camped on the trails of their close friends in the Senate, trying always to get commitments from them. Each day any news of any man's state of mind which an opposition senator picked up was passed on to Senator Gerry, and he prepared weekly lists of the Senate, showing the progress of the fight. Every day or so the steering committee of Democratic oppositionists met secretly, sometimes in a senator's office, sometimes in a convenient committee room, sometimes in one of the dingy little hideaways in the Capitol building to which Senator Clark and one or two others had keys. The meeting calls were sent out and other committee duties were performed by a regular secretary, Ben Stern, who was drafted from his everyday job as secretary to Senator Van Nuys. Liaison with the Republicans was constantly maintained, chiefly through the close working partnership between Senator Wheeler and Senator Borah, the old lion of Republican insurgence, the great veteran of the League of Nations fight, who was, after Wheeler, the most important figure in the opposition. Altogether it was a beautifully designed, smoothly running machine.

So ended the first two weeks of the court fight, for the opposition, with its formal organization under Senator Wheeler, and for the President, with the formal announcement of his decision that the Senate would be the best first battleground. Except for the fantastic last days those weeks were the most important period in the whole battle.

The administration had revealed surprising weaknesses—lukewarmness within the ranks of the Democratic faithful, an inability to hold the liberal allies all in line, above all the overconfidence in the President which blinded him to the true state of his affairs. The opposition had shown astonishing strengths—an intelligent unanimity of its conservative rank and file, an ability to attract the deserters from among the liberals previously allied to the administration, a capacity for effective organization. Two of the vital questions confronting the opposition had been answered—sufficient liberals were fighting the court plan to dilute the conservatism of the opposition rank and file, and the conservatives had shown sufficient sense to let the liberals lead the battle. Two great tactical advantages still helped the President—the Democratic party tie, and the need for a solution to the court problem—and it was pretty clear that unless the second advantage could somehow be taken from him he would win in the end.

The first two weeks of fighting were comparable to the so often decisive period in modern warfare, when one side attacks, the other, unprepared, defends, and all is helter-skelter for a while until the lines can be tightened, positions consolidated and trenches dug.

TRENCH WARFARE

February 19–April 12, 1937

THE TRENCH WARFARE period of the court fight began with the formal administration announcement that battle would be first engaged in the Senate, and lasted roughly two months. Where legislative conflict in the House takes the form of a quick, violent siege, soon decided one way or another, the unruly, unruled, loquacious Senate is ideal terrain for political trench fighting. When both sides are immobilized in a political struggle, neither has much to do but talk, and the senators are specialists in talk. The real events of this two-month trench warfare period were a series of bitter disappointments and unlucky mishaps for the administration, all tending to show a surprising weakness in the political reserves the White House was relying on. But talk was the period's most conspicuous feature. Steady barrages of oratory, long gas attacks at the hearings of the Senate Judiciary Committee were the publicly aggressive efforts of both sides.

The oratorical barrages had started long before February 19. Both sides had taken to the radio only a day or so after the President announced his plan, but now, as recruiting came to a standstill, the oratory

106

greatly increased. It is easy to make fun of such public speaking as the country was treated to during the court fight. Turgid, repetitious, crammed with non-sequiturs, richly ornamented with appeals to prejudice and self-interest, couched in an English which would have made Edmund Burke weep for very horror at the fate of the language—most of it was all these things. But it gave the country a chance to think the issue over. By sheer force of its repetitions it dinned the arguments for and against into the ears of the electorate, and by so doing turned the wheels of that intricate, slow and occasionally inefficient piece of public machinery, the Democratic process.

In the debate the opposition had one theme with half a hundred variations. "You must not pack the Court," cried the opposition, "because it will destroy the Constitution, because it will destroy the independence of the judiciary, because you have no mandate, because it will set a bad precedent, because you are a bad lot, because . . ." And so it went. The immediate result was a sharp split within the general staff at the White House.

On one side was Homer Cummings, who wanted to stick to the indirect approach he and the President had schemed out together. Obviously the hope that they had cherished, that the ground of argument might be shifted from court packing to the reorganization of the judiciary, had been frustrated at the start. But Cummings clung to his hope, arguing for continued emphasis on the law's delays, the refusals of petitions of certiorari, the age of the justices and all the rest of it. His trouble was that he did not cling very hard. He made one radio speech on the note which he considered correct; he told the President what he thought about the matter, and then he went off to Florida for a few weeks of sun, sand and sea.

Cohen, Corcoran, Assistant Attorney General Jackson and the other members of the inner circle, who stayed on in Washington, had the President's ear. Into it they poured their vociferous insistence that the opposition's strongest arguments could not be calmly ignored. They pled with the President to have the courage of his court packing. They pointed out that, after all, the Supreme Court features of the bill embodied its primary purpose, that unless resentment against the Court could be capitalized the fight was lost, that the President would seem worse than an ostrich if he followed the policy he and Cummings had laid down. The President did not hold out for long, and when Cummings returned from his vacation he found that the approach by indirection had been brutally jettisoned. The result of the whole business was exceedingly bad feeling between Cummings, who had no great love for the inner circle and regarded his plan with paternal pride, and the members of the inner circle, who had no great love for Cummings and were inclined to curse him for getting them all into a tight spot. Thus was born the first of the jealousies and suspicions which were to poison the relations of all the general staff around the President before the fight was done.

With the question of direct vs. indirect approach out of the way, the White House general staff concluded that their first job was to "sell the court bill to the country." The problem was much discussed at their almost daily meetings in the White House offices. At first they had great hopes for the formation of a sort of citizens' committee for the measure, headed by some such reassuring figure as Joseph P. Kennedy, the New Deal's tame capitalist. That scheme fell through. Then they turned to the Democratic National Committee. Jim Farley and Charlie Michelson were ordered to stage a great propaganda campaign. They set busily to work, writing speeches and arranging for their delivery, procuring the insertion of the more stirring addresses in the *Congressional Record* so that they might be printed and distributed broadcast in conveniently franked envelopes, going through all the other motions of political mass proselyting.

Even so the general staff's best resource in their effort to "sell the court bill" had not been brought into play. The President still kept silent. It has already been seen that he had a notion that the opposition would talk itself out and that then, just at the psychological moment, he would step in with a couple of rousing speeches, rally the country, rout his enemies, sweep up the pieces and pass his bill. What happened was just the reverse of the President's hope. In the first weeks of the court fight, when the present excitements of the struggle had not yet dimmed the memory of the election, members of Congress greatly feared the effects the President's talks to the nation might have on their constituents. Had he followed up his first surprise attack with a couple of hard-hitting speeches the opposition might not have been able to recruit its numbers, organize its ranks and harden its spirit. As it was, it had been allowed ample time to do all these things.

Corcoran, Jackson, West, Keenan and the others in the inner circle saw how things were going, and they made every effort to open the President's eyes. At first he would not listen. He insisted on his original plan to say nothing about the court bill at the Democratic victory dinners on March 4, to go to Warm Springs and to speak only after his return from his vacation there. But he could not play at "I see no evil" for very long. There were too many evidences of the correctness of his advisers' argument. The whole plan was changed. It was decided that he would make a fighting speech on the court bill to the celebrating Democrats on March 4 and follow it up with a "fireside chat" on March 9, just before the departure for Warm Springs was scheduled.

Cohen and Corcoran were chosen to be the principal contributors to both speeches, and work began. The initial move was the complete abandonment of the indirections of the message. No more was to be said about cluttered dockets or courts unable to get through their work; only the briefest mention was to be made of the failings of aged judges. The first speech was to be a loud rallying call to all the groups which had been relied on to support the court plan: the Democratic faithful, the farmers, labor, the liberals, the millions of people hopeful for adequate social security. All these were to be trumpeted to the colors and united behind the plan. In the second the President's personal leadership was to be emphasized and his great personal popularity brought into play. He was to answer the silly outcry against him as a potential dictator with a plea that the people trust him personally, as they had done in the past. Great hopes were built on the two speeches; as the President hinted in the first one, if they went over well enough it was planned to repeat the dose until the 27,-000,000 of November were all but up in arms and marching behind the court bill.

The first was duly delivered on March 4, before thirteen hundred Democrats who had paid a hundred dollars apiece to be present. The cream of the party's job holders was gathered in the big ballroom in the Mayflower Hotel, along with a scattering of lobbyists —one or two of these latter sat at the head table—and selected large contributors to the party's money chest. Some force had been used to pry the cash out of the faithful; the national committee's follow-up letters after the first invitation had plainly intimated that everyone receiving a government salary of more than so many thousands of dollars a year was expected to pay for tickets as a sort of job insurance; but by and large the job holders knew the party's value to them without having to be told about it.

Besides the thirteen hundred diners at the Mayflower, there were thousands upon thousands more at eleven hundred other victory dinners going on simultaneously elsewhere in the country. The spectacle at the Mayflower, the consciousness of the eating and drinking cohorts gathered together in eleven hundred other hotel dining rooms, barbecue grounds, excursion boats and the like, added up to a single overpowering impression. The diners, slightly drunk with prosperity and success and, here and there, more than slightly drunk with taxable liquors, the party bigwigs, the fattening lobbyists, the proud fat-cats, the smiling President—they all seemed to be saying at the tops of their voices, "Nothing can beat us."

The President twisted it a little, when the time came for his speech, to make it "Nothing can beat us if you follow me on the court plan." He told the listening Democrats that they had become the majority party in the nation because they had been willing to satisfy the desire of the majority for social legislation to meet the pressing problems of the time. He warned them that if they permitted the Supreme Court to stand in their road the people would find other, bolder representatives. He outlined the New Deal program and paid his respects to the Court.

"You know who assumed the power to veto and did veto that program," he cried.

The cheering swelled to a crescendo, then faded, and he went on, appealing to each group, group by group, warning each one that until the Court should be subjugated its desires could not be satisfied, "defying anyone" to say "exactly what, if anything, we can do" for the industrial worker, the farmer, the advocates of cheap power and flood control, of social security, low-cost housing, unemployment insurance and pretty much every other form of social legislation, "with any reasonable certainty that what we do will not be nullified as unconstitutional." It was the direct appeal with a vengeance, the direct appeal heavily reinforced by the trick of the carrot before the donkey's nose, and just to make it stronger he recapitulated the whole in his last paragraphs.

"Here is one third of a nation ill nourished, ill clad, ill housed—now! Here are thousands upon thousands of farmers wondering whether next year's prices will meet their mortgage interest—now! Here are thousands upon thousands of men and women laboring for long hours in factories for inadequate pay—now! Here are thousands upon thousands of children, who should be at school, working in mines and mills—now! Here are strikes more far reaching than we have ever known, costing millions of dollars—now! Here are spring floods threatening to roll again down our river valleys —now! Here is the dust bowl beginning to blow again —now! If we would keep faith with those who had faith in us, if we would make Democracy succeed, I say we must act—now!"

Such was the first speech. The Democrats applauded it to the echo, and the members of the opposition trembled and awaited the second. The second fitted neatly into the first. Where the first had been a frank appeal to the appetencies of natural supporters, the second was a reasoned attack on the Court and defense of the court plan, charged with emotion by the President's personal plea to his followers to trust him. As direct as the first, it ended with the vox humana stop pulled out all the way. The perfect voice came from ten million radios, full, rich, friendly, speaking as a friend:

"You who know me can have no fear that I would tolerate the destruction by any branch of the government of any part of our heritage of freedom. . . . You who know me will accept my solemn assurance that in a world in which democracy is under attack I seek to make American democracy work."

But the plea failed. A few letters and telegrams came in to senators of the opposition; there was the usual deluge of mail at the White House, but there were no signs that the speeches had changed the situation in any important fashion.

An angry White House argument had raged around the second speech. Several advisers, including Charles West, had been anxious to have the President announce his willingness to accept a constitutional amendment as a substitute for his bill if and when the opposition could agree on one and guarantee his getting it. Corcoran and Keenan and some others had thought the time unripe for such a gesture. They had argued that the fight was going their way, that it was time to drive ahead, and they had convinced the President. Now the drive ahead had failed; it looked as though the argument's losing side had been right after all.

Had West and his allies won, the result they had predicted—immediate disunion in the opposition—would almost surely have been obtained. There was hardly an anti-court plan senator who did not have his own private amendment. Wheeler's was for a sort of recall of judicial decisions by Congress, by a two-thirds vote after an intervening election. Borah's, a revision of the Fourteenth Amendment, definitely allowed the states all the powers over social legislation which the Court had denied the federal government. Burke's was for a straight judicial retirement age. O'Mahoney's required a seven-to-two majority of the Court to invalidate an act of Congress. And so they went. Nine chances out of ten, the opposition group would have been torn to bits in fratricidal combat if the President had asked them all to agree on one of their numerous amendments. His failure to make such an easy and meaningless gesture appears to have been one of his most serious tactical mistakes.

There was no question of tactics in the outstanding speech of the opposition, which was delivered twenty days after the President's fireside chat. There was nothing tactical about that address at all. It came straight from the heart of Carter Glass, of Virginia, full of an anger so intense that it came near being noble, charged with the force that can be derived only from absolute conviction. It was all but written in his blood, for he was a sick man when the court plan was announced, his wife was already sinking into her final illness, and his many years had laid their hand on him at last. Yet all through February and all through March he labored over his speech. It was his duty as he saw it to do all in his power to defeat the President, and, having seen it, he did it, although his hand trembled, the heavy lines in his face cut deeper and deeper, and sometimes it seemed as though he could hardly go on. There was something splendid in the old man's effort; a Tory, he would go down fighting for his Toryism. He was all of a piece and meant to remain so to the end. When the night came at last you could hear the history of the speech in the aged voice uttering the raging words.

"Confessedly I am speaking tonight from the depths of a soul filled with bitterness against a proposition which appears to me utterly destitute of moral sensibility. . . . Political janizaries paid by the federal treasury are parading the states in a desperate effort to influence the public against the Supreme Court of the United States. . . . [They would] pick six judicial

sycophants . . . , judicial marionettes to speak the
ventriloquisms of the White House. . . . The men
and women of America who value liberties . . . should
exercise their constitutional right of petition and, with
all the earnestness of their souls, protest to Congress
against this attempt to replace representative government with autocracy. . . . There has been no mandate from the people to rape the Supreme Court or
tamper with the Constitution. . . . He is no friend to
the President who would subject him to that biting
indictment, . . .

> *"He shall break his judges if they cross his word;*
> *He shall rule above the law, calling on the Lord.*
> *Strangers of his counsel, hirelings of his pay,*
> *These shall deal out Justice—sell—deny—delay.*
> *We shall take our station, dirt beneath his feet,*
> *While his hired captains jeer us in the street."*

Thus it was that Glass spoke out. The White House,
however, was infinitely more concerned over another,
earlier event. The general staff could bear with what
they thought of as the impotent fury of an old man, but
when the farm lobby failed them they knew it was serious. The farmers, the liberals and labor—these were
the great allied groups the President's strategy had depended on, and already the liberal united front for the
court plan was broken.

It was in the interval between the President's fireside
chat and Glass's speech that the general staff was finally
forced to face the new depressing reality—farm support had not materialized. The President had counted
on it unquestioningly. He had recalled the farm leaders'
outburst in November, when they turned a crop insurance meeting into a rally for the revival of the AAA.
He had planned a careful application of the carrot-
before-the-donkey trick to them. Shortly after the dis-

closure of the court plan he had let it be known that the AAA would be revived as soon as the court bill was passed. He had called the three most powerful leaders to the White House at about the same time, had put his case before them and had obtained one commitment. Edward A. O'Neal, president of the Farm Bureau Federation, biggest and most influential of the three organizations represented by the trio, had come out warmly for his plan.

O'Neal's endorsement of the plan was, however, purely personal. Simultaneously he privately told the President that he could not hope to speak for the Farm Bureau, and warned him that sentiment in the Farm Bureau's member organization might actually prove very strong against the plan. He promised that, if this should be the case, he would bend every effort to prevent positive anti-court plan action by his followers, but further than that, he said, he could not go.

Secretary of Agriculture Henry A. Wallace had been called to arms to mobilize the farm groups. Before the leaders, O'Neal himself, the elderly, slow-moving Louis J. Taber, president of the Grange, and E. E. Everson, president of the radical Farmers' Union, the secretary had waved the AAA decision as though it had been a red flag and they a pair of bulls. He had reminded them of all the New Deal's kindnesses to agriculture. He had promised kindnesses to come. He had pled and exhorted and warned them that the future would be dark if the Court were not curbed. But he could do nothing with them.

Taber, a solid conservative, prepared a statement against the bill, sent it to the head of each state Grange and asked for the state Grange heads' endorsements on it. Of the thirty-five state Granges, only four were opposed to the statement. One did not vote. The remaining thirty heartily backed Taber. The statement, which

bitterly excoriated the court plan as a threat to fundamental liberties, was accordingly issued one afternoon
in late February. The same day at lunch Wallace had
his last try at bringing Taber round. His failure was a
blow, of course, but the Grange had backed Landon, so
the general staff recovered from it. Their recovery was
only temporary.

First Everson, the radical, joined Taber. Then came
word that a poll of the member groups of the National
Co-operative Council, a progressively inclined association of farm co-operatives, had shown a large majority
against the plan. And finally the general staff learned
that O'Neal's private warning to the President, about
the real state of sentiment in the Farm Bureau Federation, had been only too accurate. That went to the
vitals, for the Federation was the favorite organization of the Agriculture Department, the cherished ally
of Secretary Wallace, the prize animal in the national
barnyard. But there was no getting away from it; it was
so.

At first the prospects had seemed good, so far as the
Federation was concerned, in spite of the O'Neal warning. The Virginia, North Carolina, Kentucky and Tennessee leaders had followed O'Neal in his support of
the bill. H. G. Lucas, president of the Texas Agricultural Association, another Federation affiliate, had been
converted by the President in person; he had hurried
home from the White House to issue a violent statement in favor of the bill and telegraph most of it to
Senator Connally. Meanwhile, however, O'Neal was
hearing from a very different group. Other state federa-
tions all over the country were writing, telegraphing
and even telephoning him to hold back. In every tone,
from the pleading to the threatening, they were asking
him to say no more and do no more in the matter. And
in one or two of the states whose leaders had imitated

O'Neal in making favorable personal statements, the same process was locally at work. The members of the Federation wanted to have nothing to do with the court bill.

The end came early in March, when the Federation's directorial board of sixteen met in Chicago. G. F. Holtzinger, of Virginia, one of those who were for the bill, arrived at the board meeting with a resolution in his pocket which would have officially put the Federation behind the President. Shortly before the formal meeting Holtzinger called on Chester Gray, the sagacious, slow-spoken Federation lobbyist. He showed Gray his resolution and asked him to edit it, since Gray was and is a sort of nonpartisan consultant in such matters to all Federation members. Gray glanced over the paper, grinned and remarked to Holtzinger:

"I guess you'd better nose around a bit before you present this, because they'll snow you under if you don't. There's only one or two members here who'll vote for it."

Holtzinger did nose around, and he found that Gray was right. No one but Ben Kilgore, Kentucky state Federation president, was ready to join him. The others were anti. They told him that they had talked to their people, that the people did not want any action for the President's plan and that they were not ready to take any. And thus the board meeting dragged on through two and a half days to its close without any formal mention of the court bill. All Secretary Wallace's cajoleries had come to nothing. After the meeting he tried once more to persuade O'Neal to use his personal influence, since he was personally for the court bill, but O'Neal told him frankly that he could do nothing in view of the feeling in the Federation. The administration was reduced to snatching at unconsidered

trifles on the farm front, and the President gave a full
forty minutes of his own time to persuading M. W.
Thatcher, leader of a minority wing in the Farmers'
Union, to go out into the Northwest and build fires
under Senator Wheeler in Montana and Senators Nye
and Frazier in North Dakota. Thatcher persuaded
easily—he was manager of the Farmers' National
Grain Corporation, a co-operative which is so heavily
indebted to the government that the Agriculture Department virtually owns it—but his efforts had very little effect.

The behavior of the farm organizations was the first
sign that there might be a popular dissent from the
court plan. Perhaps the leaders may not have known
what farm feeling was; if they were so unable to gauge
the opinions of their followers it is hard to see how
they had survived so long in the highly competitive business of running pressure groups. Secretary Wallace and
his cohorts at the Agriculture Department continued
to insist that the leaders were mistaken, but the leaders'
unanimous testimony was that the farmers were either
not interested in the court plan or angrily opposed to
it. The confident President went off to Warm Springs
convinced that Wallace was right and the farm leaders
wrong. He was magnificently unperturbed, even by the
far more serious indications appearing at this time that
labor pressure might not be all that was expected. The
President was beginning to pay the penalty for his decision to consult no one, to take no partners, but he did
not realize it.

Meanwhile the Senate Judiciary Committee hearings had begun on March 10, the day after the President's fireside chat. Preparations for the hearings had
started as soon as the decision had been reached to open
the battle in the Senate. Corcoran and Keenan were
charged with the work of preparation, and their first

step was to look the ground over. They found a distinctly disappointing situation.

The Judiciary Committee chairman, Ashurst, and Senators Neely, of West Virginia, Logan, of Kentucky, Dieterich, of Illinois, Pittman, of Nevada, and Hughes, of Delaware, were definitely committed to the President's bill. Besides these Norris was lukewarm and pushing his substitute, while McGill, of Kansas, was publicly uncommitted but privately inclined towards the bill. Definitely against were King, of Utah, Van Nuys, of Indiana, Burke, of Nebraska, Connally, of Texas, Borah, Austin, of Vermont, and Steiwer, of Oregon. O'Mahoney was privately strongly against, but he also was searching for a substitute which he could back. And, finally, Hatch, of New Mexico, and McCarran, of Nevada, were uncommitted either way. That gave Corcoran and Keenan a total of eight votes they could count on, eight they could count against and two undecided.

As though that were not bad enough, they saw at once that there was no really useful man among the administration supporters, except, of course, the lukewarm Norris, who was too anxious for a substitute to give them any help on the President's bill. One or two of the administration senators were able, some of them were enthusiastic, but there was not one with the quick wit and sharp tongue required for good hearing work. Here again the President was paying for the extreme secrecy of his preparations, for the cleverest cross-examiner in the Senate, Hugo Black, had been removed from the Judiciary Committee in January when he took the chairmanship of the Committee on Education and Labor. Corcoran and Keenan had to rely on the harsh, heavy-handed Neely, the coarse, clumsy Dieterich and McGill, a perfect small claims court lawyer.

And then Corcoran wanted to hasten the whole business, and haste and Senator Ashurst have never mixed well. Corcoran had a peculiar theory of legislative strategy born, no doubt, of his inherent contempt for the whole legislative process and of a long experience watching administration measures jammed through a subservient Congress. His idea was that after a measure had been before the Congress for two weeks everything that possibly could be said had been said; that after two weeks all discussion was repetitious, and that all that mattered was pressure. Considering the fact that the New Deal had hardly once been defeated on a major measure before the court bill, it may seem strange that he was convinced that the anti-New Dealers could bring the strongest pressure. Nevertheless he was.

Therefore he and Keenan told Ashurst to allow two weeks for presentation of the administration case and asked him to try to persuade the opposition senators to limit themselves to two weeks as well. At first they hoped that this arrangement might be made, but they reckoned without Burke and Van Nuys and Connally, who were handling the hearings for the enemies of the bill. The three had been chosen for the task at a meeting of the opposition committee members just before the hearings opened, and they made an admirable team. Connally, with his japish wit, was a perfect crossexaminer; Van Nuys, industrious, co-operative and fervent, was a first-rate detail man, and Burke was hunting a blood trail.

All three men were fighting the fight of their lives. Connally, a big man with a black string tie, oldfashioned clothes and long hair, whose air suggested he was one of nature's senators, had broken a long tradition of perfect Democratic orthodoxy to oppose the court bill and risk the mortal enmity of the President. Van Nuys, short, owl-eyed and bespectacled, with a simple, schoolmasterish manner, was already in trouble with the ruthless, dictatorial Democratic machine in Indiana when his opposition to the court bill marked him down as the object of the most wrathful malevolence. As for Burke, he was the court bill's most determined opponent in the whole Senate.

A prosperous Nebraska lawyer, Burke had dabbled in politics as the ally of the lobbyist-Democratic National Committeeman, Arthur Mullen, and the Mullen machine sent him to the Senate in 1935. Although the President, persuaded by Mullen, had given Burke a leg up in his campaign by quoting some words of his as the perfect definition of the New Deal, Burke left the administration reservation very shortly after his arrival in Washington. His opposition to the Utilities Holding Company Bill aligned him with the conservative Democrats, and his abilities soon made him a leader of that group. A short, heavy-bodied man with a slow, deep voice and an infinite capacity for taking pains, he was always a dangerous opponent. In the struggle over the court bill he surpassed himself, for he had a religious conviction that the right was on his side. He fought with the persistence of a bulldog, the rage of a bull and the calm disregard for rules of an angry woman.

When Corcoran's and Keenan's suggestion that the Judiciary Committee hearings be limited was put before Burke, Van Nuys and Connally, they flatly refused to make any agreement. They were not agreeing to anything with Keenan and Corcoran, not even the time of day. Then Corcoran and Keenan desperately urged Ashurst to force the committee to limit the hearings by resolution. The courtly statesman met their urgings with a polite, cheerful wail.

"Gentlemen, gentlemen, you should know how hard it is to get senators to agree to anything," he always answered. "Senators have their own minds, gentlemen;

they like plenty of time to express themselves. No, no, I can't get a motion like that through. No haste, no hurry, no waste, no worry—that is the motto of this committee."

Corcoran and Keenan, thoroughly exasperated, gave up for the time being and turned to the preparation of their case. The first witness was to be Cummings, the second, Assistant Attorney General Jackson. After them would come Professor Corwin, William Draper Lewis and other legal luminaries, the labor leaders, and Thatcher as a farm leader. They discussed the list of witnesses, and the order in which they were to appear, with Jimmy Roosevelt. As the general staff system was, he reported the plan in outline to the President and brought back a presidential approval. The approval was obtained; everything was ready, and Cummings took the stand on March 10.

Cummings made the indirect argument he favored. Jackson came after him with the direct approach approved by the inner circle and succeeded in presenting the most convincing defense of the bill offered during the whole court fight. The other witnesses followed in a succession which was daily made slower by the admirable organization of the opposition. The American Bar Association had offered its services to the enemies of the bill; Burke had taken advantage of the offer to suggest the establishment of a permanent research staff in Washington. Two or three important older lawyers and the cleverest young men from the largest law offices in the country had been assigned to the job, and promptly undertook the work of supplying the opposition senators with ammunition for use in the hearings. There was scarcely an administration witness whom the legal researchers had not caught in some sort of inconsistency, even before he came to the stand. The record of each was fully in the hands of Burke, Connally, Van

Nuys and their friends. Each witness was questioned exhaustively, and the sarcasms of Connally, the dogged hammering of Burke, the elaborate attacks of other opposition senators, all consumed about as much time as the actual testimony. Corcoran and Keenan fumed, privately convinced that the opposition was filibustering, but they could do nothing.

When the two weeks were up, less than half the administration witnesses had been presented. The opposition was not quite ready. Burke suggested that the administration take another week, give the opposition two weeks, and go on thereafter, each taking alternate weeks. Corcoran spurned the suggestion, in which he saw an effort to trap the administration into helping the opposition with its suspected filibuster. Corcoran and Keenan irritably closed the administration case on the spot—a serious error, for it allowed the opposition to hold the headlines thenceforward for an unconscionably long time.

While the administration witnesses were still on the stand the unwearying senators of the opposition had begun preparations for the cruelest stroke, purely from a debating standpoint, of the whole court fight. From the fight's start many of them had been anxious to bring the justices into it on their side, and the difficult problem was talked back and forth at the gatherings of the steering committee, among the opposition members of the Judiciary Committee, and whenever opponents of the court plan met together. The irrepressible Justice McReynolds ventured on a hinting speech at a fraternity dinner, naming no names but imputing poor sportsmanship to those who refused to accept the finality of the Court's decisions, but this was far from being what the senators wanted. At last it was decided to present to Chief Justice Hughes a formal request to testify before the Judiciary Committee.

Accordingly Wheeler, as leader of the opposition, King, of Utah, as the Judiciary Committee's senior Democrat, and Austin, of Vermont, as the representative of the Republicans, called on him one day, after the hearings had already begun. The Chief Justice received the three senators with his usual Jovian affability, and they made their argument, in which they put some emphasis on Cummings' denial of the Court's capacity to do its work. Although they had small hopes of any sort of success they optimistically suggested to the Chief Justice that Justice Brandeis ought to appear along with him. Hughes replied that he personally was willing enough to testify but must consult his colleagues before promising anything. A day or so later he sent a curt word to Wheeler that he could not appear. No explanation was offered, and the subject seemed to be closed.

As the time grew nearer and nearer for his own appearance before the Judiciary Committee as the opposition's opening witness, Wheeler became steadily more anxious to get some positive expression from the Court. He was to take the stand on Monday, March 22. On Saturday the twentieth he decided to try a long-shot chance. Justice Brandeis was an old and close friend of his; he went to call on him.

To Brandeis he put his case as forcefully as he could. Admitting the difficulties involved in the actual appearance of a member of the Court before the Judiciary Committee, he pleaded with the great old justice to make some substitute suggestion. Brandeis, who was far from unwilling to be helpful, thought for a while. Then he replied that, of course, it was quite out of the question for the Court to take any stand on the actual purpose or content of the bill to curb it, but that the procedural argument raised by Cummings and the President might afford an opening.

The whole elaborate fable about petitions of certiorari, the incapacities of aged judges to do their work and the rest of it could be destroyed, he said, and remarked that in his opinion the best recourse would be to a letter from the Chief Justice. Wheeler promptly asked Brandeis to say the same thing to Hughes. Brandeis refused, but gave Wheeler permission, after some urging, to telephone Hughes from his house, and to say that he was calling from there. Shaking with excitement, Wheeler picked up the telephone and got Hughes on the wire. To Hughes, Wheeler made the same argument he had made to Brandeis.

"You can't just lie down and let them do this to you," he said.

At first Hughes objected, but Wheeler vehemently reiterated his arguments. No doubt the fact that Wheeler had the tacit consent of Brandeis behind him gave an extra persuasiveness to his demands. At any rate, Hughes was brought round. The letter was promised. Then the Chief Justice asked for more time. He would need until Tuesday at the least, he said. His secretary and his clerks were gone, the week end had begun, and it would be too difficult to get the letter ready by Monday. To these objections Wheeler answered that the letter ought to be the very first item in the opposition case. Hughes saw the point. Finally he consented to haste and routed out his secretary. The document was composed in the last hours of that Saturday afternoon, and on Sunday Justice Brandeis and Justice Van Devanter, the other senior member of the Court, were shown what Hughes had written. They approved it, and it was recopied with the addition of a last paragraph indicating their approval. On Sunday evening Wheeler received the letter, and next morning he read it before the committee.

The committee's administration members were

utterly astonished and dismayed, for the letter was a masterpiece of exposition, striking down point by point all the procedural arguments in which the President and Homer Cummings had sought to conceal their real purpose. Of the petitions of certiorari, the Chief Justice said that the Court had been overgenerous in granting them, and so clearly explained the system on which they were handled that disagreement with his contention was all but impossible. Of the increase in the Court, he remarked that it could only decrease the Court's efficiency, and quoted justices of the past to prove it. And so it went. The indirections exposed by the letter had already been tacitly abandoned by the President, but in the public mind they were still his first line of defense. The effect of the Hughes letter was to show up for good and all as utterly hollow the smooth propositions with which the President had offered his bill, and the opposition's gain in the debate was tremendous. The President and the general staff at the White House were correspondingly furious with Hughes, whom they immediately convicted of playing unforgivable politics.

With the Hughes letter coming on top of the failure of the farm support, the poor response to the President's two speeches, the disunion among the liberals and the successful organization of the opposition, the general staff began to suffer from a severe attack of nerves. At the start, although they feared the effects of overconfidence on the President, the staff members had also been overconfident. They, too, were easily reminded of the November election. They, too, were inclined to doubt whether they could ever be beaten. Intelligent men as they all were, brilliant as some of them were, they lived too much in the President's aura to escape the influence of his thinking.

One result of their overconfidence was bad judgment,

which showed itself in such poor decisions as Corcoran's and Keenan's to close the administration case before the Judiciary Committee. Another was loose and ineffectual organization. Although they conferred so constantly, they also disagreed constantly, and there were many occasions when the President was not ready or available to settle their differences. Each staff member tended to act on his own. And then, while they continued rather overconfident, the attack of nerves brought on by their successive disappointments made some of them touchy and overbearing. For example an entirely faithful administration senator dared to utter a strictly private criticism of White House strategy. A member of the staff heard of it, called him and treated him to such a telephonic denunciation as made his hair stand on end. Such little things occurred often, and they were not helpful.

Some members of the staff were inclined to see a traitor at every Senate desk. They called any rebellious Democrat a traitor, and the unhappy time was now at hand when their vision of numerous treacheries— treacheries by their definition only, it should be said— was to be justified. Already before the end of February another serious miscalculation of the President's started home to roost. He had expected that his party's atrophied conservative wing would drop off in the court fight. Many conservatives had left the party, but the mildly Tory Southern oligarchy which controlled Congress had remained faithful. At first the President might not have cared whether they left him, too, for he feared their influence in 1940, the time for which he was reorganizing his party, far more than he feared the influence of the Copelands and the Gerrys. At first he might not have thought the Southerners useful to his court fight; now he knew they were, and now they were leaving him.

The Southern oligarchs had done the President's bidding from the start of the New Deal; their supersession in favor of the White House general staff can hardly be explained at all except in terms of 1940. Unfortunately, although they had been superseded, they retained an immense influence in Congress, and their attitude in the struggle was eagerly watched by other senators and representatives. They were a curious and interesting lot. The foxy old Texan realist, Vice-President Garner, with his sanguine complexion, his bushy eyebrows and his wonderfully persuasive ways, was more popular in Congress than any other man, and more powerful than any but Joe Robinson. Pat Harrison, of Mississippi, the big, gangling, witty chairman of the Senate Finance Committee, had long shared with Garner the exacting duties of administration fixer in the Senate, while James F. Byrnes, of South Carolina, sharp-tongued, shrewd, close-mouthed, had helped as general handy man.

Except for Byrnes, who was an intimate friend of the President's, they were all regarded at the White House as dust-stained practical politicians, unwarmed by any flame of true believing, with more than a suspicion of the political hack about them. Again with the exception of Byrnes, they all joined in distrusting the President and some of his objectives, but their distrust had always before been subordinated to their tolerance of him as the leader of their party and a completely engaging man. Their attitude towards the President was well summed up by Garner one day during the Utilities Holding Company Bill fight. A number of the unhappy Democrats whom he had installed in the House leadership when he was Speaker came to him, to complain of the cruel pressure to which the President was subjecting them to get his bill. The representatives criticized both the President's character and his judgment with some freedom, until Garner interrupted them.

"Now look here," said Garner, "it doesn't matter what kind of a fool you think he is; he's your fool just as long as he's President and the leader of your party."

But now, just when their attitude began to be important in the court fight, the tolerance of the Southern oligarchs was exhausted. They had an uneasy consciousness that the President might like to cast them out of their places of power in the Democracy, but the real heart of the trouble was in the New Deal's financial and labor policies. As long before as the end of January, Garner, Byrnes and several others of the most solidly faithful had been much agitated by the continued spending and the still unbalanced budget. As they saw it, if the New Deal were permitted to continue along the same financial course, the end could only be another depression and concomitant political ruin. They presented their case to the President with some vehemence. At a White House meeting attended by Garner, Robinson, Harrison, Byrnes, Speaker Bankhead, Garner's protégé, House Leader Sam Rayburn, and one or two others, they demanded that the President set $1,000,-000,000 or $1,200,000,000 as the outside limit of the 1938 relief appropriation, and when he argued for $1,500,000,000, one of them polled the meeting in his presence and demonstrated to him that his whole congressional leadership was firmly opposed to him in the matter. At first he promised to make the cut they asked; then Works Progress Administrator Harry L. Hopkins wrought with him for a while, and he changed his mind without letting Garner and the others know.

As though this were not a sufficient irritant, the sitdown strike problem was also embittering the relations between the President and the leaders. The strikes had

started in midwinter. Garner especially had been tremendously aroused by them, and before the President
left for Warm Springs on March 11 he had seen him,
discussed the matter with him and obtained a promise
that if the problem showed signs of becoming more
acute the administration would take drastic action.
While the President was in Warm Springs the problem
did grow considerably more acute, yet no action was
taken. Garner, distraught, called Charles West to his
office, outlined his view of the situation, intimated that
he did not believe the whole picture was being given the
President and insisted that West telephone the President at once, transmitting Garner's views. Still there
was no action, and Garner flew into a fury.

The new Guffey coal bill was soon to come up in the
Senate. Senator Byrnes, who was acting in concert with
Garner, offered an amendment to it, making sit-down
strikes illegal in the mines and, when the proponents of
the bill howled with rage at the prospect of delay which
the amendment offered, transformed it into a general
resolution censuring sit-down strikes. Much disturbed
at these occurrences, the President hastened back from
Warm Springs, arranging beforehand to have Garner,
Robinson and several others see him at the White
House immediately on his return. A general leaders'
conference was first called, then canceled, as the President feared it would look too official and might commit
him to something. The conference was cut down to just
Garner and Robinson, and they were asked to come to
the White House on the evening of March 29, when
the President was scheduled to arrive home.

When he did arrive his staff gave it out quite untruth-
fully that the leaders, not the President, had asked for
the conference. Garner and Robinson were anything but
pleased by that, and Garner felt he had been fooled by
the President all through the business. He went into

the meeting in a hard mood. Discussion of policy towards the sit-down strikes began. Soon it grew heated. Garner began to lose his temper. The President began to lose his. Before very long both men had forgotten their self-control and were using such language to one another that Joe Robinson, horrified, shouted them down and forced them to end the conference.

The net result of the whole business was that by the end of March Garner was crusading against the President on the labor and spending issues and carrying along with him most of the really powerful senatorial members of the Southern oligarchy. The effect on the court fight was immediate. Harrison, Byrnes, Garner and Robinson had ruled the Senate together. Now the first three were in opposition on labor and spending, and therefore disinclined to give the President the help he would otherwise have had from them on the court bill. The attitude Garner took on the court bill was plainly indicated in an argument he had with Burke, of Nebraska, whom he had been instrumental in putting on the Appropriations Committee. The relief appropriation was about to come up. Garner wanted Burke to desert the court bill hearings and fight the President's request for $1,500,000,000 for the WPA in the Appropriations Committee. Burke refused, saying he considered the court fight the most important he had ever been engaged in during his Senate service.

"Why, you're wasting your time on this court matter," replied Garner angrily. "Don't you know that inside ten days there'll be a request before your committee for a blank check for $1,500,000,000 for relief? Don't you know you can't beat $1,500,000,000?"

Indeed, in those days there were many bitternesses seeping through the Senate democracy, weakening the morale of the administration forces. If the spending and labor controversies alienated the most powerful of

the Southerners, such minor happenings as the incident
of the critical senator, the touchy member of the general staff and the telephone infuriated other Democrats. The still wavering moderates were half sleep-
less with their unabated doubt and dismay. The Democratic members of the opposition were fighting in a no-
quarter-asked-or-given style quite unfamiliar in the
clubby Senate. And such Democratic leaders as had
stuck by the President, like Joe Robinson, were on edge
with worry and exasperation. There were unpleasant
little incidents, such as the quarrel between Robinson
and Senator O'Mahoney.

It took place when the pair were lunching one day
with Joe Guffey and Joe Keenan in a private room at
the Capitol. The court fight came up in the talk.
O'Mahoney objected to something that Robinson said
and, by way of twitting him with his troubles with Huey
Long, remarked that he could "put a couple of damp
towels round his head and go to work and be a pretty
good Huey Long himself." Robinson turned purple,
and for a second the other men present thought he
would strike O'Mahoney. Instead he abused him while
his breath lasted, and in such brutal fashion as men use
when they wish to hurt another and care little how they
do it. O'Mahoney, white and trembling, could scarcely
answer. Guffey and Keenan hurled themselves into the
breach, and, as Robinson was a little shamefaced when
the fit was past, the thing was patched up. But it showed
well enough how the whole atmosphere on Capitol Hill
was being poisoned with conflict.

So March ended, with the disappointments for the
administration piling up and morale in the ranks growing steadily worse. Nevertheless, the President was still
supremely confident. If the farm pressure had not materialized, there was still labor to be depended on. If
the liberals were not united, if Garner and his friends

were disapproving, there was still Robinson's promise
of a sure majority of fifty-four to be remembered. And
if the opposition had proved surprisingly strong, there
was still a court problem to be solved and no alternative
for its solution but the bill on which the President had
the power to insist. Thus the President reasoned, and
although he was now underestimating the difficulties of
his situation far more seriously than at the start, he was
still right in believing that, as the situation stood, he
could pass his bill.

The very mainspring of his strength, however, was
the need for a solution of the court problem; after all
the disappointments it was essential. And the one possibility which the President did not contemplate was the
solution of the court problem before the court bill could
be brought to a vote.

A Switch in Time Saves Nine

SHORTLY BEFORE 1 P.M. on February 5, 1937, the lawyers and sightseers crowding the benches of the Supreme Court room observed a curious phenomenon. A page slipped through the curtains behind the justices' dais. Quietly, very quietly he hurried down the row of justices, handing a paper to each of the nine. Each glanced at what he had been given; Cardozo read most of it, and Sutherland and Stone took the trouble to read it through to the end. A tiny incident it would have been anywhere else, but that strange chamber, so like the interior of a classical icebox decorated by an insane upholsterer, has a routine which seems to have been fixed at the moment of the creation of the world. The justices' brief inattention was as striking as a small noise in a very large, very silent empty space. The lawyer at the rostrum, disconcerted, paused for a second in his exposition. A murmur ran down the benches. What could these documents be which so interested the justices? What were these papers?

They were copies of the President's message, the Attorney General's letter and the court bill. A court attendant had obtained them at the Capitol across the plaza a few minutes after the message was read in the Senate. He had hurried back and sent them to the bench at once. No wonder the justices had been inattentive to the case before them. For some, here was living proof of the correctness of their course. For others, here was the bitter fruit of their own actions.

There could have been no sharper interruption of the long judicial controversy which had divided the Court against itself for two decades and arrayed the justices in two furiously disagreeing factions during the crucial years of the New Deal. This history is no place for legal technicalities; it should suffice to say that the substance of the controversy, some of whose effects have already been examined, concerned the interpretation of the general welfare and commerce clauses of the Constitution.

The conservatives of the Bench, Justices McReynolds, Butler, Sutherland and Van Devanter, had placed a progressively narrower interpretation on the two clauses, until the federal government's powers to provide for the general welfare and regulate interstate commerce were all but whittled away by decisions based on such constitutional restrictions as the "due process" section of the Fourteenth Amendment. The liberals, Justices Brandeis, Stone and Cardozo, had steadfastly opposed their brethren, repeatedly predicting that if the Court rendered government impotent to deal with the difficult problems of the time the Court would destroy itself. While Chief Justice Hughes, whose principal object was the maintenance of the Court's prestige, gave the liberals an assistance sometimes tempered by his desire to avoid too even divisions on great questions. Justice Roberts' support of them allowed the conservatives to control the Court throughout the first years of the New Deal. The result was the series of decisions, in the Agricultural Adjustment Act, Guffey

Coal Act and other great cases, by which the New Deal program was completely nullified.

It has already been seen what hatred there was between the two sides; how one accused the other of permitting prejudice to prevail in constitutional interpretation; how one warned and the other ignored the warnings in the belief that with the election of November 1936 the New Deal would pass off like a bad dream. The President's judiciary bill confronted both sides three months almost to the day after the country had so signally failed to waken from its dream. Curiously enough, as Justice Stone is said to have remarked, the President's bill proved to be the first major measure since the NRA on which the justices' opinion was unanimous.

Naturally Justice Roberts and the four ultraconservatives regarded it as a constitutional outrage, for it was as direct a criticism of their own actions as an angry man's smack in the face for a scolding wife. Naturally the Chief Justice, with his religion of the Court's prestige, detested and feared it. But the liberals might have chosen to accept the bill as the best justification of their fruitless warnings. They might have said, "We told you so," and let it go at that. They did not. Stone and Cardozo were deeply disturbed by the bill. They considered it an effort to subject the Court to political control, and they thought the threatened destruction of the Court's independence several degrees worse than a mere temporary dominance of special economic predilections. In a sense they enjoyed the discomfiture of the conservatives; they believed that the Court had brought the bill on itself, but they hated it all the same. As for Brandeis, he was bitter.

Brandeis, the moralist, saw in the bill an offense against the good morals of government. He thought the court packing bad enough, but he was almost more distressed by the indirections of its presentation. When Senator Wheeler suggested that Tom Corcoran and Ben Cohen were responsible for the bill and the message, he took the suggestion as a personal affront. The brilliant pair had been intimate with him. Like so many of the other young New Dealers, they had thought it a rare privilege to sit at his feet and hear his wisdom, and he had admired them for the useful public servants they were. Could they have hatched such a scheme? Brandeis could not bear to believe it, but Wheeler's story was circumstantial. To relieve his anxiety he asked another of his young friends to find out the truth, and when the message came back that the bill and message had emanated from the Attorney General's office he was overjoyed.

Meanwhile the Court was compelled to find an answer to the cruelly urgent question, What to do? More great New Deal cases stood on its docket; once again the justices were required to decide on the powers or impotency of government to deal with the problems of a troubled world. Would they reiterate their arbitrary insistence on government's impotence, or would the liberals now suddenly prevail? Would the Court save itself by reversing itself, or would it preserve its consistency and damn the consequences? Once again, as it had when the justices were compelled to pass judgment on the early actions of the New Deal, the final verdict depended on Roberts. The four conservatives were die-hards; the words they had spoken were too bitter to be eaten. But Roberts was a moderate; he had left his moderation for a while, but now, perhaps, he might return to it.

In the three months intervening between the election and the presentation of the court bill, the urgent question had already been half answered. An immediate reaction to the election had taken place in the Supreme

Court chamber. The previous spring McReynolds and
his followers had treated government lawyers as
though they were thieving schoolboys. Now the justices
of the right were polite and sympathetic when they
questioned the government men. Moreover, the justices
had exhibited their awareness of their own political
miscalculation in ways more tangible than politeness
and sympathy.

A retroactive tax on profits from silver speculation
had been imposed when the Silver Purchase Bill was
passed, and in November it was contested before the
Court. Although the government side was admirably
presented by Assistant Attorney General Jackson, an
adverse decision seemed certain, for several years
earlier Justice McReynolds had written an opinion committing the Court to a flat veto on all retroactive taxa-
tion. Nevertheless, when the silver tax opinion was
handed down in January, it was found that the justices
had decided unanimously for the government. The
shrewder New Dealers concluded that the extreme cap-
tiousness of the pre-election Court was a thing of the
past.

In January also occurred the moment which may be
described as half answering the question so urgently
put to the Court by the President's bill. It must have
been on a Saturday, for Saturdays are the Court's conference days, when the justices meet to discuss and vote
on cases. The case before the Court that Saturday was
a challenge of the constitutionality of the state of
Washington's minimum wage law, and the challenge
was based squarely on Justice Roberts' opinion of the
previous spring, invalidating the almost precisely
similar New York statute. Every justice there must
have recalled that it was that opinion which had troubled even the reactionaries, provoked the President's
"no man's land" comment and put the Court in the posi-

tion of disapproving all social legislation from whatever source, federal or state. The atmosphere in the grandiose conference room must have been somewhat tense when the Chief Justice, as the custom is, put the question first to Justice Cardozo, the Court's junior member. Cardozo voted to uphold the Washington law, just as he had voted to uphold the New York law. Next was Roberts, the very man whose opinion had struck the New York law down. Yet Roberts agreed with Cardozo.

Thus it was that the conservative domination of the Court came to its close *before the disclosure of the President's court plan.* Probably it will never be known how Roberts' self-reversal affected the justices. Some of them may have known it was coming; Roberts may have made his decision to take a hint from the election returns without consulting any of his brethren—these are matters of mystery. There may have been jubilation and astonishment, open anger and loud bluster in the conference room that day. Or there may merely have been silent acquiescence. The known facts are that the vote occurred in January and that Roberts switched. They are the only known facts. At the time, of course, no facts were known at all, for the vote was secret.

Knowledge of the facts now merely serves to confuse the picture of what happened within the Court after the disclosure of the President's bill. How far had Roberts meant to go when he reversed himself on the New York statute? Had he intended simply to let the Court retreat from the untenable position of disapproving all social legislation, from whatever source, to the more defensible one of holding only the federal government powerless to deal with social problems on the ground of states' rights? Or had he intended to throw wide the door for the federal as well as the state governments? These are questions which cannot be answered. One can but guess at what really occurred, but one or two guesses appear to be fairly well supported by the evidence.

It seems probable, in the first place, that all the justices realized that their only chance to save the Court lay in more self-reversals. It also seems probable that some of the conservative justices looked with sympathy on the self-reversals so long as they were not required to participate in them. And finally it seems probable that the most important result of the disclosure of the court plan was to make Charles Evans Hughes Chief Justice of the United States in fact as well as name.

For all the imposing weight of his prestige, he had never been Chief Justice in fact before. Baptist clergyman's boy who made incredibly good, hero of the Armstrong Insurance investigation, ex-governor of New York, ex-justice of the high bench, ex-candidate for the presidency, only really successful American diplomatist for a couple of decades—he was all these things when President Hoover named him to the Court, but he could not tame the Court's conservatives. He is said to have tried. If he did, such efforts as he made were futile, and although every sign indicated that he was well aware of what the Court's blockade of the New Deal must eventually mean, he was condemned to public isolation in the center of the bench. After the AAA decision it was common gossip in Washington that he had changed his vote to join McReynolds and the others in striking the AAA down; and lying as Washington gossip often is, his known distaste for even divisions on important questions, the dangers the Court would have run by offering one of its criticized five-to-four decisions on the act beloved by the farmers, and the previous and subsequent tenor of Hughes's own opinions all suggested that there was at least

something tactical in his stand. There had been other
humiliations, but the days of humiliations were past
now.

Now the justices turned naturally to him; they united
behind him; they promised to follow him so far as they
could. That, at least, is the best supported reconstruction of what occurred; above all there is considerable
testimony that Roberts, the man with the deciding vote,
definitely accepted Hughes as his leader. Having gone
from disconsolate and fruitless hovering between the
two factions to dominance of both, Hughes promptly
assumed the heavy responsibilities arising out of the
situation.

His first unpleasant task was writing the majority
opinion upholding the Washington minimum wage law.
It was not easy, although he had dissented in the
previous New York case, for there was still Roberts'
change of front to be explained. To meet the situation
he prepared a majestic judgment nullifying not only
the New York case decision but the ancient precedental
Adkins case decision also; grounded the whole in the
novel argument that judicial interpretation must take
cognizance of the changes of the times, and put a good
face on the thing by blaming the state of New York's
lawyers for failing to attack the Adkins case's validity.
There followed the puzzle of the Senate Judiciary
Committee hearings, which he solved with such perfect
success, and after that again came yet more weighty
matters.

Early in February the justices had heard five Wagner
Labor Relations Act cases, and not long thereafter the
Alabama suits involving the Social Security Act were
brought before them. On the Court's decisions on
these two laws hung the whole future of the court fight.
Each law implied a great extension of the powers of
government; each drew the issue squarely between the

liberals and the conservatives. The Wagner act, enforc-
ing collective bargaining and permitting the federal
government to designate the workers' bargaining
agent, ran directly counter to the Guffey Coal Act holding that labor relations were of local concern only. The
Social Security Act was a far more striking example of
that "coercion" of the states which the Court had seen
in the AAA. To sustain the Wagner act the Court
would have to abandon its narrow and crippling
interpretation of the interstate commerce clause. To
sustain the Social Security Act the Court would have
to allow some real meaning to the general welfare
clause. Yet if the Court balked, the court bill would
surely pass. Thus the justices were brought face to face
with their dilemma.

Once more one would like to know what happened in
the Court's conference room when the justices met their
dilemma. When Hughes put his question to Roberts on
the Wagner act, was he already aware that the reply
would approve the act's validity? Had he perhaps persuaded Roberts that to uphold a state minimum wage
law was not enough, that the Court must allow the
national government a free hand; and if he had, did he
by any chance betray what had occurred by some brief
alteration in his Olympian demeanor? Did the liberals
allow themselves the wicked pleasure of hinting that
much trouble might have been avoided if Roberts had
voted with them from the start? Was McReynolds the
only justice who seems to have wished the Court to die
hard, openly infuriated? Above all, how did Roberts
behave? Did he put his vote on the practical basis that
circumstances forced it on him? Or did he pass it off
with legal explanation? Did he seem to be conscious
that his switch would save the Court, or had he somehow rationalized it until he himself believed his course
consistent? One would like answers to all these ques-

tions; unhappily answers are not available and very likely never will be. Again the known facts are only that the Court voted to sustain both the great acts and that Roberts' voice was deciding.

Naturally these facts were not known at the time. Whether the Court's vote on the Wagner act was delayed or the justices who had the task of writing the opinions worked very slowly, an unconscionable time elapsed between the argument of the cases and the disclosure of the decision. Decision Monday followed decision Monday, and Washington waited interminably to hear which painful horn of their dilemma the justices had chosen. Each Monday the court chamber was jammed to the doors, and each Monday the crowd went home disappointed. The President and his general staff were not disturbed by the long wait. They were convinced that in the end the Court would have to find against the New Deal, and they cheerfully seized the opportunity presented by the justices' inaction to accuse them of indulging in a sit-down strike. The waiting put the opposition, on the other hand, in a state of anguish, for every man in it hoped that the Court would avoid committing suicide, but none could see how.

Then on March 29, just a week after Wheeler had read Hughes's letter to the Judiciary Committee, came another decision Monday. Once again the court chamber was crowded when the Chief Justice marched in at the head of his little black-robed procession; this time the crowd heard something for its pains. The Court upheld the Railway Labor Act; it upheld the revised Frazier–Lemke Farm Mortgage Moratorium Bill, both with unanimous decisions reminiscent of the decision in the silver tax case. And then the Chief Justice read his opinion on the Washington minimum wage law. That was the great moment. News of the January

vote was out at last; at last it began to seem possible
that the Court would avoid the expected judicial hara-
kari.

The news was out, but its implications were scarcely
noticed. A few thought the Court might duck a decision
on the Wagner labor act, a very few dared to half
predict that the act would be upheld. But the great
majority believed with the President and his general
staff that the Washington law decision was no more
than a tactful preface to the Wagner act's destruction.
The White House expectations were based not only on
the unanimous opinion of the administration legal experts, but also on the belief that there had been a leak
from the Court itself. This last was one of those
fantastic things which can only happen in Washington.
Justice McReynolds had said something at a private
party. On its way through the city's whispering galleries
the remark had been magnified, so that the report
reached the White House that McReynolds had sworn
that nothing, not even the President's threat to pack
the high bench, could frighten the conservatives from
their position blocking the New Deal's path. It is of
such silly stuff that great political miscalculations are
made. The President and his general staff found that
they had made one on Monday, April 12, when Chief
Justice Hughes spoke the death sentence of the President's court plan before an astonished audience in the
Court's chamber.

That day the courtroom was jammed as usual with
lawyers, sightseers, wives and friends of justices in
their special space, reporters in their side boxes, and
all the rest of the motley mob from which the Washington commedia dell' arte draws its spectators. As
usual the justices filed in on the dot of twelve, and as
usual the Court's business began with a few minutes of
dignified official piddling. Then the Chief Justice gave

the signal, and the reading of the Wagner act opinions started.

Of the five Wagner act cases, the Jones and Laughlin case alone involved the great problem of the federal powers in all its extension. The steel company's suit to keep the National Labor Relations Board out of its plant was supported by the Court's previous holdings that all production, whether in mining, manufactures or agriculture, was a purely local matter. The attorneys for the steel company had confidently quoted an impressive list of precedents; Solicitor General Reed, on the other hand, had been forced to argue that the Court's previous position was mistaken, on the grounds that such production as Jones' and Laughlin's was national in its effects on the complex economic structure.

Hughes himself had written the majority opinion, and he read it magnificently, giving its every phrase an overtone of infallibility which made the whole business sound like a rehearsal for the last judgment. As the justices' habit is, he began with an exposition of the facts of the case. An examination of the constitutional arguments came next. Thence he launched into a discussion of the interstate commerce clause and its applicability to Jones' and Laughlin's activities. The steel company lawyers on one side of the courtroom and the government lawyers on the other listened eagerly, overcome with an equal horror and astonishment. Surely the Chief Justice could not be approving the Solicitor General's argument. Surely he could not be discarding all the earlier doctrines of the Court's majority, opening a broad road to labor regulation by the federal government and setting up a brand-new reading of the commerce clause. Surely he could not be allowing all the federal powers the Court had so firmly denied. But he was. The liberals had won the long controversy at last.

And thus, with the government lawyers choking with incredulity and fear and the Chief Justice enthroned in triumph on his assaulted bench, ended the court fight's most extraordinary scene. With such a leading actor and such a setting—those squabby Numidian marble columns, those inept bas-reliefs, those overpompous crimson velvet and makeshift white cotton curtains— it was as perfectly staged and cast a little incident as American history can show. Its only defect was a trace of overtheatricality. Its ironies—the Court's self-salvation by self-reversal, the Court's destruction of the President by giving him what he wanted—were just a trifle too cosmic. There was just a suspicion of the Eugene O'Neill touch. Nevertheless, it was the turning point of the court fight, and after it everything that the Court did, even the announcement of the Social Security Act's validity, was the purest, weariest anticlimax. After it the President once more resumed the center of the stage.

III. REAR-GUARD ACTION

THE FIRST CHANCE

April 12–April 19, 1937

IN THE CAPITOL news communicates itself as rapidly as a malignant contagious disease. A few seconds after the tickers bring notice of an important event to the press galleries, reporters are in the lobbies to hear the leading senators' and representatives' opinions of it. Five minutes later everyone—solons so obscure that they are known only for the scandal of their private lives or of their grammar, pages, clerks, tourists, even lavatory attendants—knows what has happened and is gossiping about it. Groups gather on the floor to jubilate or deplore; the smokers in the cloakrooms irreverently supply the human background; and the political organism quickly digests the latest fact and adjusts itself to it.

The news of the Supreme Court's self-reversal on the Wagner Labor Relations Act was subjected to the same disseminative and assimilative process, but it was so big, so extraordinary, that the lawmakers were startled out of their usual calm. The senators of the opposition virtually held a cheer meeting, and if they had built a bonfire on the Senate floor no one would have been surprised. Their leader, Wheeler, looked

like a cat which had subsisted on a canary diet for
several weeks; he alone had predicted that the justices
would prefer to avoid self-destruction, and some suspected that his prophecy was based on an advance
judicial hint, for the senator was seeing a good deal of
the members of the Court in those days. At any rate,
whatever the source of his optimism, he was openly
enchanted to see it confirmed, and he and his allies
gathered at once to plan the conversion of those wavering senatorial moderates whom the news would naturally most effect.

Among the supporters of the President, on the other
hand, word of the Court's action produced an instant
consternation. Every loyal senator foresaw how easy
Wheeler and his friends would find their recruiting
among the moderates; the administration men were as
aware as Wheeler that nothing but the need for a
solution of the court problem had held the vitally important moderates in line, and now the problem had
solved itself. Compromise talk spread like wildfire
through the administration ranks. Senators told one
another that now the President could be contented with
two or three extra justices and piously hoped that he
would agree to modify his demands while a compromise
could still be easily arranged. Senator Byrnes privately
put the question that was in every mind: "Why run for
a train after you've caught it?"

The situation was pretty well summed up by Joe
Robinson, only the day after the decision was handed
down, when he summoned Joe Keenan to the Hill to
talk the next move over with him. Keenan joined
Robinson in the leader's dingy little office in the
frescoed bowels of the Capitol building. He found him
at his desk, with papers spread all around him, and a
copy of the majority opinions in the Wagner act in
the middle of the mess. Robinson greeted Keenan and

told him that he thought it very important to think the matter through carefully before acting. Keenan agreed, and Robinson picked up the print of the Wagner act opinions and analyzed them, point by point. He came out with the conclusion that the justices had given the President most of the important things he desired. The Guffey act decisions' limitations on labor legislation had been reversed, he pointed out; the whole interpretation of the commerce clause had been immensely broadened; it was now possible to forge ahead with the President's program without worrying about the Court.

"The thing to do, Joe," he told Keenan, "is to settle this thing right now. This bill's raising hell in the Senate. Now it's going to be worse than ever, but if the President wants to compromise I can get him a couple of extra justices tomorrow. What he ought to do is say he's won, which he has, agree to compromise to make the thing sure, and wind the whole business up."

Meanwhile the President was also reacting to the news, and in a very different fashion. For two years he had wanted a liberal Court. Two months and a few days before, he had taken radical steps to get a liberal Court. Early on the afternoon of April 12 he learned that he had a liberal Court. His first reaction was an old-fashioned fit of temper, which was only intensified by his astonishment.

He and his advisers had been counting on reactionary decisions, consistent with the Court's previous course. It has been seen how rumors of an offhand remark of Justice McReynolds' had increased the assurance of the advance verdict by the administration legal experts. So confident had the President been of the Wagner act's invalidation that, when his confidence was disappointed, he could see nothing but duplicity in the Court's change

of front. Never inclined to think his opponents wholly
unspotted from the world, he had reserved a particular
distrust for the conservative and middle-of-the-road
justices of the high bench. In the long line of arbitrarily
conservative decisions which provoked him to his court
bill, he had seen not only a blockade of his program but
a personal injury to himself. And now he took the
Court's change of front in some sense personally. It
was more than an effort to avoid institutional suicide.
It was an attempt to beat him on his bill. It was
political, purely. It was not reliable. It was engineered
by the Chief Justice, whom he and his advisers agreed
in regarding as their most dangerous, implacable
enemy. Altogether it was not to be tolerated.

In this mood the President approached the problem
posed for him by the Court's action. In the first place
he was distinctly not inclined to agree with Robinson
and the other senators that truce or compromise could
be called a victory in his fight. Quite aside from his
personal annoyance with them, he thought it necessary
to give a crushing lesson to the congressional rebels,
and he did not believe that truce or compromise would
teach them much. Spurred on by the overconfidence
which is the sad, repeated theme in the court fight's
story, blinded by it to the dark chance of defeat, he
longed to press forward, past a mere bloodless success,
to a resounding triumph over the high bench and its
defenders. And then, in Senator Byrnes's phrase, he
had not quite caught the train he wanted.

The truth seems to be that the President wanted
something more than a liberal Court, something which
he disclosed, in a conversation after the Wagner act
decision, to Professor William Zebina Ripley and
Senator O'Mahoney. The old liberal from Harvard
and the young politician from Wyoming had been summoned to the White House to have their fears about

the court plan soothed away. They found the President at the big desk in his sunny oval office, among the flags and ship pictures. He radiated good humor, greeting them genially, waving them into chairs with his long cigarette holder, asking them to tell him everything that was on their minds. The two men took up their tale together. Both of them said they could understand why he had made his first attack on the Court, but they asked why he would not compromise when he had got the liberal majority he desired on the bench. For proof they pointed to the great decision.

The President's reply was to explain that a five-to-four majority was not enough for him. He said he wanted a Court which would "co-operate" with the White House. He needed six new justices who would be friendly and approachable, men with whom he could confer, as man to man, on his great plans for social and economic reform and experiment. In his days as governor of New York, he recalled, he had a close relationship with several members of the New York Court of Appeals, and it had worked very well. He thought that where great questions were involved it was in the public interest to have the Court and the Executive work things out together, rather than to have a long interval of uncertainty between the Executive's action and the Court's reaction. It was the same thing he had suggested so unsuccessfully to the Chief Justice, early in his first administration. And even then the idea had not been a new one. He had revealed it to two friendly newspapermen shortly before his 1933 inauguration.

Nevertheless, his latest revelation of it scarcely had the desired effect on Senator O'Mahoney and Professor Ripley. Their ideas of the American constitutional structure were rather more conventional than the President's. As they listened to the President calmly explain-

ing what he wanted they could not forget the doctrine
of separate powers. They answered him as best they
might, but they were so astonished that when they left
the cheerful office they took the trouble to compare
notes on what they had heard. Eventually what they
had heard was heard by others, and the leaders of the
opposition to the court plan accepted it as the best
proof of their fears.

Besides the President's state of mind, there was also
an outside factor which had its weight in his decision
to press on. His administration had been definitely
committed for two years to give Joe Robinson the first
Supreme Court vacancy which occurred.

The commitment was made after one of those amazing congressional sessions in which Robinson had procured for the President all the long list of statutes he
demanded, and had procured them as the President dictated them—almost without the change of a comma.
Near the session's close Jim Farley lunched on the Hill
with the Senate leader. His mission was to express the
President's gratitude for Robinson's good work, and he
laid the gratitude on thickly, in his best Postmaster
General fashion. As politicians will when they are
grateful, he suggested that Robinson might look for a
quid pro quo.

Stirred by Farley's kindness and excited by his
promises, Robinson revealed his life's ambition. Almost
since his childhood, he said, he had wanted to sit on
the high bench as a justice of the Supreme Court of
the United States. He asked Farley to find out for him
whether he might hope. Farley was reassuring and
promised to look into the matter. A few days later he
told Robinson that he had talked the matter over with
the "proper party" and had found that Robinson could
positively count on succeeding to the first place made
vacant by the death or resignation of one of the nine.

Robinson was jubilant. At once he told the great news to his friends. In the little group around him the matter was regarded as so entirely settled that one of Robinson's intimates even went to Republican Senate Leader Charles L. McNary, of Oregon, to ask whether Robinson's appointment would arouse partisan opposition. McNary, another Robinson crony, understood the inquiry came from the President, so definite was the messenger's language in regard to the appointment, and delightedly sent back the reply that the Republicans would take the greatest pleasure in voting to confirm Joe.

Thus the assumption that Robinson would get the next available justice's robes was an important factor in the whole Senate situation. Robinson himself, knowing that Jim Farley had never gone back on his word in a political deal yet, did not doubt for an instant that the President himself had given the promise. Meanwhile the President, although he constantly avoided speaking out in the matter to those who mentioned it to him, was perfectly aware that there would be an unprecedented explosion on the Hill if Robinson did not get the place he was counting on.

The two-year-old promise to Robinson and the President's overconfidence were the minor and major themes of the central action of the court drama. Always his optimism drove the President too far onward, and whenever he showed signs of wanting to call a halt there was his promise to Robinson to spur him on. In the choice of course at the time of the Wagner decision the promise to Robinson was merely an influence. Later it was to be deciding.

The trouble was that the President and the political intellectuals around him could not forget Robinson's conservative past. They lumped him in with all the other powerful Southerners whom they disdained and distrusted, although they were still, in those days, going along with the New Deal for reasons of political convenience. They suspected that the Southerners would revert to their original conservatism just as soon as political necessity permitted it, and they felt that there was no place imaginable in which Robinson would be more likely to revert than in the protected security of the high bench. They recalled, too, how Robinson had joined the other Southerners in their midwinter lecture to the President about budget balancing, public economies and labor policies.

At the same time the White House knew that Robinson must be given the first vacancy arising from the retirement, resignation or death of one of the sitting justices. More than one vacancy in the near future could hardly be counted on. Therefore additional justices were necessary to offset the Robinson appointment when it had to be made. There was, of course, the possibility of compromise on two extra justices instead of six. But here again it was remembered that the court plan was supposed to have comfortable majorities in both houses of Congress. If additional justices were necessary, then why back down at all? Why not drive forward to one of the greatest victories any administration had ever had? So the President reasoned.

Nor was the President's reasoning modified by the reasoning of the general staff, whose attitude at this time was well expressed in their reception of Keenan when he reported his conversation with Robinson to them. Keenan presented Robinson's views on compromise to the next general staff council, putting especial emphasis on Robinson's worries about the future. On his own hook he suggested that the President prepare another fireside chat, to reiterate his demand for permanent reforms of the judiciary conformable to his bill, but to announce that, in view of the Court's new stand, he was now willing to accept only two new justices. If there was no call for the general staff to listen to Keenan, certainly Robinson's opinion should have carried some weight. He was the President's best lieutenant, his most unvaryingly faithful congressional follower and his most reliable adviser. Yet Corcoran, James Roosevelt and most of the other members of the general staff pooh-poohed Keenan's report. Dear old Joe Robinson, they said, had a tendency to be a "defeatist", and they pointed out that there was no positive proof that the bill would lose many votes by the Court's self-reversal.

This general disinclination to compromise was strengthened by forces inside and outside the little group. Outside was Cummings, not averse to compromise itself but always insistent that the principle of his bill be preserved. Unfortunately it was difficult to work out a compromise preserving the Cummings principle, and that meant one voice against most proposed halfway measures.

Three more, and probably more influential, voices were those of Tom Corcoran, Ben Cohen and Assistant Attorney General Jackson. They feared compromise for a reason of their own. As they saw it, if any court bill was passed it would make the administration responsible for the future actions of the high bench. They did not believe that the mere addition of two extra justices would produce a dependable high bench. They foresaw that a time might come when the new Court of eleven would render an unpopular decision, and then, they predicted, the whole business would rebound sharply into the President's face.

"If you're going to pack a court at all you've got to really pack it," was the way Jackson put it.

Keenan still further complicated the situation by favoring a compromise which the others detested. Able, industrious, well-intentioned man though he was, Keenan was far from being such an idealist in governmental matters as some other members of the general staff. There was nothing of the liberal intellectual about him; his blood would never have run cold at a critical editorial in the *New Republic* or the *Nation*. He had been charmed by the so-called "pork-barrel compromise" suggested by Senator Charles O. Andrews, an elderly Florida Democrat just arrived in the Senate from his state's Supreme Court, who had been terrified by the President's bill. Andrews wanted to increase the size of the Supreme Bench to eleven, and he rationalized the increase by providing that each justice should represent one of the ten federal judicial circuits, with the Chief Justice at large. In a long after-dinner conversation Keenan had started by trying to convince Andrews of the President's bill's wisdom, Andrews had ended by convincing Keenan of the wisdom of his bill. Keenan thereupon began pushing it at the White House, and Corcoran and Assistant Attorney General Jackson, who detested the pork-barrel flavor of the Andrews measure, opposed him with all their strength.

And finally Jackson had a theory that the Court's self-reversal in the Wagner labor act decisions really did not mean anything. He had himself presented the government side in the Social Security Act cases. He was aware of the great principles involved in them; he knew that to uphold the act the Court would have to add a new interpretation of the general welfare clause to its new interpretation of the commerce clause; he could not believe that even now the justices were ready for so complete an about-face. Therefore he argued that the only thing to do was wait and see, that the time for compromise would be at hand when the Court had plainly demonstrated there was meaning in the promise of the Wagner act decisions.

With the chance of adverse social security decisions to gild his hopes and the advice of his general staff to reinforce his own inclinations, the President naturally decided to spurn all compromise suggestions and fight onward for his bill. His mind was made up only a few days after the Wagner act decision was handed down, and nothing could shake him in his resolution. When he revealed it to his unhappy congressional leaders he gave them plainly to understand that nothing had happened to make him more receptive to suggestions. When some protested he ignored their protests. He told the puzzled voters, who were also asking Senator Byrnes's question, that a mere five-to-four decision of the Court, hanging on one man's whim, was not enough. He ordered his weary troops back to the ramparts and then, so confident was he, began planning a fishing trip in the Gulf of Mexico.

FORWARD WHERE?

April 19, 1937

THE PRESIDENT'S WORD was "forward." But forward where? Like Wellington abandoning half-fertile Portugal to hold his lines at Torres Vedras, the justices had retreated to an impregnable position. All their proud legal conquests of the past decades, all that great area of economic legislation over which their readings of the commerce and welfare clauses had given them the final authority of veto, had been surrendered, ignominiously perhaps, but seemingly forever; and they were entrenched once more behind the ancient fortifications of their court as an established and respected institution. The Napoleonic legions, tramping wearily over the denuded, inhospitable countryside towards the grim Peninsular mountains, had no harder task ahead than the President's supporters struggling forward to storm the Court's redoubts.

In his preparations for the fight the President had counted the liberals, the farmers and labor as his sure allies. In the first two weeks after the attack the liberal united front had broken. In the first month the farmers, who had been expected to march to war with an invalidated AAA benefit check for their battle standard,

162

decided to stay at home and till the fields. Now the Senate moderates, those partisan followers whom the President had counted not as allies but as his own troops, were beginning to desert the administration.

The court problem had solved itself. The need for a solution which had held the moderates in line was gone, and within ten days after the Wagner act decisions Joe Robinson made his first gloomy report. He had promised a majority of fifty-four for the bill; suddenly he could promise it no longer. Where there had been thirty senators in the administration's camp, thirty in the opposition's and thirty-five in doubt, there were suddenly thirty-five and then forty-five opposed. Sometimes the doubting senators went to Robinson to tell him that they doubted no longer; sometimes Robinson heard of their defections from their friends among the administration faithful. He did all that he could to drive the deserters back into line. He pled, he exhorted, and he threatened, but without effect. Their answers to him followed a simple pattern:

"I'm sorry, Joe, but I don't see any need for this damn bill now. I don't like it and I'm not going to vote for it."

And while Robinson's reports from the front grew blacker and blacker, the President was paying a heavy penalty in still another sector of the battle for his failure to consult anyone, his refusal to take partners and make allies before the fight began. Labor was sulking in its tent. The Achilles of the administration forces was withdrawn from the struggle, and the all-powerful lobbyists of the two great workers' organizations, who should have swarmed over the Capitol, terrifying the timid legislators with reminders of primaries and elections to come, were lolling comfortably in their offices, their feet on their desks, smoking their excellent cigars.

Of all the subplots of the court drama, the story of labor was the most interesting. It was also the most disconcerting to the President. It has already been seen how he expected the A. F. of L. and the C.I.O. to reunite in support of his bill, as they had in support of him during the election, although the two warring factions had flown at each other's throats as soon as the votes were counted. He formed his expectation at the beginning of January, and, in the face of a labor situation growing daily more acute, he never abandoned it. The C.I.O. enrolled the workers of half-a-dozen mighty industries; the A. F. of L., always hampered by its conservative craft unionism, fought back as best it could; the sit-down strikes began in earnest; and still the President failed to realize what it all implied.

His first lesson in caution was administered by the A. F. of L., in which one powerful group had fought him even during the presidential campaign. These die-hards, led by Big Bill Hutcheson of the Carpenters' Union, who had served the Republican Campaign Committee as chairman of its labor division, viewed the President with an infinite distrust. Before his advent they had enjoyed an indolent security on the comfortable summits of their tightly organized craft unions. For labor in general, for the great mass of workers, they had cared nothing, yet they had been accepted as the leaders of the labor movement. Now their unions were engulfed in a larger movement; their importance was at an end; their very security was threatened by the impetus to unionization given by the New Deal. They were not grateful to the President, whom they rightly held responsible for their plight; they were far from ready to help him on his court bill.

Soon after the disclosure of the bill the executive council of the A. F. of L. met in Washington, in the large, gloomy chamber, like a cross between an old-fashioned company board room and a one-train-a-day New England railway station, where the A. F. of L.'s destinies are usually settled. The matter before the meeting was the A. F. of L.'s attitude towards the court bill. President William Green and a large majority of the solid, prosperous-seeming, middle-aged men around the table favored supporting the bill. They believed, quite correctly, that some reform of the Court was in the interest of labor. They judged that most industrial workers would favor the bill. And they thought it would be extremely dangerous for the A. F. of L. not to go along with so immensely successful a popular leader as the President, at a time when the President had it within his power to destroy the A. F. of L. by throwing the weight of his influence behind the C.I.O.

The cigars were lighted. The room began to fill with acrid smoke, and the discussion started. Hutcheson angrily opposed the project to support the President. A beefy, heavy-jowled man, he spoke loudly and emphatically. He was backed up by John Coefield, of the Plumbers' Union, and by the red-baiting A. F. of L. vice-president, Matthew Woll, a little man whose plump, sharp face peers out between the wings of his high collar like the face of some small animal in a hedge. The argument grew heated and prolonged itself. In the end, of course, the majority prevailed, and the court bill received the emphatic official endorsement of the A. F. of L.

The trouble was that, gratifying as official endorsements can be, they were not what the court bill needed. Three or four clever lobbyists with a good strong pressure group behind them, scaring hell out of the all-important waverers, were the real necessity, and these the A. F. of L. failed to produce. Being no more than a congeries of independent organisms, allied only by mutual self-interest, the A. F. of L. has depended on a tradition of mutual toleration to hold it together. Although a minority may be very small—smaller even than the Hutcheson group in opposition to court bill endorsement—the practice has always been to respect the minority's views. Thus the A. F. of L. support of the court bill was emasculated by the stand of the Hutcheson group. A. F. of L. unions passed resolutions echoing the executive council's endorsement of the bill; pious, loquacious William Green talked to a few senators and appeared solemnly before the Judiciary Committee; the A. F. of L. lobbyists put in a good word for the bill when they found time, but the heat was never really turned on.

The President's great reliance had not been the A. F. of L., however; it had been the C.I.O. and its leader, John L. Lewis. The C.I.O. owed its existence to the New Deal labor policies, and Lewis, his new position as a powerful national figure. Lewis had been the prime mover in labor's fight for the President in the 1936 campaign. At the frank solicitation of the White House—conveyed by one of those obscure left-wing officials whom the White House so often employs as messenger boys—Lewis had drawn on his organization's funds to make the handsomest contribution received by the Democratic National Committee. Surely Lewis and the C.I.O. could not fail the President now, in this new time of need!

Lewis, the man who had to make the decision in the matter, was as remarkable a human phenomenon as American labor has produced in its long struggle with the most obstinate employing class in the world. Outwardly his history and characteristics were those of a typical leader of America's workers. Born of a family of poor coal miners, introduced in his early youth to labor in the mines, he used a rude oratory to lift himself on the shoulders of his fellows to a minor position

in their union. Married to a woman of superior education and attainments, he acquired from her a cultiva-
tion of mind which proved a useful asset to his rhetoric
as well as to himself. He rose rapidly through the ranks
of the United Mine Workers, and by 1920 he was the
union's president and a man of such growing influence
in the councils of the A. F. of L. that four years later
he was able to impose his candidate for the presidency,
the former mineworkers' secretary-treasurer, William
Green. While his importance within labor's ranks increased, his national stature suffered the same shrinkage
which the decade after the World War brought to the
stature of all labor leaders. In those years he was
known as a red-baiter, and he was a stalwart Republican.

The dawn of the New Deal once more altered his
fortunes. Among the tame and far from daring men
around the A. F. of L.'s council table he stood out as
a model of energy and enterprise. Under the aegis of
the NRA, while his brother leaders sat for the most
part supine, he recruited hundreds of thousands of new
workers to his union. And then, with his eyes opened
to labor's new opportunity, he began a clamor for the
unionization of the mass industries on mass lines, not
by the small craft units on which the A. F. of L. was
chiefly founded. His former subordinate, Green, the
die-hard, Hutcheson, and all the craft union leaders
fought him furiously. At one point he and Hutcheson
came to blows on the floor of an A. F. of L. convention.
In the end, disgusted with the A. F. of L.'s refusal to
seize the opportunity presented by the administration's
friendliness to labor, he rallied to his standard such
other leaders of mass unions as David Dubinsky and
Sidney Hillman, of the garment and textile workers,
and formed the C.I.O.

Such was the story of John L. Lewis—a typical labor

success story. Even in his private life he was typical.
Finding it hard, as other labor leaders had, to see why
he should deny himself what every executive of every
manufacturing company was permitted without comment, he assumed the trappings of American bourgeois
existence, the good car, the chauffeur, the comfortable
Colonial house in Alexandria and the rest.

Where he was not typical was in his character. You
could see something of it in his appearance. That squat,
troglodytic body, that large, broad face of an unhealthy
but irritable bulldog, that prognathous chin and ridiculous nose, those small, sharp eyes and overpoweringly
beetling brows fitted him well for his new role of
bogieman in the house of American capitalism. They
also expressed a good deal of the dynamic personal
force, the recklessness and daring, the shrewd cunning
and fertility in expedients and talent for negotiation
which he brought to his task of organizing the un-
organized American workers. He was ambitious, immensely ambitious, but ambitious to succeed through his
movement and not by betraying it. He had a peculiar
vision of the strengths which American labor might
attain if it would but organize, and he meant to be the
engineer of that attainment. As befitted one who had
campaigned for Warren Gamaliel Harding and Franklin
Delano Roosevelt with an almost equal enthusiasm, he
was no partisan in politics; he saw politics only in terms
of what they might mean to him and to his C.I.O. Of all
men he was deeply suspicious, but of politicians above
all. When one fervent New Dealer urged him simply
to place his own and the C.I.O.'s fate in the President's
hands he remarked brusquely:

"I've been sold down the river by too goddam many
politicians to trust any of them."

Indeed there had never been a warm personal feeling between the President and this man on whom he

counted so nonchalantly to become his ally. The President has no overwhelming passion for great powers near the throne, and Lewis had made himself a great power. Although the President had helped him, he knew very well that he was creating a force he could not control. He showed his feelings rather amusingly one day when a friend remarked on Lewis' Alexandria house of that time being the old home of George Washington's physician, Dr Ball. The friend said that he understood Dr Ball had killed Washington, to which the President replied rather wryly that he trusted that the house's present occupant would not prove equally fatal to Washington's thirty-first successor.

As for Lewis, he liked the President rather less than the President liked him. The blarneying Roosevelt manner—what someone has called "Mr Roosevelt's man-to-man blather"—irritated him profoundly. He quickly perceived the President's slight nervousness lest he become a Frankenstein's monster, and it made him all the more determined to become just as little controllable, every bit as independently powerful as the President feared he might. For him the President was merely a political convenience, and, knowing his own and his C.I.O.'s value to the White House, he was never overeager to cultivate the Roosevelt good will. Similarly the President, knowing the New Deal's value to the C.I.O. and to Lewis, was not overeager to go out of his way to please the labor leader. The bond between the two men was merely the bond of their usefulness to each other.

Thus the President failed to take Lewis into partnership when he was maturing his court plan. True, he allowed Lewis to know that something was afoot, and that the something was a bill and not an amendment, long before any others but his most intimate advisers knew it. A day or so before the delivery of his message

on the state of the Union—very near the time of the
January 5 meeting at which the members of his
Cabinet asked what the message meant and got no
explanation—the President saw Lewis at the White
House. One of the subjects which they discussed was
the Supreme Court problem, about which Lewis, who
favored an amendment, felt very strongly. Lewis
pressed the President, and the President in his smiling
way told Lewis to leave the matter to him, promising
that some action would be taken in the near future.
Still Lewis was not content, and the President hinted
that the action he contemplated was legislative in character and indicated that it would be vaguely fore-
shadowed in his message.

But that was all the President did. While there was
still time, while the President was still able to go to
Lewis and say, "This thing is in our mutual interest;
let's go into it together, however we may feel about
other matters," he preferred to make no sign. He
chose to go it alone, to produce the court bill as his
personal rabbit out of his personal hat. He did not
see the danger in risking no one's prestige but his own,
for his overconfidence blinded him. The result was
precisely what might have been expected.

By February 5, 1937, the bond between the President and Lewis had been seriously weakened. Lewis
felt, with some justice, that he could take part of the
credit for the President's huge majority in November.
He remembered the large and solicited contribution.
He considered that it was time for the President to
deliver, in terms of assistance for the C.I.O. in its conflict with the A. F. of L. The President did not deliver,
and although he maintained a public silence which irritated John Garner into rebellion on one hand, he was
known to feel that the C.I.O. was going too far in its
organizing drives, which deeply annoyed Lewis on the

other. The result was that when the court bill was announced the labor leader cheerfully decided to let the President dree his own weird for a while. He made his emphatic statement, endorsing the bill; he publicly commanded Labor's Nonpartisan League to fling itself into the fight; but, like William Green, he failed to put the heat on.

Lewis' decision was perfectly natural. After all, there was nothing pressing about the fight for Lewis. The court had still to act on the National Labor Relations law; he could wait and see. Meanwhile, if the President wanted anything done, he could come to Lewis and ask for it. There was an infinity of things which Lewis wanted in exchange. It is interesting that Lewis was all the more reluctant to fling himself into the fight without a definite quid pro quo, because he saw very clearly that since the President had taken no partners or allies at the start, all the prestige of victory would go to him alone. To put it brutally, Lewis himself was somewhat disturbed at the prospect of absolute White House predominance which a presidential court bill triumph would have implied. If the President had no great desire to see Lewis too powerful, Lewis' ardor to see the President's power immensely increased was still less burning.

And so Labor's Nonpartisan League was left to muster what labor pressure it could, and left by Lewis in the knowledge that it could not muster much. The League had been organized during the election, with the short-term object of supporting the Democratic ticket and the long-term one of providing an effective instrument for political action by the workers. Lewis and Sidney Hillman had been the moving spirits in the League's organization. Lewis was the chairman of its board, but Major George L. Berry, leader of the pressmen and an A. F. of L. man, had been

installed as president to express the unity of labor
behind the Democratic ticket. Berry was a singular
political figure. In appearance he resembled an inex-
pensive rocking horse of German manufacture, one of
the stumpy ones with the hair painted on in large
black-and-white dapples. His shape had the same
peculiar ungainliness, his features the same strange
prominence, and like the rocking horse's, his locks,
which he wore glued rather sparsely across his bald
spot, seemed to be painted on. In conversation or in
oratory a torrent of faintly ungrammatical but richly
pious platitudes was his invariable contribution. In
politics cunning was his stock in trade. Such was the
Lochinvar on whom the President was forced to rely
for the labor pressure behind his court bill.

Worst of all, Lochinvar Berry had a horse which was
lame in all four legs. He had had great ambitions for
Labor's Nonpartisan League, by which he hoped to be
carried to high eminences. Unfortunately he regarded
the support of both factions of labor as essential to
success, and although the League was founded on a
union between the A. F. of L. and the C.I.O., the A. F.
of L. was suspicious of the League from the first.
A. F. of L. leaders had a not unnatural tendency to
murmur to one another that the League was a "Lewis
stooge." With his hope of keeping one foot in each
camp in mind, Berry voted for suspension of the C.I.O.
unions at the A. F. of L.'s Tampa convention in the
fall. His idea was that he could explain to Lewis later
that the rebellious C.I.O. groups were going to be
suspended anyway, and that he had cast his vote as he
did only to conciliate the angry moguls of craft
unionism and to preserve the League's usefulness.
Although he tried hard, he could not make Lewis see
his action in that light. Lewis was hopping mad, and
long before the presentation of the court bill he had

begun to freeze Berry out of the League—a task which was made easier by the fact that the C.I.O. was the financial angel of the organization. Thus the League was divided. If Berry men had one plan, Lewis-Hillman men, led by E. L. Oliver, who was to succeed Berry as president of the League, always had another. There was constant friction, constant work at cross-purposes, constant irritation, and things were made no pleasanter when Lewis calmly stopped the League's office rent and most League salaries in the middle of it all.

Where Lewis and Green, for their own reasons, had had no great desire to put the heat on for the court bill, Berry positively longed to. He was well aware that if he succeeded he would become a major hero of the New Deal. Yet he could not succeed, not only because of the internal dissensions in the League, but also because he could get no real support from the A. F. of L. or the C.I.O. The A. F. of L. leaders had not been in the least conciliated by Berry's vote at Tampa. They still regarded the League as a Lewis stooge and would have nothing to do with it. Consequently Berry tried frantically to get Lewis' help. He knew he must have some help, for without labor union backing the League was a mere paper organization. He hoped against hope that he could somehow draw Lewis into the fight, perhaps by calling on him for advice. Lewis, for the reasons already rehearsed, would have no more to do with him than the A. F. of L. He purposely made it quite impossible for Berry to go to him for advice, and Berry was left to carry on alone.

The result was no more effective than the ringing official endorsements of the court plan by the C.I.O. and the A. F. of L. The loquacious Berry promised great things. With his gift for pious metaphor he compared the whole business to a holy war, and he swore that labor would take a leading part. And then, after the first loud pronouncements, no more happened. To be sure, the League ground out a deal of run-of-the-mine propaganda. Letters to local union and central body leaders; statements; little pamphlets on "Packing the Court or Petting the Sweat Shop" and the like; even a "Supreme Court Battle Hymn" modeled on the "Battle Hymn of the Republic"—such things as these the League produced in great quantities.

Then Berry telephoned senators, and so did Oliver, and the League arranged for a number of official endorsements of the court plan by unions and labor groups back in the districts. The League even held a convention in Washington early in March, at which Bob La Follette spoke, and many a threatening fist was waved at the legislators opposed to the court plan. The trouble about it all was that it was just so much sound and fury. A few of the more timid members of Congress may have been frightened by it—many a senator would make a pregnant doe look as brave as a catamount—but all the sensible ones realized that it lacked the authentic note of "You vote our way, or else."

It took some time for the general staff at the White House to grasp what had happened. Not being seasoned politicians, they failed at first to note the absence of labor lobbyists on Capitol Hill. But when they did they were far more frantic than George Berry. One or two of them took refuge in the irritation they so often feel against prospective but disobedient supporters. It was about this time that one began to hear it whispered from the President's inner circle that really, John Lewis was going so far that he would queer the whole pitch of the labor movement. Others tried various expedients.

The chief one was to prod Lewis with a series of messages through various third parties, all to the effect that it was as much to his interest to join the fight as it was to the President's. By March, however, the sit-down strike situation had grown so much worse that no one at the White House could go to Lewis and plead with him directly. His immediate answer would have been to suggest some tangible return, and the President was in no position to offer the return that Lewis wanted. Lewis paid no attention to the indirect messages. The members of the general staff could do nothing but curse him and his imported labor weapon and wait for the court to invalidate the Wagner labor act.

Had the Wagner labor act been invalidated, there can be no doubt that Lewis' lobbyists and Green's lobbyists would have flown to Capitol Hill like a nestful of angry wasps. The labor act, with its guarantee of the right of collective bargaining, was the great legal buckler behind which the C.I.O. organizing campaign was being carried on, and the A. F. of L., if it did not like the C.I.O. organizing campaign, then believed that the labor act was also an immense protection for its craft unions. Both Lewis and Green had been waiting to see what would happen to the act. When it was sustained by the Supreme Court they both concluded that their official endorsements of the President's bill would do for the present.

The nature of their decision was finally made publicly obvious in the Patriot's Day meetings arranged by Berry for April 19, just a week after the Wagner labor act decisions were handed down. Berry had grandiosely announced the meetings as mighty mass rallies, at which the nation's embattled workers would terrify the court bill opposition by mere force of numbers. Unfortunately he had also allowed them to become entangled in local political situations in several districts, and he had decided to address all the meetings simultaneously by radio himself—which profoundly annoyed both the

A. F. of L. and the C.I.O. The consequence was that word went out from the C.I.O. and A. F. of L. headquarters in Washington that the meetings were poison. Workers, who had no one in their unions to urge them to attend, stayed away in immense hordes, and the meetings were a resoundingly hollow failure.

A good sample was the one in Omaha, Nebr. It had been predicted that all Nebraska labor would unite to demand the immediate resignation of anti-court bill leader, Senator Edward R. Burke. A resolution demanding Senator Burke's resignation was indeed passed at the meeting, but he might have been more impressed if the meeting had been attended by more than a few hundred voters. Large, empty halls, however thickly festooned with bunting, have never frightened a politician yet.

Thus the desertion of labor, the last and most powerful of the allies on whom the President had counted, was finally assured by the Supreme Court's switch. To add the last touch to the picture of the desperate situation in which the President found himself after his decision to press forward, the administration was taking a severe licking in the extraordinary public debate of the court issue that had raged over America since the presentation of the President's bill.

With the exceptions of slavery, prohibition and perhaps the League of Nations, no previous issue had ever caused the American people to be inundated with such deluges of propaganda, oral and written. The air, a new forum of public disputation, resounded nightly with the oratory of both sides. The press, whose editorial pages never ceased their banshee wailing, opened its news columns to the fullest reports of anything anybody, down to the local undertaker, had to say about the court bill, for or against. The mails were choked with pamphlets, and huge crowds turned out for pretty

nearly any meeting which had not been arranged by
George Berry. And throughout the whole controversy
the opposition had a distinct edge.

Their most important advantage was in the opposition group in Congress. More men in the group spoke
well than among the administration's supporters; more
men in it were fervently convinced of the righteousness
of their cause. There were times when the administration oratory's torrents dried up for a while, but the attacks on the bill were never interrupted. And the steering committee of opposition senators, smartly commanded by Senator Wheeler, was careful to arrange
that very few but Democrats, and, if possible, chiefly
Democrats of liberal tinge, should do the really prominent attacking. At the frequent semisecret meetings of
the steering committee the great stump-speaking tours
across the country, which senators resorted to as they
never had before except in the League of Nations fight,
were energetically encouraged and sometimes arranged
for. One opposition senator might know of a speaking
opportunity here; another of an empty platform there.
Senators who were setting out on cross-country oratorical marathons were warned, and these dates were
added to their schedules.

And then there were the hearings. It has been seen
how their angry suspicion of a filibuster and their confidence that victory would be theirs in the end had led
Tom Corcoran and Joe Keenan to resign the hearings
to the opposition. The anti-court plan senators took
full advantage of the opportunity, using it to hold the
headlines and the attention of the country for considerably more than a month. The presentation of opposition witnesses was managed by the same trio who had
been named to organize the heckling of the administration's testifiers—Burke, Van Nuys and Connally, with
Burke supervising the work. It was hard work, too.

An amazing succession of witnesses was put on the
stand, and even so not half of the fairly distinguished
men and women who volunteered to appear were
called. College presidents like Dodds, of Princeton, law
deans like Smith, of Columbia, journalists like Dorothy
Thompson, representatives of the churches, Everson,
of the Farmers' Union, Taber and the lobbyist, Fred
J. Brenckman, for the Grange, leaders of women's and
fraternal organizations, prominent former members of
the administration like Raymond Moley, anyone in fact
whose words might impress, intimidate or persuade a
senator, or affect the public mind—all were brought to
Washington to testify. Much assistance in the hearing
work was given the senators by the Bar Association's
Washington committee of bright young lawyers and
eminent old ones. Some witnesses' expenses were paid
by the Bar Association, while for others traveling
money was secretly put up by the Republican National
Committee.

Indeed the Republican Committee did a deal of quiet
work for the opposition, and although the general staff
at the White House suspected what was going on they
could never lay their hands on the proofs they longed
for. Besides paying the expenses of a number of witnesses National Chairman Hamilton had his research
staff put in some time finding good men who would take
the stand. Under the National Committee's amateur
brain truster, Dr O. Glenn Saxon, the Republican researchers specialized in academic testifiers and were
actually responsible for the appearance of a large number of the opposition witnesses with university background. Other small jobs were done by the committee.
If it was desired to have a witness's qualifications looked
up the Republican researchers were as ready to do it as
the Bar Association men. If material on any important
aspect of the court problem was required, then one of

the Republican senators asked for it but often passed it on to his Democratic colleagues.

But the senators were by no means the only organizers of propaganda. All over the country the class which the President has nicknamed the "economic royalists" were aroused to a pitch of wildest excitement by the court bill, and, being rich, their instant reaction was to spend very large sums of money on the fight. There was a good deal that was rather funny and a good deal that was rather nasty about this aspect of the struggle.

The ease with which the bogus "Associations to Preserve Our Liberties" and the like skimmed the cream off the idiocy of the rich was opulently ludicrous. And single individuals did their amusing bits, behaving the while as though they were so many Dutch boys, each with a finger in the dike. One Baltimore businessman spent a good many thousands of dollars circularizing literally scores of thousands of men and women with bitter letters against the court bill—but the men and women he chose to circularize were taken from the Republican National Committee's lists of dependable workers, so that his effort was about like making a perfervid recruiting speech to an army already in the field. Then there were odd little incidents, like that of the secret dinners of anti-court plan Democratic members of the House. Seven of the dinners took place, on the chain-letter principle, beginning with a small one at which each diner agreed to bring another diner to the next, and continuing in the same fashion until eighty-nine representatives were present at the seventh. They were paid for with two thousand dollars which one of the leading independent steel masters passed in cash, through a prominent Republican intermediary, to one of the Democratic representatives who organized the first small dinner.

Nor were bogus "Associations to Preserve Our Liberties" the only groups conducting a more organized propaganda. During the 1936 campaign the Republican National Committee had had a religious adjunct which called itself "America Forward." This outfit was just about to be finally liquidated when the court fight began. The announcement of the court bill promptly revived it. Under the direction of the Rev. Dr Ralph E. Nollner, a Methodist of the old and angry school, it took a fairly important part in the struggle. Dr Nollner was financed from Republican sources. He had some help from the eminent Lutheran divine, Dr Theodore Graebner, professor of philosophy at Concordia Seminary, St Louis. They joined in stirring up the churches against the bill, and Dr Nollner arranged for scores of broadcasts by anti-court plan ministers on local radio forums all over the country. He claimed that more than two hundred of these clerical air attacks had taken place during the hundred and sixty-eight days of the fight. If he was not exaggerating, his work may have had much to do with the prevailing feeling in the Senate that the churches were generally strongly opposed to the court bill.

The most effective independent propagandist organization was put together by the newspaper publisher, Frank E. Gannett, who managed to collect considerable sums of money for his National Committee to Uphold Constitutional Government. As with the other "committees", a large share of its funds came from the so-called economic royalists, among them Mr Gannett himself, but it differed from most of the others in that it gave its contributors something very definite for their dollars. Altogether several tons of propaganda must have been distributed by it. It sent out literally hundreds of thousands of copies of Senator Glass's famous radio speech, and prints of other important opposition addresses were also sown broadcast about the country at its expense. Some of its most effective work was done with small newspapers, to which it supplied quantities of printable, mildly newsy copy. Occasionally its doings were slightly naïve, as when it telegraphed all the Republican county committeemen in Nevada that if they would only give the Democratic Senator McCarran their endorsement for re-election, he would come out against the court bill the next day. But in general it accomplished as much as such committees can accomplish. Here again, incidentally, the Republicans helped. The Republican Michelson, William Hard, was detached from the national committee's service to act as liaison man between the Gannett group and the secretary of the opposition steering committee, Ben Stern.

Unlike the Baltimore businessman, a few individuals also accomplished something. One was Garrett McAnerney, a leading San Francisco lawyer, who virtually closed his office during the struggle to devote his whole time to propagandizing the Pacific Coast. His efforts gained an added weight from his position as one of the leading counsel of the Roman Catholic Church, but there were others without such an advantage who succeeded in stirring up considerable opposition sentiment. And besides the avowedly propagandist organizations and the private volunteers, the Grange added insult to injury by conducting a campaign against the court bill on the radio and in the farm press, and some fraternal and many established women's organizations hurled themselves into the fray. In the ladies' clubs the bosoms heaved with indignation, and female speakers toured the country, shouting the battle cry of freedom until their very millinery quivered.

Taking it as a general proposition, of course, it is a question how much good all the anti-court plan propaganda did, for the same groups and individuals were carrying it on as had exerted themselves to elect Alfred

M. Landon to the presidency. While overmuch importance should not be given to it, except as a fascinating political phenomenon, yet two things about it ought to be remembered. In the first place, where the propagandists had been unhappy and confused in their support of Landon, they were united and furious in their attack on the court plan. And in the second, besides the straight propaganda there was the open public debate already described, in which senators and representatives quite untarred by the reactionary brush were the opposition's principal spokesmen.

The opposition might have been less successful if the administration had given it any real competition. The fact that the administration did not is one of the most puzzling facts about the court fight. In the debate, of course, the administration was somewhat hampered. Its great voice, the President's, had been silenced by the poor response to his first two speeches, and although he hankered to take the issue to the country in a nationwide campaign trip, the unhappy example of Woodrow Wilson always prevented him. And of outside assistance the administration received almost none. The extreme left-wing groups, among them the Communist party, were vociferous in the President's support, and such influential liberal periodicals as the *Nation* and the *New Republic* lent a much more useful helping hand. But that was about all. Yet the administration had been forced to make its own propaganda on other issues and had shown an amazing expertness in handling the problem.

How the White House general staff sought from the first to "sell the court bill to the country", how a citizens' committee was briefly contemplated and how the task was finally turned over to the Democratic National Committee has already been related. The committee, shrewdly commanded by Jim Farley, with the great

expert, Charlie Michelson, in charge of its publicity
division, had done a magnificent job in the past. It
might have been expected to repeat the performance,
but it did not, and that was the real trouble. Instead it
was weak, fumbling, almost, it seemed, halfhearted.
All the motions were gone through, of course. A "Committee for Public Information", ostensibly unconnected
with Democratic headquarters, was formed and began
to issue handouts. Radio time was arranged and
speeches were written for senators. Pamphlets were
distributed, generally under frank. Such appropriate
groups as local Democratic Clubs, labor organizations,
farmers' associations and the like were circularized.
Postmaster General Farley himself wandered about
the country, announcing at every stop that the court
bill was "in the bag." Yet it was all wasted effort. The
national committee did its stuff, but the stuff did not
get over.

A reason for this curious ill-success may be found
in the surprising maladroitness which was exhibited in
some instances. Several speeches were poorly written.
One was so bad that Senator M. M. Neely, the hard-
driving, loud-shouting, highly verbal senator from West
Virginia, whose passion for brightly colored costumes
is only equaled in intensity by his subservient loyalty to
Joe Guffey, positively refused to deliver it. Then there
was the matter of recruiting. Under ordinary circumstances Farley and Michelson would have taken an important part in the recruiting work, but they did little
in the court fight. Farley, who is usually a man of a
Ulyssean variety of devices, proved a singularly unin-
ventive warrior—so much so that once, when a member
of the general staff took a list of waverers to him to
find out what individuals would be best able to bring
pressure on each senator, Farley's answer was simply
"Roosevelt" for nine out of ten of the names on the

list. And there were instances of downright carelessness, as when Joe Keenan had persuaded Senator Mc-
Carran to speak to one of the Berry Patriot's Day
rallies and asked Michelson to make the detailed ar-
rangements. Had McCarran spoken, he would have
been committed to support of the bill; Michelson forgot to prepare a speech or even get in touch with him,
and in the end McCarran left the reservation for good.

Faced with all this—with deserting Senate moderates and a gloomy Robinson, with suddenly conservative farmers, sulking labor and disunited liberals, with
failure in debate and all the rest—the President still
harped on his old theme, "The people are with me. I
know it." Unfortunately the very worst of his troubles
was that, apparently, they were not.

There is an old and excellent Washington saying,
"Congress never gets very far from the country,"
which embodies a principle that may be applied to the
court fight. In Congress the Supreme Court's self-
reversal had caused the moderate New Dealers to
desert the President, giving the opposition's liberal-
led, conservative coalition a clear majority of the votes.
Apply the principle of the saying, and in the country
you have the millions of middle-class Americans, whose
political thinking is precisely that of the moderate New
Dealers, who voted for the President in droves at the
November election, deserting him on the court issue
just as the senators did. That is at least the most credi-
ble explanation of the striking signs of national chilli-
ness towards the court bill.

A GAY COMMANDER
AND A DESPERATE STAFF

April 19–May 18, 1937

THE PRESIDENT and the men around him had rarely fought a losing fight. In all the New Deal years only one important measure had given the President a fore-taste of defeat—the Utilities Holding Company Bill, and in that conflict Senators Wheeler and Black and Representative Rayburn rallied the troops, reformed the lines and triumphed when the White House was ready to give in. One or two more were chancy; the rest had been ridiculously easy. The New Deal had won its victories in Congress with the same splendid facility which wreathed the Italian arms with laurels in the Ethiopian campaign—and on about the same fighting terms too.

But now the terms were different. Now the White House was confronted with the disagreeable necessity of fighting a losing fight, and the White House was sadly unprepared. In supreme command was the President, a general who had flung away his binoculars, used his ordnance map for scrap paper and turned his back on the battle. He would not believe that the fight was a losing one, for he simply would not listen to pessimistic reports from the front. If they came into him he heard them out, smiled, puffed at his cigarette and changed the subject.

185

He had a reason for everything. When word continued to come from Robinson that votes were slipping away every day or so, he talked of "defeatist" leaders. When particular defections were brought to his attention, he pointed out that the labor pressure had not been put on this man, or that another man had ridden into office on his coattails and could never muster the final courage to vote against him, or that still another was suffering from personal pique and should not be regarded as typical. In the end he always told his advisers to wait and see, predicting that when the bill came to a vote he would have a surprising majority. Thus the blackness of the situation was explained away, by a sort of Maskelyne and Cook vanishing act which deceived the magician instead of his audience.

With such a commander the general staff at the White House could not do much. The little system they had evolved continued to operate. The staff councils still took place daily at the White House. Jimmy Roosevelt still reported the proceedings to his father and procured the President's approval for contemplated steps. Individual members of the staff saw him from time to time, to talk the situation over. Votes were still counted, pressures discussed and schemes canvassed. Indeed they worked very hard and very faithfully, this little group of men whom the President had preferred above his orthodox lieutenants on Capitol Hill. They sensed their responsibility, and they did their best to live up to it. Their only difficulty, which most of them loyally failed even to formulate in their minds, was simply that the President did nothing to unify or give direction to their efforts. As one of them did put it, "It was as if they were under a spell."

There was no orderly daily pooling of information, no way for the members of the staff to know precisely where to concentrate their forces, no certainty in the struggle anywhere. They could not even manage an accurate list of their own supporters—and this in a fight in which the opposition had admirably prepared, carefully checked, semiweekly lists from their whip, Gerry, who was able to say at a moment's notice whether any senator was sure, inclined to the opposition, wavering, inclined to the administration or sure for the administration.

Robinson and Keenan both tried to make lists. So did Corcoran. Time and again the whole downtown group gathered at the White House to check the Senate over. But Robinson carried all his information in his head, and some of it was confidential and not to be revealed even to the White House. And some senators talked double, giving one impression to Keenan and Corcoran and quite another to James Roosevelt when they called on the President. And other senators would not talk at all, and no two could agree how they should be counted. The result was that these staff efforts to read the roster of the troops invariably collapsed in endless and futile argument. The administration actually never possessed a reliable list of its friends and enemies until the very final weeks of the struggle.

This may seem incredible, but it is true, and if you will think of the situation for an instant you will see its effects written plain all over the administration's strategic wallowings in the weeks following the Wagner labor act decisions. The vital class in the Senate were the Democratic waverers. The Court's change of front had caused them to desert the administration, yet it cannot be said that the President was entirely without grounds for his suspicion that when the test of a vote came they would be inclined to return to the administration fold. The trouble was, nothing was ever done to prepare for their return. Without a reliable list there was no way in which the general staff could con-

centrate its efforts where they would do the most good.
Few temperaments could have survived unruffled in
such a hopeless situation. The feeling which the general staff members had, that they were constantly making passes in the air while their opponents were landing
their blows on the button every time, is not conducive
to calm co-operation. Consequently disunion began to
grow up among them. Robinson was a man apart; he
never joined their councils, and he preferred to work
alone like the independent potentate that he was. When
they wanted information from him they had to go to
him, and this annoyed some of them. But the disunion
affected the White House group itself. Personal irri-
tations, disagreements, all the petty unpleasantnesses
which will trouble any small human society, were suddenly magnified by the untoward pressure of events
into angers and even suspicions.

There were really unpleasant incidents—several of
them connected with the failure of the Democratic
National Committee's propaganda campaign. Michelson, whose wise way of feeding the public what it
wanted had restored life to the democracy after the
terrible years of the twenties, was an old-line Democrat, a survivor from an earlier regime. He was suspected at the start of disliking the court bill in a way
that none of the others did, not for its strategic defects but for what it meant in terms of change in the
government. Very likely the suspicion was groundless.
Whether it was or no, it caused tension as soon as the
failure of the national committee's efforts was clear.

Michelson and his assistant, Roddan, still sat in on
the staff conferences, but when they were not present
the other staff members talked of the orations he ghost-
wrote for administration supporters of the court bill
as "Charlie's Shirley Temple speeches." Such occurrences as the neglected chance to nail down McCarran

with a Patriot's Day address, and Farley's stock answer of "Roosevelt" when he was asked who should
bring pressure on senators, set the other members of
the general staff to murmuring among themselves. So
much feeling naturally found its expression on one
occasion when Neely refused to deliver the speech
Michelson had written for him.

"What's the matter, is he yellow?" Michelson asked
when Neely's refusal was reported in the staff council
of that day.

"No, he just doesn't want to deliver your speech,
Charlie," was the meaningful reply, shot back with an
angry emphasis.

The speeches which Jim Farley was making all over
the country caused a real row. Several of the other
members of the general staff thought the Farley
speeches ill conceived and silly. The constant prediction that the "court bill was in the bag" when it obviously was not sounded like shadowboxing to them;
what was worse, such statements by Farley bounded
back in the face of the administration. Michelson wrote
the Farley speeches. He was held jointly responsible.
The explosion came one day when the general staff was
once more canvassing the problem of the waverers.
Keenan was especially concerned about it.

"Why doesn't Jim Farley put some pressure on these
men?" he asked Michelson at last.

Michelson and Roddan answered together that Big
Jim was doing his best, that he was speaking all over
the country. That was the spark which detonated the
general irritation. The others asked furiously if
Michelson and Roddan could not think of better ways
for Farley to bring pressure on senators than by
futile oratory. They demanded to be told if better
methods had not been found in the past, and they
proclaimed themselves unable to see why they were

not being used now. They pooh-poohed the idea that
any senator would be affected by a mere speech in
his home district, and they ended by telling Michelson
point-blank that he could not mention a single instance
in which a Farley speech had had a good effect. Michelson
and Roddan, who must have been somewhat disconcerted
by the outburst, rather weakly replied that
they thought that Senator Dennis Chavez, of New
Mexico, had been influenced by Big Jim's talk, but
could produce no other name.

Whether or no Farley and Michelson were backward
in trying to round up the senators, the other members
of the general staff were not. Horribly handicapped
though they were by the lack of an adequate list of
troops, they tried hard to make old-fashioned political
heat supply the place of all the pressures, from labor,
from agriculture, from the electorate, from the Court
itself, which had so sadly failed them.

All through April and May, while they were making
their last convulsive effort to hold their troops in line,
the Capitol corridors buzzed with stories of administration
heat. Plenty of them were false or overdrawn,
but plenty of them were true too. The bargain with
one senator from the industrial Mid West, who was
allowed to nominate a federal judge or so for his promise
to go along, was almost a matter of public record,
and it was generally known that judicial patronage was
being rather freely used in other cases. Nor was the
patronage doled out exclusively judicial. The appointment
of an obscure clergyman of Scandinavian origin to
an important diplomatic post may be traced to the court
fight, and so may a number of other, less surprising
pie slicings.

Projects were another weapon. One simple-minded
senator was frightened out of his wits by the threat
(obviously hollow), that if he voted wrong the WPA

would simply stop operating in his state. Another was surprised by a flood of letters from mayors and county officials back home, all simultaneously asking him to hurry down to the office of Works Progress Administrator Hopkins to see about new sewer lines, new street pavings, new parks, new dams and all those other blessings which the relief organization can shower on the local communities. There was no mention of the court bill in the letters, but the senator drew a rather natural inference from the great number of them and the peculiar simultaneity of their arrival, just at a time when the pleasing prospect of lining his constituents' pockets with WPA dollars might have been expected to influence his decision on the bill.

In still another case punishment was administered and reward was given at the same time. Long before the court fight Senator Wheeler had been working hard to get the $17,000,000 Buffalo Rapids Dam project for his state. It had been virtually promised to him, and when he went into opposition Montana was not deprived of its dam. Instead Senator James Murray, Wheeler's colleague and the reputed author of the immortal phrase, "pap, patronage and projects," was called down to the White House, officially informed that the dam would be built and allowed to announce the new candy from the White House steps. And months later, when the President was in Montana during his autumn trip through the Northwest, he spoke much of the Buffalo Rapids Dam and other great projects in the state, but always credited them to Senator Murray and the Montana congressman, although Senator Wheeler had been the moving force in obtaining most of them.

The actual distribution of patronage and projects were by no means the only weapons in the administration's armory. Political fires back home were industri-

ously built under recalcitrant senators. Their enemies
were publicly accorded handsome treatment by the administration. Members of their local party organizations were warned that unless the senators changed
their stands the organizations themselves would be
lodged in the doghouse. All sorts of minor propaganda
groups, like the Thatcher wing of the Farmers' Union,
were set to yapping in the districts.

The quality of the whole business was summed up
by the unfortunate Jim Farley's remark to a group of
newspapermen in the hall of the White House offices.
He had just seen the President, and he was asked how
the court fight was going. Senator O'Mahoney's opposition had not become public at the time, and Senator
McCarran was only known to be inclined to oppose.
Farley chose the two senators for the text of a little
sermon on how most Democrats would eventually return to the administration fold. He flatly predicted they
would both vote for the court bill.

"When Senator O'Mahoney comes round for help
on a sugar bill," he said, "his conscience won't be both-
ering him then, will it? Neither will Senator McCarran's when he wants something for his state. It's all in
the point of view."

The three sentences, spoken off the record but printed
all the same, made the general staff angrier than ever
with Farley, for they confirmed O'Mahoney in his intentions and drove McCarran off the reservation for
good, in a tearing fit of temper. Unfortunately, if
Farley's words summed up the quality of the administration effort to put the heat on, their results also
summed up the results of the effort. The issue was too
big; the senators were too much excited by it to be
affected by the petty political bullying and legal bribery
which are ordinarily so useful to all administrations.
While the members of the general staff were learning

this disappointing lesson, they were simultaneously moving heaven and earth to blast the court bill out of the Judiciary Committee. They wanted to bring it to the floor and get a vote on it as soon as possible, on the theory that they might be able to hold their forces together if they could but hurry the fight to a prompt finish. By a sad chance for them, however, the man they had to deal with if they wanted to expedite their bill was still Henry Fountain Ashurst. His motto remained, "No haste, no hurry, no waste, no worry," and his attitude was well described by his own later statement that "when this fight started I knew it would kill someone, and I made up my mind it wouldn't be me."

Born in a covered wagon at Winnemucca, Nev., by the side of the old California trail, Ashurst arrived in Arizona while yet a child. His parents' choice of domicile was fortunate for him, for he early proved to have one of those alloyed-silver tongues which are the best equipment for the practice of politics and the law in a small state. After a good education he accordingly opened an Arizona law office in 1904. A mere law office could not hold him long. He entered politics early. Borne upward by his oratory and a native shrewdness, he arrived in the Senate in 1912. He found the Senate so agreeable that he never left it, and he was serving his fifth term when the court bill fell on him like a hundred of brick.

His exterior was gloriously senatorial. Tall, with aquiline features and flowing gray locks, usually clothed in a full-bottomed, folksily shabby cutaway coat, he seemed the ideal American statesman until you observed the genial indecision of his lower face and the odd, careless twinkle in his eyes. His rolling periods, ornately garnished with flowers of semiclassical learning and delivered in a faintly precious voice, sounded like a statesman's sentences until you heard the quaint, high Ashurst giggle punctuating them. That little giggle was the key to the Ashurst character.

He loved the pomps of senatorial existence, but he also found them funny. He had a passion for small jokes and an easy life. He dearly liked to wear a literary air, and for years he had kept a diary of doings in the Senate for the benefit of future generations. Above all he was fond of enjoying himself, and he managed to get enjoyment out of most things. Endorsing the President's court bill after calling court packing the "prelude to tyranny" would have embarrassed most men; not so Ashurst, who thought it the best fun in the world and used to carry with him printed copies of an address on the beauties of inconsistency, for distribution to all and sundry. When witnesses before his committee were caught in contradictions he always told them that inconsistency was "one of life's greatest virtues."

Poor Tom Corcoran and Joe Keenan never knew where to find such a man. Time and again they thought they had pinned him down; time and again they heard his mocking giggle and realized he had eluded them. First the hearings ran on to seven weeks, and then the Judiciary Committee went into an executive session which seemed interminable until it did terminate on May 18, three months and thirteen days from the date of the bill's introduction. Uncertainty was breeding ever wilder suspicions in the inner circle, and the President's advisers, confronted with Senator Ashurst's committee's endless delay, suspected him of conducting an indirect filibuster against the court bill. Meanwhile the senator enjoyed himself to the full, being courtly and giggling at his own courtliness by turns. It was during this period that he received a letter from a constituent, fulsomely praising his heroic stand on the President's bill. He replied in two words:

"Which stand?"

The executive sessions, into which the Judiciary Committee subsided when the hearings ended in mid-April, were watched with a breathless interest by the general staff and the members of the opposition. When they started in the committee's dankly comfortable room in the Capitol's lower floor, the line-up on the committee was eight to seven, with three undecided. The original administration sextet, Ashurst, Neely, Logan, Dieterich, Pittman and Hughes, had been joined by McGill and Norris. Norris was still pushing his seven-to-two decision substitute for the court bill, but he had made it definitely known long before that he would vote with the President if it were his only chance to do something about the Court. As for McGill, the nasal-voiced hectoring to which he had subjected opposition witnesses had made his position clear as soon as the hearings were really under way.

The opposition still had their seven votes: King, Van Nuys, Burke, Connally, Borah, Austin and Steiwer. The whole thing hung on three senators: McCarran, O'Mahoney and the sensible, clever, quiet-spoken Carl A. Hatch, of New Mexico. All three were Democrats. Hatch and, until then, O'Mahoney were faithful New Dealers. As has been seen, O'Mahoney was bitterly opposed to the court bill from the very day of its announcement, but he had kept his opposition to himself and tried frantically to get a compromise accepted. The hearings were over or just ending when he paid his call on the President with Professor Ripley and heard the Rooseveltian lecture on the beauties of a cooperative Court. Apparently that White House visit convinced him of the futility of his compromise efforts. Shortly after it he presented himself to a meeting of the opposition steering committee, announced that he would oppose the President's bill whatever happened, and asked to be accepted as a fellow worker. Wheeler and the others welcomed him with open arms, and he immediately became a regular attendant at the secret, smoke-heavy meetings, at which the anti-court plan Democrats canvassed their situation and discussed the future with all the harsh realism which good politicians practice in private.

O'Mahoney had already made one speech against the bill when Farley offered his tactless prediction to the newspapermen at the White House and added McCarran to the opposition. Like O'Mahoney, Mc-Carran had wanted compromise. He had been ready to go along on a two-judge increase of the Court, and he had tried hard to get the administration to accept his scheme. He, too, had been firmly turned down, but he might still have been dealt with until his paroxysm of rage at Big Jim's gaff. He gave the opposition its ninth vote, while the administration still had eight. Hatch became the key to the situation.

During the executive sessions of the committee the administration men labored endlessly with Hatch. The object of the sessions was to examine every proposed substitute for the court bill and to study all the bill's own aspects, in preparation for the day when the committee would vote. Much of the time was given over to the presentation of compromises. Norris argued valiantly for his, and the committee listened with the deep respect which every senator and group of senators, whatever their political opinions, invariably accords to the great old man. Andrews, whose notions had so pleased Keenan, offered his, and a great many other senators of all shades of political coloring offered theirs. Hatch was one of them.

He had begun to think very early in the fight that he could not vote for the President's bill. There was something about it he could not stomach; in Joe Robinson's phrase, it was "pretty raw", with its frank request for

a round half dozen of extra justices. In his inconspicu-
ous way he had made up his mind during the hearings,
and he had informed the administration leaders on the
Hill and the members of the general staff at the White
House that he could not vote for the measure in its
first form. He, too, demanded compromise. His suggestion was that the judicial age limit be set at seventy-
five; that coadjutor justices for members of the Bench
who had passed that age be appointed as under the
President's scheme, but that the President be permitted
to make only one such appointment in any single year.
Like all the others, his compromise had been turned
down flat at the White House. Thereupon he simply
told the general staff members that it was as far as he
was willing to go, and asked them not to expect his support. Thus the President's no-compromise stand, born
of his overconfidence, lost him the majority in the
Judiciary Committee he could surely have obtained if
he had been ready to give ground after the Wagner
labor act decisions.

All through the April weeks when compromise could
only have been beaten by a successful filibuster the
President refused to listen to any talk of it. The same
forces were at work against it as had been immediately
after the Wagner labor act decisions. Cummings was
ready, even eager for compromise if it preserved the
principle and the lower court features of his precious
bill, but any measure meeting his requirements was sure
to run head on into the objection raised by Cohen, Corcoran and Jackson that "if you're going to pack a court,
you've got to really pack it." Their efforts to head off
compromise were made all the more intense by Keenan's continued advocacy of the Andrews scheme for
a "pork-barrel court", which they so cordially detested.
They made the efforts not from any failure in realism
—all three of them saw pretty well how the situation

stood—but because they honestly believed that the court bill's death by inanition, or even a defeat on the open floor of the Senate, would be preferable to what Cummings and Keenan wanted.

Naturally, with things going as they were, the general staff searched for stratagems to turn the tide of battle. The best of these was born of the Cohen-Corcoran-Jackson attitude towards compromise. This trio, in whom were concentrated as much sheer ability, solid information and disinterestedness as the government has had at its service in a good many years, were accustomed to taking the long view. They figured the situation out rather simply. While Tom Corcoran and perhaps Ben Cohen might have liked to see great powers concentrated in the White House by a court bill victory, all three regarded the New Deal program as the most important thing to consider. Because of the President's carrot-before-the-donkey trick and the complete lack of interest in any other legislation while the court bill was before Congress, all the big measures which it had been hoped to pass during the session—the wages and hours bill, the farm bill, the little TVA bill and the rest— were slowly expiring unnoticed. With their belief in the primary importance of the general New Deal program as their point of departure, the three therefore hatched their scheme. As they planned it, the court bill was to be relegated to the background, while the other great measures, and especially the farm, labor and TVA bills, were to be pressed at once.

The carrot-before-the-donkey trick had not worked. The farm, labor and liberal groups had failed the administration. Now Corcoran, Jackson and Cohen frankly hoped that by paying off these natural allies in advance a much more vigorous support might be obtained from them. Moreover, they expected that three such important pieces of legislation would take a deal of time to get out of the way—the wages and hours bill alone, which Corcoran and Cohen had written, would have been accomplishment enough for an ordinary Congress—and they believed that the opposition to the court bill would be weakened by the long period of inactivity. Meanwhile, if the Supreme Court should suddenly invalidate the Social Security Act, as Jackson rather thought it might, the court bill would be waiting in cold storage for an immediate revival. Their scheme was perfect in all its details. They thought they had even provided against a filibuster, for in the event the court bill could not be revived early, the delay would pinch the debate on it between the final action on the other measures, and the hot, weary, fantastic hours which end a session.

Having evolved the scheme, they proceeded to push it energetically, with the tangible result that work was begun in Congress on the big general program measures they wished to see pass. But as for relegating the court bill to the background, that was impossible. In the first place a bill which had roiled up feeling in the country and the Congress to the extent the court bill had, could no more be relegated to the background than a tremendous catfight in a quiet back alley. While the bill continued to exist it occupied everyone's attention, just as a catfight does. Nor was it even feasible to try to call a momentary truce in the struggle over the bill. Congressional leaders have a deeply rooted distaste for unfinished business, and Joe Robinson was adamant. He would not have the bill left hanging, and that was the end of it. He hoped the President would compromise. He hoped the Court would switch again on the Social Security cases. He hoped something would happen to turn the tide of battle. But as for stopping in the middle, that he would not do. Winning or losing, he would fight on, and so he told the general staff.

So other schemes were desperately canvassed, and a few were even tried out. One such was to break the Senate deadlock by turning to the House. There Maury Maverick had got his name tacked onto the President's original bill by seizing a mimeographed copy, scribbling his signature on it and dropping it in the bill hopper a couple of minutes after the measure arrived at the Capitol. Maverick is not overpopular with his more conservative fellows, and dealing with a Maverick bill seemed an unnecessary handicap.

Therefore the first step in the scheme was to get Representative Fred Vinson, of Kentucky, to introduce a slightly revised bill. The general staff figured it would be easy to obtain enough House members' signatures to a petition to bring a Vinson bill out of the hostile House Judiciary Committee. But Speaker Bankhead and Majority Leader Sam Rayburn were so infuriated by the effort to make the House do the dirty work, as they put it, that this scheme, too, was abandoned. And so were all the others. It was no time for stratagems. Nothing less than a complete reorganization of fighting line-up, such as a compromise would have brought, or a tremendous aid to recruiting, such as adverse decisions in the Social Security cases, could save the administration and the President.

Meanwhile the opposition was making new recruits almost daily. Wheeler, the perfect leader of such guerilla warfare as the opposition had to carry on, was everywhere at once, buttonholing his friends, mocking his enemies, urging on the propagandists, confirming the Republicans in their all-important resolution to keep silent. He and Borah still held their unnoticed conferences, and two slyer veterans to plot the destruction of an overconfident President could not be found in the Senate. He and the buttoned-up, efficient Gerry still went over their lists. He still presided at the regu-

lar gatherings of the steering committee, which grew
more determined and more cheerful with every report.
And other senators were only slightly less energetic in
the fight. Gerry's files bulged with the material collected
by the senatorial espionage service the opposition had
organized. Everywhere waverers were beset by the
members of the opposition, who wheedled, persuaded,
threatened and cajoled until the waverers wavered no
longer. By the beginning of May the steering committee concluded that they commanded an absolute majority of the Senate.

The administration had its spies, too, and Robinson's
reports of the state of affairs grew gloomier and gloomier. Yet the President maintained his optimism unconcerned. His response to pessimistic predictions was
still the same polite attention, the same smile and the
same firm refusal to take them seriously. He still repeated that the people were with him, he knew it, and
he supported his belief that when the test came he
would have the Senate votes, too, with the peculiar
notion that he could always win over sufficient senators
by appealing to them personally. So unshakable was his
overconfidence that on April 28, with defeat already
staring him blankly in the face, he cheerfully left Washington for Texas and a little fishing under the Gulf sun.

Almost simultaneously a new upsurge of worry over
the condition of affairs caused Corcoran, Jackson and
Cohen to revise their first scheme. The spectacle of the
Democratic party publicly disintegrating on the Hill,
the immediate neglect which had been the lot of the
great measures they favored in spite of all the pressure
behind them, and the desire to find an expedient which
would meet with Robinson's approval, led them to
abandon the idea of action on the court bill even at the
end of the session. Cohen and Corcoran were the chief
originators of the new strategy; Jackson merely dis-

cussed it with them once or twice. But all three agreed
together that it would be best to let the court bill drop
completely for the present, with an announcement that
it would be taken up at the following session. They had
three reasons for wanting to keep it alive at all. First
they hoped that with the passing months the administration might be able to consolidate its position, rally
its forces and perhaps win its bill. Second there was the
need to save face, which could be neatly done by declaring that the Court's switch had made immediate
action unnecessary. And third there was their belief
that the Court's switch was not a dependable indication
of its future course, that "a sword of Damocles" had
to be hung over the justices' heads to keep them in line.

The President had already left on his fishing trip in
the Gulf when Corcoran, Cohen and Jackson produced
their modified scheme, which was subsequently approved
by West and Keenan. It was while he was away also that
a move to save the situation was made by the congressional leaders. Even Joe Robinson had been pretty
much out of touch with the President all through
April. He had done his routine duties and let it go at
that. Then, while the President was catching his tarpon
in the bright Southern waters, he and his friends could
stand it no longer.

Early in May Joe Robinson, Pat Harrison and Alben
W. Barkley, of Kentucky, invited Jimmy Roosevelt to
lunch with them in the private office of Colonel Edwin
A. Halsey, secretary of the Senate. At the lunch Robinson and Harrison and Barkley told Jimmy the un-
varnished truth as they saw it. In the first place, they
said, if the President continued to insist on his original
plan for six additional justices he would be beaten. In
the second, they pointed out that the bill, with all the
bitterness it had aroused, was raising hell with the
Democratic party. They besought Jimmy to make the

President see reason, to persuade him not to pull his house down about his ears out of pure obstinacy. They asked to be allowed to handle the bill themselves, and they promised to do their level best for the President. Finally they insisted that Jimmy take their message to the President before his return to Washington. Robinson was the spokesman.

"Mr Roosevelt," he said, "you tell your poppa that he'd better leave this whole thing to us to get what we can out of it. We'll do our best for him."

How Jimmy Roosevelt reacted to this interview is not known, but it must be remembered that the view that the congressional leaders were defeatists had important currency at the White House, being shared by the President himself. Indeed the tag "defeatist" was the President's explanation of his failure to rely on his congressional leaders' advice. He once told an adviser that in September, during the campaign, when the Democracy's congressional bigwigs visited him in Hyde Park, he had had to spend a whole afternoon allaying their fears and convincing them that a triumph was in store. Why humor such proved pessimists? the President asked. Either because he was infected with his father's opinion or because he simply did not wish to act on his own responsibility Jimmy Roosevelt called a luncheon meeting of the inner circle for the next day.

The whole group gathered at the White House. Corcoran, Keenan, West, Michelson, Roddan and Early were all there, and Attorney General Homer S. Cummings had also been invited. Jimmy told them of his talk with Robinson, Harrison and Barkley, and in this case the inner circle agreed with the leaders on the Hill. All the men at the luncheon urged Jimmy to give Robinson's message to the President without softening it in any detail. Some of those present were so eager to see the word passed on that they even tried to reach

the President by telephone, but they found he was at
sea. The next suggestion was for Jimmy to fly to Gal-
veston, but it was thought that such a step would be too
conspicuous. At length it was decided that Jimmy should
go out to Indianapolis with Jim Farley, to meet the
President on his way home.

A good many members of the inner circle were
lighter hearted when they left that luncheon table, for
they saw a dawning hope of a solution. Corcoran must
have believed the great chance to promote the scheme
of letting the bill go over had come at last. The meeting broke up quickly, and only Cummings lingered on
with Jimmy for a moment. It is significant of the state
of mind in the inner circle that some of its members
suspected that Cummings, being the proud author of the
court bill, persuaded the President's son to forget the
advice of the meeting and to soften the leaders' message
after all. Actually Cummings did nothing of the sort.

The suspicion of Cummings was occasioned by the
fact that the President returned to Washington with
his determination to fight on quite undiminished. His
first action was to call in Robinson, Bankhead and Rayburn and to announce to them once more that the fight
must continue. Once more he laughed at their fears,
and this time he emphasized his intentions by putting
the court bill at the top of his list of legislative "musts."
What is more, he used a sort of indirect threat to gin-
ger up their efforts to get him what he wanted. Naturally such delicate matters are vaguely put, but he left
them with a clear impression. They understood him to
say that they could and should get him the court bill,
but that if they failed he would still be content, for then
he would be able to take the issue to the country in
1938 or even in 1940.

The veiled intimation that the President might not
be through in 1940 upset the leaders pretty completely.

So did the President's statement to them that they did not know what was going on in their own districts. Sam Rayburn had won every election for a couple of decades and might have been presumed to know pretty well what his people were thinking, yet the President told him flatly that he was wrong in suspecting they were not overly enthusiastic for the court bill. As for Robinson, he was convinced that his message had not been passed on to the President by James Roosevelt, and consequently deeply irritated. Altogether they were not a happy trio when they left the White House, with the President's final injunctions ringing unpleasantly in their ears.

Events moved very rapidly in those days. The President got back from Texas on May 14 and saw Robinson, Bankhead and Rayburn the same afternoon. His orders to them were a disappointment to the members of the general staff, for although Corcoran, Cohen and Jackson still opposed compromise they did not want to have to present their own scheme to an adamantine President. Nevertheless, the trio and their ally, West, did not give up.

After waiting a day or so they broached the scheme and found, somewhat to their surprise, that it met with a fairly favorable reception. In the brief interval, perhaps, the congressional leaders' fears had had time to sink into the President's mind. Moreover, letting the bill go over to the next session was more appealing than the immediate compromise Robinson sought. As Corcoran was careful to point out, it not only allowed for face-saving and conceded nothing; it also positively promised to give the President the bill he longed for at the next session.

At any rate the President was far more amenable. He said that he liked the scheme and would consider it very seriously. He gave the impression that he might well resort to it in the near future. The men who had hatched the scheme breathed sighs of relief—sighs which were breathed too soon. The trouble was that while the excited discussions were in progress the opposition had already prepared the event which was to prove the scheme's destruction. To be sure, it was also the event which gave the President his second chance to save himself, but the President was ready for the Corcoran-Cohen-Jackson scheme, where he was completely unready to seize his chance.

Throughout most of the fight the opposition senators were in pretty close touch with certain members of the Supreme Court, and one strong faction among them, headed by Senator Burke, desired to use these contacts to prevent any resignations or retirements from the bench. They were the bitter-enders, greedy for an absolute victory over the President. The two most influential members of the opposition, Wheeler and Borah, were, however, of a different opinion. Their one desire was to prevent the packing of the Court, and they believed that a retirement or so would weaken the President's case almost as much as the Court's change of front in the Wagner decision had done. Borah, an intimate friend of Justice Van Devanter's, knew that the justice was anxious to retire. He told Wheeler about it, and they decided to turn the justice's desire to advantage. Borah dropped a hint to Van Devanter that his retirement would strengthen the opposition, and, after some consideration, the justice decided to leave the bench. The thing was planned in the utmost detail. At the senators' slightly devilish prompting, Van Devanter even decided to send his letter of resignation to the President on the very day of the Judiciary Committee's preordained unfavorable vote on the court bill.

Naturally Wheeler learned of Van Devanter's decision from Senator Borah. He promptly made an over-

ture to the administration. Through a third party he
passed the word of the coming retirement along to
Charles West, with a message that the time had come
to compromise. Wheeler's suggestion was that the
President announce himself satisfied with Van Devanter's retirement, so long as he got long-term reform in
the shape of the Wheeler amendment permitting Congress to override court decisions by a two-thirds vote
after an intervening election. The suggestion was refused, partly on the ground that Wheeler, regarded as
the blackest of the Democratic traitors, ought not to
be allowed to get any glory out of the court fight.

For the day or so they had to wait the general staff
at the White House hoped against hope that Wheeler's
news was untrue. They saw with agonizing clarity
what the news meant—that if the court bill was to be
put over to the next session Joe Robinson would have
to be elevated to the bench alone, without offsetting
appointments.

As for the President, he was a shade less confident
now. He still walked widdershins around his problem,
but he was ready to admit that it was there. And who
could help but admit it? It seemed, it almost seemed as
though a suddenly unfriendly Fortune had pettishly
determined to make the President see she could be
fickle. The liberals had proved "perfectionist"; the
farmers ungratefully apathetic or hostile; the powerful
labor movement he had called forth out of nothing had
deserted him in his hour of need; all the laurels of triumph had untimely withered—and still the President
had smiled. And now, when his smile was fading, this
last blow threatened, to teach him, as it were, that
equanimity has its place like everything else.

The Ghost of Justice Robinson

THAT WAS a pleasant May in Washington. While the prospect darkened at the White House the children of comfortable Democratic job holders played loudly in the streets of the spreading suburbs; ladies were already lunching in Georgetown's gardens; and half Iowa and most of Kansas, vacationing with a new prosperity, gaped at the preposterous, slightly faded prettiness of the cherry trees in the sun, along the rim of Major L'Enfant's formal waters. May 18 was another bright day, and the President, who is sensitive to the weather, must have enjoyed the brightness pouring through his windows as he breakfasted in bed.

One of the letters on his tray that morning was from Justice Van Devanter—an unfamiliar correspondent indeed. It contained the announcement of the justice's intention to retire at the close of the Court's spring term. The President read it, thought it over, and within an hour he had dictated an acknowledgment, curtly, in dry but polite terms. And then, at ten o'clock, the Judiciary Committee met for its final executive session, to pass judgment on the President's court bill. Norris', Hatch's, Andrews' substitutes for the bill were

208

voted down one by one, and so were all the others.
Ashurst moved a vote on the bill itself, and the inevitable response came all up and down the table. A
few minutes later the President was informed by telephone from the Capitol that the senators had decided,
ten to eight, to report his great measure unfavorably,
with the formal recommendation that "it do not pass."

The committee's action merely underlined the significance of the Van Devanter letter. After the Wagner
labor act decision the President had publicly stated that
a mere five-to-four liberal majority on the Court was
"too uncertain." He had argued that no majority of
one could be depended on. That argument was now also
destroyed, and, so far as the public could see, there was
no reason why the President should not be content to
supplant Justice Van Devanter with a liberal and abandon his court bill. Thus Van Devanter's retirement was
all the more exquisitely embarrassing, for of course
Robinson had to be appointed, and yet the President
could hardly explain that the opportunity to fill Van
Devanter's vacancy did not satisfy him because he did
not consider his ablest and most faithful lieutenant, the
leader of his party in the Senate, sufficiently liberal for
the place.

And yet, embarrassing as it was and disastrous as it
was to prove, the Van Devanter retirement offered the
President his last real chance to save himself. The key
to the situation was to be found that same afternoon
in the Senate chamber, where the news of the vacancy
on the high bench caused an extraordinary scene to be
enacted. Joe Robinson, grinning and thoroughly happy
for the first time in the history of the court fight, held
a sort of reception at his desk in the front row. One
after another his colleagues, both Democratic and Republican, hustled up to congratulate him on the promotion which they believed the Van Devanter retirement

would surely bring their friend. They slapped him on the back, they put their arms around his shoulders, they pumphandled him energetically, they called him "Mr Justice." The whole Senate was aware of the administration promise to Robinson, and pretty nearly every senator was determined the President should redeem it.

With the Senate in such a mood the President would have had no trouble in obtaining a quick compromise. All that needed to be done was to invest Joe Robinson promptly and publicly with Justice Van Devanter's cast-off robes and announce that with that "great liberal", the Senate majority leader, on the Court, only two additional justices were required. Thus a bold face might have been put on the matter; the Senate's deep affection for Robinson might have been capitalized, and the President would have won all along the line. By May 18 feeling on both sides was so strong that even the passage of a two-judge bill would have been a triumph.

Unfortunately the White House was too obsessed with the implications of the Robinson appointment, and the President was still too unwilling to look the facts of his situation in the face, to see where the advantage of the Van Devanter retirement lay. In the first place the President is far from fond of having political I.O.U.s brusquely presented for immediate payment. He is like those enormously rich men and women who always pay their bills but like to do so in their own time, and grow furious if their creditors presume to suggest that monthly settlements are advisable. And the behavior of the Senate was, in effect, the brusquest possible presentation of an I.O.U. for the giving of which the President was extremely sorry.

As though the scene in the Senate itself were not enough, Pat Harrison and Jimmy Byrnes called at the White House only a couple of hours after the Van Devanter retirement became known, to tell the President that it was essential that he put Joe Robinson into the vacant place at once. They outlined the situation in the Senate to him precisely as it has been outlined above, and they called for the immediate compromise it made possible. Their visit threw the President into a real rage. He suspected that Joe Robinson had arranged for it, and he felt that his hand was being forced. In addition to this personal anger of the President's there was a second factor—the reaction of the liberal groups to Robinson's candidacy. Although they praised him warmly enough in public, several of the left-wing legislators sent private messages to the White House that the appointment would be a disastrous concession to conservatism. And the liberal intellectuals of the urban East, men and women like the editors of the *New Republic* and the *Nation,* raised a great howl against it. Thus the two groups whose opinion the President most regards were attempting to hold him back from accepting the Byrnes-Harrison suggestion.

The net result was that the White House behaved as though it found the situation produced by Van Devanter's retirement so hopelessly uncomfortable that it knew no way to turn. Steve Early tried to be jaunty with his comment, "One down and five to go," but there was no jauntiness in private. Towards Robinson the President and his advisers behaved as if they were a newly rich family, ashamed to allow a shabby poor relation to dine with them in public. Otherwise, for several days, they merely wriggled on the hook. One or two of the general staff began to put the word around that Robinson would not be appointed, although they never had any such assurance from the President. When that set off a violent explosion in the Senate they hurriedly sent out a contradictory report that the job was safe for old Joe. Meanwhile neither they nor the President said anything to Robinson. It seems incredible now, this failure to do handsomely what had to be done anyway, but the White House's nervous irritation at being put on the spot and the still persisting blindness to the true state of affairs made it almost inevitable then.

At any rate the failure to do the handsome thing proved quite disastrous. The chance for a quick compromise was ignored. The pleasure of the Senate at seeing old Joe get his heart's desire was not capitalized. Instead the President enraged Joe Robinson by making no sign to him. To be sure, Jim Farley did telephone him after a few days and tell him to "think no more about it", that the place was surely his; but what Robinson wanted was a public recognition of his services. Meditating on his four and one half years of complete faithfulness to the President, nursing his grievance, he made up his mind in anger. If the White House made no sign to him he would make no sign to the White House. If the President desired to communicate with his strongest officer on the Hill he would have to make the overture.

Among his friends Robinson was perfectly frank about his hurt and his decision. Several days after the Van Devanter retirement Senator Byrd, of Virginia, asked him if he would like the Virginia congressional delegation's unanimous endorsement for the Supreme Court; Joe was almost childishly pleased with the offer. Byrd and Carter Glass quickly arranged the matter together, and the endorsement was made public the same evening. Next day, as soon as Joe saw Byrd, he hurried up to thank him.

"Harry," he said, "I can't tell you what it means to me to have fellows like you and Carter Glass come out for me. It's moved me very deeply these last few days to see how many friends I have. Why, I tell you, Harry, everybody's told me they're for me except that fellow

in the White House, and I swear I won't say a word
to him until he says it first to me."

The result was that Robinson was completely out of
touch with the White House for two vitally important
weeks. In a way the situation was ludicrous, but to the
main actors in it, it was tragic. As the days passed and
Joe still kept the White House in a sort of one-man
Coventry, the President and his advisers grew more
and more nervous. After all, Joe Robinson was their
chief strength in the Senate, and they could not allow
an estrangement to grow up. At the same time they had
come to a definite decision that there must be a couple
of extra court places for recognized liberal thinkers to
balance Joe's appointment, and that was horribly embarrassing to have to explain to Joe.

At first they thought it would be best for the President to call in Joe and tell him frankly what had been
decided. Then they realized that their delay had so
infuriated Robinson that if the President took any such
line with him, an explosion loud and violent enough to
blow the court plan and the administration's congressional machine sky high together, would surely follow.
So they had recourse to the old device of a mutual
friend. A messenger was sent to Joe to explain the
White House attitude. It was a pretty bitter pill for
Robinson to have to swallow, hearing that the President believed that other appointments were needed to
make his own look respectable. But after some grum-
bling he swallowed it.

The White House settled down to wait for Robinson, but Robinson never showed up. Nothing less than
a definite invitation to call on the President would satisfy him, and so the days slipped by and a new bitterness and rebellion spread in the Senate. The circle at
the White House was distracted by divided councils,
and no one could agree on a general estimate of the

position of the fight. Some consoled themselves with
the faint hope that the justices of the Court, although
they had already once refused to commit suicide, would
obligingly do so soon by throwing out the Social Security Act. And then, on May 24, the act was upheld,
and this time, while the decision sustaining the unemployment insurance clauses was by a five-to-four vote,
seven of the justices approved the act's old age pension
sections. It was the coup de grâce, the final disappointment which made the President admit at last that Fortune could be hideously fickle.

Yet the decision produced no unity in the councils at
the White House. Some advisers urged immediate compromise, and Cummings still clamored for the preservation of the "principle" of his precious bill. Cohen,
Corcoran and Jackson, however, stuck to their original
view that when "you're going to pack a court, you've
got to really pack it." They still saw great dangers in
compromise, and they still preferred to allow the court
bill to go over to the next session, even if it meant
brazening out the solitary appointment of Joe Robinson. They urged their view on the President with all the
persuasive force at their command, and the President,
who was also immensely busy with other matters, could
not make up his mind.

Meanwhile Robinson's continuing estrangement from
the President was growing desperately serious. At
first, perhaps because of the nervous irritation over the
whole Robinson matter, it had been hoped that the definite invitation on which Joe insisted could somehow be
avoided. Finally the White House made up its mind
to take its medicine. Once again the inner circle canvassed the situation. Luckily a patronage matter in
which Joe was concerned was hanging fire. It was decided that Jimmy Roosevelt should visit him in his
office, ostensibly to talk the patronage matter over, and

that an invitation to the White House should be slipped
casually into the conversation after Joe had been
promised whatever it was he wanted. Accordingly
Jimmy did visit Joe. Joe received him pleasantly
enough, and the patronage matter was soon settled.
Then Jimmy remarked:

"Father's been wishing you would come to see him,
Senator. In fact he's rather hurt that you've stayed
away so long."

Joe replied gruffly that he had been embarrassed
about visiting the President, that he feared to seem to
seek the Van Devanter place. Jimmy replied that Joe's
feeling was ridiculous, that the President would never
think anything so foolish, and, as the prearranged
scheme was, he reached for the telephone. In half a second he had his call through to the White House. In
another he had the President on the wire. The President made a great joke of Joe's hesitations and asked
him to call that very evening after dinner.

Even then the President had not made up his mind.
Almost immediately before Joe Robinson marched into
the White House the President had talked with Corcoran and Jackson, and they had used all their brilliance, all their information and all their influence on
him to persuade him finally to their view. They had
urged that an outright defeat would be better than a
dangerous compromise. They had pled with him to
accept defeat and make an issue of it, or, better still,
adopt their scheme to let the bill go over. And the
President had met their arguments in such fashion that
when they left him they had hopes.

The President's decision must have been made during his talk with Robinson. Its course was simple
enough. After rather elaborately affectionate greet-
ings on the part of the President and slightly gruff ones
by Robinson the President asked the Senate leader to

tell him just how he thought the situation stood. The state of affairs explained to Robinson by the messenger was taken as a foregone conclusion. Even now the President did not specifically mention the Van Devanter succession to old Joe. The discussion centered around the court bill. Robinson told the President that the Senate would surely beat him on his six-justice bill and urged compromise. The President asked how the compromise should be arranged, and Robinson suggested that he be allowed to settle the thing as best he could. The President assented, and after a brief discussion of possible compromises the talk was over. Joe Robinson left the White House a happy man. When he hinted to newspapermen on the steps that compromise was in the air he was beaming from ear to ear.

The President's talk with Robinson that night of June 3 marked the end of a phase of the court fight just as clearly as the Wagner labor act decisions did. After the labor act decisions the tide had turned against the President, but he had thought he could stem its flow by ordering it back. Now at last he realized that he was wrong. He acknowledged the possibility of defeat, but he could not bear the public humiliation which a resort to the Cohen-Corcoran-Jackson scheme would have brought upon him after the Van Devanter retirement. He preferred compromise, and, to get it, he relinquished his personal command of the fight and passed his field marshal's baton to Joe Robinson. He had acted at last, but he had acted too late. His last chance was gone, frittered away in the two weeks of aimless, fruitless waiting between the Van Devanter retirement and the final decision.

IV. DEATH OF THE BILL

FULL RETREAT

June 3–July 1, 1937

O<small>N THAT JUNE EVENING</small> when Joseph Taylor Robinson assumed command of the court fight he was sixty-five years old, and he had led his party in the Senate for fourteen years. In his youth he had looked what he was, one of those boy orators of the back country for whom, at the turn of the century, politics was the natural vocation. Now age's chemistry had applied its solvents to his huge bulk; he suggested the senator, but a senator of the late Roman Empire, oddly masquerading in the dignified but uninteresting costume of a respectable banker in an American small town. That broad, heavy face, with its brutal jaw, its small, cunning eyes, its pride of place and power, might have been reproduced direct from the bust of an Iberian *novus homo* in the Vatican.

Curiously enough his character was no less remarkable than his appearance. He had a peculiar personal force, an energy and strength which made it easy for him to dominate. Subtility and delicacy were absent from his make-up; he could never use the stiletto, but he was a past master with the bludgeon.

While his character was remarkable, his intellectual equipment was distinctly ordinary. Abstract thought was not his forte, and he was quite destitute of any inconvenient set of guiding political principles or the great notions of what ought to be done which such a set of principles might have produced. His tastes were simple. He loved the rough-and-tumble of legislative combat and the practical details of partisan manipulation. Encompassing the defeat of his enemies by a good, forthright political deal in private, or bellowing his defiance at them in public were equally to his taste, and he delighted in the dignity of Senate membership and his own achievement of leading his party in the Senate for so long. He had a passion for his work, and after his work he liked best killing very large numbers of very large birds or animals or fish and consuming immense meals and swapping interminable anecdotes with other powerful, practical men. He was a big, hearty, successfully ambitious fellow, and he took himself and everything he did with the utmost solemnity.

He was a professional officeholder, and his career was a Horatio Alger story of his singular profession. Born in comparative poverty, but marked out for early success by his gift of verbose, impassioned public declamation, he had risen with an amazing rapidity. In 1913 he achieved the unusual distinction of serving the slightly breathless Arkansas voters as representative of the 6th District, governor and senator, all in the space of fourteen days.

Once in the Senate his success was inevitable. His very ordinariness of mind endeared him to his colleagues, who have even more than the usual distaste for the unpleasing sensations of intellectual inferiority. Their admiration was earned by his steadfastness in the code of the "honest politician", who may vote against his beliefs every morning but will run the danger of defeat to keep his given word. He avoided the political isolation which comes soon or late to more consistent senators by a perfect party regularity; whether his party's thinking veered far to the right or left, he always followed it. And that extraordinary personal force of his, the sheer strength of character and courage in a fight which no one could deny him, set him apart from and above his fellows. He was a big man, but a big man governed by conventional ambitions and provincial habits of mind, and thus an ideal Senate leader.

His relations with the President had been peculiar. When the New Deal began, he had been suspected at the White House for the conservatism of his previous record and associations, and he was always underrated by the President's circle of intellectual advisers, who could not understand or appreciate his qualities as a practical politician. This atmosphere of disdain deeply irritated him, and all the genial, airy Rooseveltian charm could not put out his smoldering annoyance at his complete exclusion from the councils in which policy was decided. Occasionally his dignity had been affronted by a disclosure of his impotence in regard to policy, and he had boiled with fury; once or twice he had been almost driven into rebellion by his rage at a presidential departure from his political code, as when the President secretly ordered the 1935 tax bill to be jammed through the Senate in a week, then publicly denied his commands and left Robinson to ride out the storm alone.

Yet he had served the President throughout the New Deal with absolute obedience, and he had used his great personal and official powers to enforce an equal obedience on the Senate. While he never really liked the President, he worshiped the Democratic party, and since the President was the party leader he was ready to allow him all authority. And he was much encouraged to subservience by his life's ambition to become a justice of the Supreme Court, which could be fulfilled only by the President's good will.

Such was the man to whom the President had relinquished his field marshal's baton, and delegated the difficult task of rallying his forces in the court fight. He had been deeply hurt when the President thrust him aside and took personal command of the battle. He was all the more overjoyed on that evening of June 3 to find his power restored, and the prospect of an early appointment to the high bench caused every fiber of his being to throb with delight. In such a state of mind he hurled himself into the battle with a furious energy and a shrewd cunning which terrified the opposition. So long as the President continued in overconfident command Wheeler and his allies had been utterly confident. Now, with the murmur running through the Senate's corridors and lobbies that Robinson had been authorized to do what he could, they feared the worst.

The very next morning after his interview with the President, Robinson began canvassing possible compromises. The President's relinquishment of personal command had shorn his personal advisers of power; Robinson disliked them, and he turned at once to the men whom he understood and who understood him—his fellow senators. A new council of war consisting of Senator Logan, the best of the reliable administration men on the Judiciary Committee, Sherman Minton, of Indiana, a young New Deal war hawk who had begun to make his name in the Senate, the assistant majority leader, Alben Barkley, of Kentucky, and one or two others, were summoned to Robinson's little private office on the Capitol's ground floor.

There, in the nicely blended atmosphere of cigar smoke and undiluted political realism which characterizes such meetings, the situation was discussed at length. Two alternatives to the President's bill were outstanding. The first was that advocated by Senator Hatch, of New Mexico, by which the President was authorized to appoint a coadjutor justice for any justice who had passed the age of seventy-five and failed to retire, but was forbidden to make more than one such appointment in any one year. The second was that of Senator Andrews, for a pork-barrel court, with ten justices representing the ten judicial districts, and the Chief Justice appointed at large.

The Andrews compromise was the more available politically, but besides the extreme distaste which Corcoran, Cohen and Jackson felt for it, it had a fatal defect. Justice Butler was from the same judicial district which includes Arkansas. He was comparatively young and very healthy, and by the terms of the Andrews bill his presence on the bench would have excluded Joe Robinson from membership in the Court. The Andrews bill was urged on Robinson by many, among others by Keenan, a close friend of Robinson's and the only intimate White House adviser with whom he maintained contact. Robinson's answer to Keenan was simple and direct.

"It's been my lifelong ambition to go on the Court, Joe," he said. "You wouldn't want me to give it up now, would you, just when I have a chance of fulfilling it?"

Keenan was moved by the rather pathetic frankness of the big man; he abandoned his advocacy of the Andrews bill and so did its other supporters. Within two or three days the Hatch compromise was settled on as the one to be offered, and Senator Logan was chosen by the little group meeting in Robinson's office to draft it into a bill. He was a big, loose-jointed, countrified-looking old man, with a queer, harsh, trailing voice and such a thatch of hair that he was once admirably compared to an African rhinoceros wearing

a native grass hut for a hat, and he got the bill-
drafting task because he had served on the Supreme
Court of his state before coming to the Senate. No
one could have contrasted more strongly with the brilliant, youthful members of the inner circle at the White
House, and his selection for such an important duty
summed up the whole change which Robinson's appointment to absolute command wrought in the court
fight.

After conferring with Robinson and the others,
Logan decided to prepare the compromise as a series
of amendments to a bill which had been engineered
through the House by Hatton Sumners and was now
pending before the Senate Judiciary Committee. The
measure embodied such minor recommendations of the
court plan as direct intervention of the Attorney
General in private suits touching the constitutionality
of federal laws. The task did not take Logan long.
Hatch had already prepared one draft of his compromise, and in any case the alterations of the original
court plan which it required were not immensely complicated. By June 11 Logan had got his measure into a
shape satisfactory to Robinson and the others, and
after a final conference in Robinson's office a master
copy was made.

Robinson was purposely leaving the unofficial White
House advisers out in the cold, and therefore he chose
to deal only with the Justice Department. On June 5,
before the senators had finally agreed on the Hatch
compromise, he had conferred with Homer Cummings.
Cummings saw that the compromise preserved the
principles of his own bill and heartily approved it. On
June 11 Robinson took the master copy of the approved draft to his friend Keenan, in whose special
bureaucratic province were all measures affecting the
courts.

The two men understood one another perfectly. With his genial manner and his unpretentious, hearty presence Keenan had none of the slightly ostentatious intellectualism which Robinson detested. And if Robinson warmly appreciated Keenan's abilities and good qualities, Keenan was capable of seeing in Robinson the distinctive force and strength which most of his colleagues of the White House general staff had so undervalued. Keenan glanced through the final Logan draft, approved it in his turn and gave it to his secretary, asking her to make two copies and to send one to Jimmy Roosevelt at the White House and the other to Cummings. While the girl was typing Keenan and Robinson talked of the court fight and of a district court job then vacant in Arkansas, for which Robinson had a candidate. After a while a message came that Mrs Robinson was waiting in the majority leader's motor, and Robinson asked Keenan to come for a drive in the country. Keenan accepted, and while the big limousine ate up the miles of Virginia road, he and Robinson continued their discussion of the district court place and the court fight. Suddenly Mrs Robinson broke in.

"Joe, why don't you take this district court job yourself and come home?" she asked her husband, placing a perceptible emphasis on the word "district." "It's taking too much out of you here. You ought to stop, after all these years."

Robinson patted her knee, laughed his loud, booming laugh and pooh-poohed her question, but Mrs Robinson was right. He was not well; he had the heart weakness which so often comes to huge, sanguine, violent men, and although he angrily ignored his symptoms the struggle was taking too much out of him. While the compromise was being prepared and perfected, he was also carrying out all his manifold other duties as Senate leader and doing the recruiting for the compromise himself. The job was cruelly hard.

Politics is a singular game, slightly squalid, all too human and played for stakes which none of the participants could afford if others did not pay the bills. But it is also a game of skill, requiring as many special qualities in the good player as tennis, for example. Of all these qualities the most important is a sense of timing, and it was just this sense, which he had always had before in such a superlative degree, that was completely deadened in the President by his overconfidence in the court fight. His whole conduct of the early part of the fight was marked by fantastic mistakes in timing; the final, crucial one had been his fretful refusal to swallow the bitter brew of the Van Devanter retirement until two weeks had been frittered away. This final miscalculation was what made Robinson's job so hard.

In those two wasted weeks all the good feeling in the Senate which the prospect of Robinson's appointment to the bench at first produced, had been curdled into a furious irritation with the White House by the spectacle of the shabby treatment accorded the leader. The Social Security decisions had destroyed for good and all the argument that "something had to be done about the Supreme Court", and the Van Devanter vacancy made it impossible for the President to declare that a mere five-to-four majority was "too uncertain." The opposition had seized the opportunity offered by the increased ill feeling and the growing doubt to obtain one or two more definite commitments against the court bill, and to harden the determination of those who had already joined them. The time when compromise would have been easy was definitely past. Now Robinson was faced with an exceedingly difficult, wearily uncertain task.

He tackled it with the herculean energy which marked all his great exploits, carrying virtually the whole burden of the work himself. Two or three trustworthy lieutenants were permitted to share with him the job of feeling out individual senators, but after that he accepted the sole responsibility. The lieutenants were Minton, Hugo Black and Barkley, and Bob La Follette also helped. All through the June days they circulated among the senators, testing their sentiments, talking compromise, reporting to Robinson. When they discovered a likely prospect for compromise he was immediately summoned to Robinson's suite in the Senate Office Building, for the leader had deserted his Capitol hideaway in the interests of the other senators' convenience. There was scarcely a morning in June when he did not see one or two or three of his colleagues and try to extract from them a commitment to the court bill.

It can be imagined how exhausting such a course of persuasion must have been, added to all the other duties which he had to perform. Each interview had to be leisurely and full; he could not seem to dragoon his followers. With each man he discussed at length the situation created by the court bill, laying an especial emphasis on the damage the fight was doing the Democratic party. To most of them he admitted that the original bill had been "raw", pointed out that the substitute was much milder and held up the partisan duty of going along. Each man had opinions to which he had to listen; each prejudices which it was necessary to conciliate. In the end Robinson always had to ask the question:

"Well, how are you going to stand?"

And in each case, however verbose the senator, however much he might hate to give a definite promise, Robinson had to try to pin him down. With many he

succeeded, with some he failed. He was so painstaking
in the work and so doubtful of the outcome that
although most leaders would only have concerned
themselves with the waverers, he took the trouble to
go through this pinning-down process with every single
one of the senators who had been committed to the
President's original bill.

His precautions were wise, for if he was pouring all
his immense energies into the fight, the leaders of the
opposition were not behind him. The first rumors of
compromise and the grudging confirmation which the
President had given them at a press conference—he
said he cared nothing about details, so long as the
"principle" he had suggested was preserved—had been
a fearful blow to the opposition leaders. But they had
soon rallied. Wheeler, Borah, Burke, O'Mahoney,
Gerry, George and the others concentrated a new fury
in the fight. Even old Hiram Johnson, sick and failing,
sniffed the air of battle like an ancient war horse, pawed
the ground and charged into the fray. While Robinson
bore the chief burden of attacking the waverers for
the administration, there were a score of forceful and
determined senators on the other side to plague them
wherever they went. Under the direction of the steering committee, the opposition espionage system, its
remarkable machinery of intramural lobbying and its
careful propaganda were all speeded up. Under Robinson's heavy pressure the opposition lost some ground,
but so little that its leaders began to regain their confidence.

In mid-June they struck their most savage blow at
the President—the majority report of the Judiciary
Committee condemning the court bill. It was perhaps
the strangest proof of all of the fantastic errors into
which the President's refusal to face the facts had led
him. On May 18 the committee had voted ten to eight

to report the bill unfavorably. Had the President
agreed to compromise on May 14, immediately on his
return from Texas, had he believed the dark report
which his own congressional leaders made to him, he
might have avoided a condemnation of the bill by the
majority. Hatch voted against the original measure; if
his compromise had been adopted before May 18 he
would have switched, and the committee would have
been evenly split. And had the Hatch compromise been
adopted immediately after the Wagner labor act decisions an actual majority might have been obtained for
it, since McCarran would certainly have accepted it
until Farley's tactlessness infuriated him.

Instead the President had waited too long to face
the facts. He had lost McCarran for good, he had lost
O'Mahoney. He had cheerfully permitted an unfavorable majority report to become an absolute certainty.
The opposition leaders had taken full advantage of the
situation. With their usual astuteness they had pinned
O'Mahoney and McCarran down by appointing them
to the sub-committee charged with drafting the report
itself, along with the committee's senior Democratic
and Republican members, King, of Utah, and Borah.

The report was prepared in the deepest secrecy, but
on a co-operative system. Burke, Van Nuys, even
Wheeler, who was not a member of the Judiciary Committee at all, submitted material to the quartet drafting the report. Each of the four committee members
assumed responsibility for a special section of the document; it was divided roughly into four sections, com-
prising a devastating analysis of the actual provisions
of the bill, a dark prediction of its effects on the
judiciary and the constitutional system, an eloquent plea
for the defense of the Supreme Court and a careful
review of the Court's place as a constitutional institution, closing with Washington's celebrated last warning

against "usurpations." In the end all the material which had been collected and prepared was turned over to O'Mahoney, to be recast in a unified whole. O'Mahoney aimed to turn out a powerful and memorable document of state, and he succeeded in his aim. The reasoning of the report was close and cogent, the style effective if occasionally clumsy. O'Mahoney had the good sense to conserve many of Borah's flashing phrases, and they gave an extra force. The whole constituted so savage an indictment of the President and his purposes, however, that it made the waverers nervous. And no wonder, for the authors of the report did not spare the most biting sarcasm and the most cruel innuendo.

"Those of us who hold office in this government, however humble or exalted it may be, are creatures of the Constitution," they replied to the President. "To it we owe all the power and authority we possess. Outside of it we have none. We are bound by it in every official act.

"We know that this instrument, without which we would not be able to call ourselves presidents, judges or legislators, was carefully planned and deliberately framed to establish three co-ordinate branches of government, every one of them to be independent of the others. For the protection of the people, for the preservation of the rights of the individual, for the maintenance of the liberties of minorities, for maintaining the checks and balances of our dual system, the three branches of the government were so constituted that the independent expression of honest difference could never be restrained in the people's servants and no one branch could overawe or subjugate the others. That is the American system. It is immeasurably more important, immeasurably more sacred to the people of America, indeed to the people of the world, than the immediate adoption of any legislation, however beneficial."

And again:

"Today it may be the Court which is charged with forgetting its constitutional duties. Tomorrow it may be the Congress. The next day it may be the Executive. If we yield to temptation now to lay the lash upon the Court we are only teaching others how to apply it to ourselves and to the people when the occasion seems to warrant. . . . This bill is an invasion of the judicial power such as has never been attempted in this country."

And of the President's rather entertaining veto of a world's fair appropriation bill, on the ground that the congressional committee set up to administer the funds was an unconstitutional encroachment on the executive domain:

"The solicitude of the President to maintain the independence of the executive arm of the government against invasion by the legislative should be an example to us in solicitude to preserve the independence of the judiciary from any danger of invasion by the legislative and executive branches combined."

And of safeguarding the rights of the citizen:

"The condition of the world abroad must of necessity cause us to hesitate at this time and to refuse to enact any law that would impair the independence of or destroy the people's confidence in an independent judicial branch of our government. We unhesitatingly assert that any effort looking to impairment of the independent judiciary of necessity operates toward centralization of power in the other branches of a tripartite form of government. We declare for the continuance and perpetuation of government and rule by law, as distinguished from government and rule by men. . . . Reduction of the supremacy of law means an increasing enlargement of the degree of personal government. Personal government, or government by an individual, means autocratic dominance, by whatever name it may be designated."

And finally:

"The Constitution of the United States, courageously construed and upheld through one hundred and fifty years of history, has been the bulwark of human liberty. It was bequeathed to us in a great hour of human destiny by one of the greatest characters civilization has produced—George Washington. It is in our hands now to preserve or destroy. If ever there was a time when the people of America should heed the words of the father of their country, this is the hour."

There followed the celebrated passage from the Farewell Address, warning that "the spirit of encroachment tends to consolidate the powers of all the departments in one, and thus to create, whatever the form of government, a real despotism", and the report closed with a brutal bill of particulars against the President's measure:

"We recommend the rejection of this bill as a needless, futile and utterly dangerous abandonment of constitutional principle.

"It was presented to the Congress in a most intricate form and for reasons that obscured its real purpose.

"It would not banish age from the bench nor abolish divided decisions.

"It would not reduce the expense of litigation nor speed the decision of cases.

"It is a proposal without precedent or justification.

"It would subjugate the courts to the will of Congress and the President and thereby destroy the independence of the judiciary, the only certain shield of individual rights.

"It contains the germ of a system of centralized administration of law that would enable an executive so minded to send his judges into every judicial district in the land to sit in judgment on controversies between the government and the citizen.

"It points the way to an evasion of the Constitution and establishes the method whereby the people may be deprived of their right to pass upon all amendments of the fundamental law.

"It stands now before the country, acknowledged by its proponents as a plan to force judicial interpretation of the Constitution, a proposal that violates every sacred tradition of American democracy.

"Under the form of the Constitution it seeks to do that which is unconstitutional.

"Its ultimate operation would be to make this government one of men rather than of law, and its practical operation would be to make the Constitution what the executive or legislative branches say it is—an interpretation to be changed with each change of administration.

"It is a measure which should be so emphatically rejected that its parallel will never again be presented to the free representatives of the free people of America."

To those words were appended the signatures of all ten opposition members of the Judiciary Committee, including the moderate Hatch, who merely added a concurrent report indicating that he believed the vices in the bill might be cured by such a compromise as he had proposed. The administration's congressional leaders, like Robinson, thought that the strong tone of the report was unwise; the President and the men immediately around him were stirred to impotent fury by its language. Although such things cannot be surely known, it is said with some authority that the resolve to be revenged on such men as O'Mahoney was born about this time. The state of mind at the White House was only exacerbated by the fact that a minority report replying to the majority had actually been prepared by Corcoran and Keenan.

This thoughtful precaution, one of the most curious illustrations of the degree to which the White House expected to dominate its congressional followers, was the subject of the last unhappy conflict between the impatient general staff and that unhasting, unhurrying legislator, Senator Ashurst. Tom Corcoran presented Ashurst with the paper which he had saved the senators so much trouble by writing, and firmly commanded him to get all the administration committee members to sign it. Ashurst, as usual, slithered out of Corcoran's reach. Actually, of course, Ashurst was deeply irritated by Corcoran's brusque departure from the usual procedure. His ridiculous semiserious pomposities are a sort of outward sign of a special sentimentality about all the Senate forms and dignities. He had cherished the deliberative procedures, the solemn formalities of his committee ever since he came to be chairman. As it was when he refused to apply strong-arm methods to the opposition to shorten the hearings, so now again all this side of him was horrified. Even Corcoran could not dislodge him from his refuge in a baroque courtliness.

"My dear sir, you do not realize how hard it is to get senators to agree," he told Corcoran. "Every senator has his own ideas; he does not like to abandon them. It might take weeks, it might take months, before I could get the senators to agree on this report. I might never get them to agree. Oh no, my dear sir, I do not think it is worth even trying."

Corcoran, who had heard precisely the same story before, ground his teeth with annoyance and expostulated energetically, but expostulating to Ashurst is like reasoning with the wind. He got absolutely nowhere, and the minority report, which embodied chiefly the direct arguments made before the Judiciary Committee by Assistant Attorney General Jackson, never saw the light of day. And so ended the important participation of the members of the White House general staff in the court fight. At this period some of its more irresponsible members drove Robinson almost mad by harrying him with messages, perfectly unauthorized by the President, to the effect that if he did not succeed in getting the desired compromise his hope of the Van Devanter vacancy would be in vain. Except for such incursions as this the general staff had nothing much more to do. Only Keenan continued to work in the closest co-operation with Robinson.

Cummings, on the other hand, had begun to take an important part again. His resurgence was natural, for the point of view represented by Corcoran, Cohen and Jackson had been definitely abandoned by the President in his June 3 interview with Robinson, while that of Cummings, who longed above all to preserve the principle of his precious measure, had become the dominating one. The unfavorable report of the Judiciary Committee majority was submitted on June 14. Three days later he and Solicitor General Reed discussed the proposed compromise at length with Robinson, and placed the seal of their approval on it.

From Robinson's office that afternoon they hurried to the White House, where they went over the new measure in detail with the President. During this conference there was a rather ludicrous incident. On re-examining the measure's provisions Cummings and Reed discovered that it appeared to abandon the so-called "flexible feature" of the court bill, by which the number of new judges to be appointed would have been governed by the ages of the sitting judges. The

discovery caused mild consternation; at first they suspected that the senators had omitted the feature on
purpose. There was some excitable telephoning, and it
was finally found that an entire clause had been dropped
out of the bill by the stenographer who copied it.

Even so the bill was far from being in letter-perfect
form, and Cummings met almost daily at the Capitol
with Robinson, Logan and the others to revise its
language. The Hatch proposal was difficult to reduce
to unambiguous legal terminology, and there were
other, minor problems. While Robinson was taking
part in these meetings, interviewing waverers every
morning and carrying on all his other duties, he was
also doing his best to heal the terrible breach which
had grown up within the Democratic party in Congress. By mid-June the situation was positively appalling to one for whom, like Robinson, partisan
regularity was an article of faith in a general worship
of the Democracy.

The most startling outward sign of what had occurred was the mid-June departure for his native
Uvalde of the old Texas fox, John Nance Garner. In
all the Vice-President's numerous years of congressional service he had never before left Washington
during a session for more than a few days, yet he
calmly packed up and went home now, just at the time
when the administration most needed him.

His departure was not a result of the court fight. His
attitude towards that, after the first brief period when
he had given the President some help, had been simply
a hands-off one. Privately he had a dislike for the court
plan and all that it implied—and he did not keep it so
completely private either. It has already been seen how
he held his nose and turned thumbs down in the Senate
lobby when the President's message was being read;
later the story of how he had forgotten himself a little

at a lunch in Robinson's private office and remarked loudly to Senator Wheeler, "Burt, you're a real patriot," was common gossip in the corridors and cloakrooms. But publicly he did not concern himself with the court fight.

What caused his defection was the President's attitude towards the budget and the sit-down strikes. After the talk with the President in which both men had grown so angry that Robinson was forced to intervene he had become a frank troublemaker on these two matters. Every senatorial move towards economy, no matter how much disliked it was at the White House, had his encouragement. Every effort to handle the labor situation firmly had his hearty approval. He made no bones about how he felt. Indeed, on one occasion, when that most articulate of Republicans, Senator Vandenberg, made a ripsnorting speech denouncing the sit-down strikes as no better than revolution, the Vice-President had left the rostrum, gone down onto the Senate floor itself and there embraced Vandenberg and congratulated him warmly in full view of the galleries. And as April and May slipped by he grew steadily more disgusted, until he announced his intention of going away.

At first the White House received the announcement with some relief. The feeling was that it would be a considerable pleasure to have the genial old troublemaker out of Washington. And then compromise was decided on, and it suddenly became necessary to preserve every appearance of Democratic unity.

The time was past when the President did not care in the least how many conservatives left the Democratic party, when he greeted the news of their defections with "a good riddance", and dreamed of forming a perfect union with such Progressives as Bob La Follette. Garner was in demand once more, and Sam Rayburn,

the earthy, sensible, smart fellow Texan whom Garner
had sponsored for the House leadership, was hastily
called on to persuade the Vice-President to stay at his
post. Rayburn did what he could, pleading the useful
influence that Garner might have on events. But Garner
had promised a beloved grandchild he would join her
on a holiday, and he had pretty well made up his mind
that he had as much chance of influencing the administration as of deflecting the course of a railroad
express. He returned a flat "No" to Rayburn's urgencies
and set out for Uvalde on schedule.

His refusal to concern himself with the court bill
and his sudden independence in regard to economy and
labor had been bad enough. No man was more influential in the Senate than Garner. Almost as many
men were beholden to him for help with committee
assignments and other favors as were beholden to
Robinson. Many more were personally devoted to him
than to the majority leader. In the President's first
administration larger numbers of senators had seen the
light on New Deal measures in the private office with
the well-stocked liquor closet which Garner called his
"bureau of education" than anywhere else in Washington. He was sharper than Robinson, more coolheaded
and even more experienced, and Robinson had found
his advice invaluable. It can be imagined, therefore,
how his hands-off attitude affected the court fight. His
final departure for Uvalde was still worse. At that
moment in the battle it was equivalent to the loss of a
well-equipped division, for it not only deprived Robinson of the council and assistance Garner would have
offered as a matter of personal friendship to him; it
also suggested to many wavering and doubtful senators
that the moment for independence was not quite past.

Garner's departure, Robinson's enforced resort to
Minton, Black, Schwellenbach, La Follette and Barkley

instead of to his two wily, immensely knowledgeable lieutenants in past battles, Harrison and Byrnes—these were the outward signs of what was happening to the Democracy in the Senate. Except for Robinson, virtually every one of the men who had managed the Senate for the President during his first term was in private or public revolt. Most of them had not yet rebelled on the court bill, but, like Garner, they were keeping severely out of the fight. And it was not only their distaste for such individual measures as the wage-hour bill, their disagreement with such White House policies as that on the sit-down strikes, which had driven them off the reservation. They were also suffering from half-undefined uneasiness. In their private conversations they came close to formulating it when they pointed out to one another that if the President won in the end, he would be the absolute boss. What was really troubling them was their sense of the degree to which the predominance of the White House would be established if victory should be achieved in the court fight and the simultaneous party struggle.

The party struggle was made all the more acute by the fact that everyone expected the majority leadership of the Senate to fall vacant very soon. Alben Barkley, the official assistant leader, a rather chesty, solemnly eloquent fellow with a private passion for barbershop song and an obedience to the President even more unquestioning than Robinson's, had White House backing for the post. The members of the general staff, left unemployed by the transfer of command in the court fight, were busily at work canvassing for Barkley, and this fact did not improve feeling in the Senate.

Moreover, the other candidates were stressing a measure of independence of the White House in their campaigns. They were Harrison, the foxy, rather lazy, golf-loving, immensely witty man who had been finally induced to run by his annoyance at the White House backing of Barkley, and Byrnes, the former White House intimate who had led the rebellion on the sit-down strikes. Before Garner left for Uvalde he had given Byrnes his support, and both Byrnes and Harrison had considerable numbers of votes. The scheme was that when the time came Byrnes would withdraw and throw his votes to Harrison, and the possibility that this stratagem might succeed greatly disturbed the administration cohorts. There was endless talk of "disloyalty" on one side, and on the other endless murmuring against White House interference in the affairs of the Senate and against the President's highhanded habit of ordering Congress about. The opposition to the court bill plumped for Harrison virtually en bloc, and the poison of bitterness spread and spread through the once clubby Senate until poor Robinson, who loved the old, friendly, easy atmosphere, was half distracted.

In those days Joe Robinson was like a great bull in the ring at that undecided moment in the contest when the banderillas have been placed. His ponderous, direct, violent way of charging at a problem was always taurine; in this fight for the first time he seemed to tire a little from the darts of his enemies. One wondered, would he end by goring the encircling matadors, or would they succeed in driving the sword of defeat home at his shoulder. Although he was already troubled and unwell Robinson continued to pour out his immense energies without stint, still conferring with Cummings, still trying to smooth things out in the Senate, still interviewing his troops. Towards the end of June he concluded that he was as near to having a positive majority as he ever would be, and in the month's last days he held a series of three battle rallies. Minton and Schwellenbach and Barkley summoned the

senators who had given their commitments, whether
vague or positive, to these meetings, which were held
in Robinson's Senate Office Building suite. About fifteen
senators attended each meeting.

The details of the compromise had not been worked
out when Robinson began his task of individual recruiting, and a good many senators did not quite know
what they had agreed to support. Therefore Robinson
opened each of the three meetings with a careful explanation of the provisions of the substitute measure.
He followed the explanation with a little speech, urging
on the listening Democrats the importance of sticking
by the President. And he ended by announcing that
unless he heard a voice to the contrary he would regard
every man present as positively committed to vote for
the Hatch compromise. Only one senator, John R.
Overton, of Louisiana, with whom the Long ring had
wrought violently but in vain, spoke out to preserve his
freedom of action. Minton and Barkley, who were
present at all three meetings, made lists of the attend-
ing senators, and these lists formed the basis of the
subsequently famous Robinson list of fifty-one names
of promised supporters.

With his meetings over, Robinson reported to the
President that he believed he had recruited a majority
for the new bill. To smooth the way for it a little he
suggested that its announcement be preceded by a grand
Democratic harmony party, and the picnic at the Jefferson Island Club off the Maryland coast was accordingly
arranged. It was at this fantastic celebration that the
inutility of personal charm in political crises was finally
demonstrated, somewhat to the President's chagrin.
The scheme was that every Democratic member of
Congress, all the Cabinet and the President would fore-
gather in masculine peace at the comfortable clubhouse
on Jefferson Island. There they would while their time

away eating and drinking heavily and enjoying those
hearty pleasures, like the pleasures of a large business
convention, in which legislators indulge when they are
collected in herds. The senators and representatives were
to come down in relays, one third on each of three days,
and the President was to remain throughout, greeting
them all, buttering them all liberally with the nice
flattery he knows so well how to apply, and conciliating
all their wounded feelings. Everything went exactly ac-
cording to schedule. Even the weather was idyllic. But
no one was conciliated, no one was charmed out of
rebellion, and the net result of the whole business was
a public spectacle in which the scoffers took infinite
pleasure.

Nevertheless, Robinson was almost cheerful. He
had had some trouble with the President—it was about
this time that he remarked to a White House intimate
that "it's too bad you can never tell a President of the
United States the truth"—but by and large things had
gone well. His endless conferences with Logan and
Cummings, Barkley and Hatch (as original author of
the compromise Hatch had taken part in the discussions
too) were over at last. All the problems in connection
with the substitute had been straightened out, and in
the last of the many concurrent conferences which the
President was holding with Cummings and Reed, the
President had signified his final assent to the substitute
measure in all its details. The majority had been recruited; the commitments had been obtained. It was
time to announce the compromise to the public.

Accordingly Cummings and Reed, Logan and Hatch
joined Robinson once more in his Capitol office on the
morning of July 1. The substitute had been printed, and
all that remained to do was prepare a statement to
accompany copies of it. The other four men deferred
to Robinson in this, and he dictated one in his usual

elaborately punctuated, opulently official, heavily verbose style. Robinson had a gift for making the least
important statement sound like a communiqué revealing
the result of a peace conference between warring
nations. This statement was important, and he outdid
himself. The others suggested several changes when
the stenographer had the copies read and passed them
round. Robinson thereupon redictated the statement,
and, since they had all heard it as he reeled it off, the
others immediately approved it. It was issued a little
later by Robinson, and the period of long-range combat promptly ended, on the hundred and forty-fourth
day of the fight. The time for hand-to-hand fighting
had come.

HAND–TO–HAND COMBAT

THROUGHOUT its first hundred and forty-four days the court fight was a war of position. Assisted by the justices, the defenders of the Court had outmaneuvered the President with the murderous precision of Marshal Saxe. In the end even the President, blinded by optimism though he was, had been forced to recognize the hopelessness of his situation and to abandon his original bill. The abandonment of the original bill, the transfer of command to Joe Robinson, had simultaneously infused the administration forces with a new courage and reduced the difficulties of their objective. They had marched on the opposition flank at its most vulnerable point, where the company of wavering Democratic senators still did not know which side they should be fighting on. They had broken the opposition lines and obtained a number of valuable recruits. And now, on July 1, with the maneuvering over and the time for hand-to-hand combat come, the two sides were so evenly matched and placed that none could tell how the fight would end.

Outwardly the administration maintained a perfectly confident front. Neither the President nor Joe Robinson

nor any of the general staff at the White House nor
any of Robinson's lieutenants on the Hill would admit
of any question as to the eventual certainty of triumph.
The attack on the waverers had been successful; they
would allow no doubt of that, and to all outward ap-
pearances they were right. The President and the men
around him enjoyed an untroubled belief in their own
optimistic predictions. Had not Joe Robinson and Joe
Keenan made the first reliable Senate list ever compiled
by the administration strategists? Had not the lists
shown a minimum of fifty-one votes for the new
measure? Could not Robinson, the man whom they had
suspected of "defeatism" in the fight's early stages,
surely be trusted not to overestimate the brightness of
the prospect? The catch, unfortunately, lay in that
weary remark of Robinson's to a White House intimate, that "you could never tell a President of the
United States the truth."

There were a number of reasons why Robinson
should have been unable to tell the President the truth
—the President's irritable distaste for gloom, the fact
that his own chance of elevation to the high bench
was partly involved in the struggle, the danger of losing
the confidence of the White House by appearing a
"defeatist" again. At any rate Robinson seems to have
disclosed his own exact opinion of the state of affairs
to no more than one or two of the persons most intimate
with him. With the President, with his own lieutenants,
with the public, he did not permit himself an instant's
doubt as to the outcome of the fight. Yet with Joe
Keenan and at least one other man he was perfectly
frank that he considered it a dangerously near thing.

Robinson and Keenan were always able to count up
to forty-four sure Senate votes, and, if they chose to
ignore the qualms from which Senator James Hamilton
Lewis was obviously suffering, they could add the

bewhiskered Illinois statesman and make it forty-five. But after that they had to go to such men as Brown, of Michigan, Russell, of Georgia, Chavez, of New Mexico, Ryan Duffy, of Wisconsin, Bankhead, of Alabama, and even Overton, of Louisiana, who had positively refused to commit himself, to make up their lists to a majority. Some of these senators had grudgingly promised support; others had imitated Overton's caution, but whether they had made promises or no, Robinson was perfectly aware that their disinclination to go along was so extreme as to make them quite unreliable. At any moment they might take into their heads to desert, and if only three or four of them deserted the jig was up. The constant strain of such uncertainty told even on the indomitable Robinson. In the four days which intervened between the announcement of the substitute measure and the beginning of the debate he and Keenan were in frequent conference. Sometimes in these long, businesslike discussions of strategy between the two friends Robinson would suddenly grow hopeless. In these moments of despair he always repeated one unhappy question:

"Where are the votes, Joe? Show me the votes."

Yet although Robinson occasionally lost heart he was always convinced that the administration had an excellent chance. The difference between what he believed and the President believed was that the President considered the chance a certainty. Meanwhile Wheeler and the leaders of the opposition had precisely the same estimate of their own prospects as Robinson had of the administration's. They were perfectly aware that Robinson had swelled the President's forces with a vital recruitment of waverers, and where Robinson was quite positive that he had at least forty-four votes, Wheeler and Burke and Gerry and the others numbered their sure supporters at forty-two. They founded their hopes on the knowledge they shared with Robinson of the exceeding queasiness with which the prospect of battle affected the newly recruited waverers.

Both sides busied themselves energetically in those five days intervening between July 1 and the beginning of the debate. The substitute bill was formally offered in the Senate on July 2, after a final meeting in Robinson's office of the group which had joined in drafting it. At the last moment there was intense excitement because it was discovered that the word "may" had been used instead of "shall" in the clauses governing the appointment of the additional judges. Cummings objected to it strenuously, on the grounds that it made the measure permissive instead of mandatory. After some bustling and scurrying the defect was corrected. Cummings went home content, leaving to the senators the task of forming the administration forces into perfect battle array. It was for this purpose that Robinson saw Keenan so often during those days. His other lieutenants, Minton, Schwellenbach, Black and Barkley, were also always at his orders, and he himself gave considerable time to circulating through the Senate, reassuring one legislator, intimidating another and arousing the partisan feelings of a third. What time he had left he gave to preparing the speech with which it had been decided he should open the debate.

Nor did the opposition, with its remarkable organization, allow itself a moment's idleness. Now for the first time the meetings of the steering committee of Democratic opponents to the court bill were thrown open to the Republicans, and the strategy of the debate itself was carefully examined. The first and easiest decision was that all of the men to open the opposition argument would be Democrats. The Republicans, who had successfully maintained their conspiracy of silence for so long, consoled themselves with the prospect of succumbing to oratory after the Democrats were done. It was agreed that every single one of the forty-two sure opponents of the substitute bill should speak his piece upon the Senate floor.

All of them were well aware that their best reserve weapon was the filibuster. Often before filibusters had succeeded with no more than a handful of senators to support them. Now the opposition leaders could count on forty-two speeches by forty-two different senators for a starter. There were, moreover, at least twenty of their number who were willing to speak until doomsday to defeat the President and his bill. Such men as O'Mahoney and Wheeler, Clark, of Missouri, Mc-Carran and Burke, and Borah, Johnson and Vandenberg among the Republicans, constituted themselves a sort of battalion of death. At the final meetings each of them announced that if necessary he would speak not once but twice on the bill itself, and twice more on every amendment.

Senator Burke, who acted as liaison officer with the Bar Association's Washington committee of distinguished old and bright young lawyers, was asked to instruct the committee members to prepare an immense number of amendments. These were desirable for filibustering purposes because of the seldom-invoked Senate rule that, while no member may speak more than twice on a bill in any single day, he may propose as many amendments as he wants and speak twice on each of them too.

The Bar Association's flying squadron had their headquarters in a comfortable suite at the Mayflower Hotel. There, one hot July morning, the clever youngsters to whom the task had been delegated set anxiously to work. Burke had given them a bale of close on two hundred official Senate amendment blanks and had told them to fill as many as they could. Their

idea was that an amendment should be a clearly
worded, strictly constitutional and wholly serious alteration of the legislation to be amended. Sweating at
every pore, they labored among their law books. They
had a few ideas already and endless head scratching
produced a few more. The ideas were carefully drafted
and redrafted until the whole group approved the
wording, when the young men typed them onto the
amendment blanks. After a day and a half of arduous
work they had exactly fifteen blanks filled in. They
were at their wits' end, and they gave up.

It was time for them to get a lesson in the processes
of democracy. Fortunately the moment of their sur-
render was a Sunday noon, and Senator Bailey, who
lives at the Mayflower, had chosen to spend the Sunday
resting in bed. The youthful lawyers telephoned Bailey's
apartment, and he told them to come right up. They
picked up a copy of the court bill and the pile of blanks
both filled and unfilled, and hurried to his bedside.
There they showed him what they had done. Bailey
burst into a roar of laughter.

He gave them the lesson they so sorely needed then
and there. Taking a copy of the court bill, he asked one
of the young men to prepare for dictation. Turning to
the section limiting the enlargement of the Supreme
Bench to fifteen, he began:

"Strike out the word 'fifteen' and insert in lieu
thereof the word 'fourteen.' Take another. Strike out
the word 'fifteen' and insert in lieu thereof the word
'thirteen.' Take another. Strike out the word 'fifteen'
and insert in lieu thereof the word 'twelve.' "

And so it went. The possibilities of the word "fifteen"
were soon exhausted, but there were plenty of other
things about the bill, from its enacting clause to its
last sentence, which Senator Bailey desired to see
amended. Under the popping eyes of his visitors he

rattled off nearly fifty amendments in less than two
hours. After that the official amendment writers
thanked Bailey heartily, returned to their own office
and dashed off another sixty. The next morning they
delivered a great bundle of a hundred and twenty-five
filled-in amendment blanks, all neatly typed and
formally worded, to Senator Burke at the Capitol. The
filibustering possibilities in the bundle were truly majestic. There were twenty senators who had formally
sworn to make two full-dress senatorial speeches on
each of the hundred and twenty-five amendments. A
full-dress senatorial speech lasts at least two hours and
may last two days. The oratory might well have flowed
on until the 1938 election if the President's and Robinson's lines had held firm.

Robinson was well aware of the formidable quality
of the opposition, and even the President realized it.
At the last moment an effort was made to dissipate the
opposition's strength, and made by the President himself. He had not held wholly aloof from the struggle
after June 3; he had revived his scheme of personal
interviews with doubtful Democrats, and he had
managed them more realistically than he managed the
early meetings by which he had hoped to gentle the
Senate into obedience. Instead of calling in the white
and gray sheep together he had summoned the gray
sheep one by one, and with some of them at least he
chose an approach less direct but more realistic than his
earlier cneerful explanations of the court bill. The
"problems of their states" were the new theme of his
conversations with the senators. He had professed a
deep interest in needs of their constituents and declared
himself anxious to be of what assistance he could. In
such fashion he had helped Robinson considerably,
although at least one waverer was downright annoyed
by the suddenness of these flattering anxieties.

Now, however, something different was required. Both the President and Robinson knew well that one of the opposition's greatest strengths was the retiring behavior of its Republican members. If the Democratic leaders of the opposition could only be induced to keep quiet, if they would content themselves with voting against the bill only, then all would be well for the administration. But in order to achieve this end the leading Democratic oppositionists had to be dealt with, and no group of men could have been less like the friendly, agonizing waverers.

The attempt might never have been made had not Senator Homer T. Bone, of Washington, a member of the left-wing Democratic bloc who had maintained a friendly contact with Senator Wheeler throughout the struggle, suddenly reported that Wheeler seemed ready to talk turkey. From the moment when Wheeler had issued his first statement against the court bill the White House had tried to persuade him to discuss the whole problem with the President. Every kind of message was sent to him, by every imaginable kind of messenger, but Wheeler had remained adamant, always taking the position that he would be glad to go to the White House when he was invited to do so, but not before. The President, who greatly preferred to have it seem that men had to come to him, could never bring himself to invite Wheeler until the Bone tip suggested that such an invitation might be immensely profitable. Accordingly the invitation went to Wheeler, through a third party, but in clear terms. Wheeler promptly accepted, and the meeting, the strangest scene in the whole long drama of the court fight, occurred shortly before midday on July 6, in the President's office at the White House. In the same sunny room, months before, the President had made his decision to try to pack the Supreme Court. Then he had gambled his prestige, his power in his party and his absolute command of Congress with perfect confidence that he would win. Now he sat at his desk between the flags with the ugly possibility of defeat staring him in the face.

The atmosphere of the meeting was heavily surcharged. In the President's mind there boiled all the mounting bitterness of months of frustration. He had gone into the fight because he believed that the Supreme Court ought to "co-operate" with him, because he was convinced that the Court had done wrong in blocking his plans for social and economic reform and because he thought it his prerogative to bring the Court into line. His long frustration had surprised no one more than the overconfident President. Moreover, he did not consider it Congress's business to oppose his broad objectives. Yet the opposition had come, and on that hot July morning he was sacrificing his pride in the hope of conciliating it.

His hope—not unlike that of the young lady from Niger who sang songs to the tiger—was the best measure of how strangely his overconfidence persisted. Not only was Wheeler completely convinced that he was doing right in opposing the court plan. He was pretty bitter himself, what with his recollection of his illtreatment by the administration before the court plan, his awareness of the sort of thing that had been said about him at the White House since he went into opposition and his knowledge of such incidents as that of the Buffalo Rapids Dam and the President's successful effort to persuade the Northwestern farm leader, Thatcher, to stir up trouble for him in Montana. Altogether he was scarcely in the mood to be mollified by the easy Roosevelt geniality, the matter-of-fact, man-to-man, I-bear-no-malice manner.

At first the President sought to make his court plan seem unimportant, to show that it was nothing for old

friends to fight over. A workable judicial system, like
the English in its flexibility and dispatch, was all he
wanted, so he said. Wheeler pointed out that packing
the Supreme Court was something else again, and took
the offensive himself. How could the President have
been so heartlessly cruel to eighty-year-old Justice
Brandeis, the first and best New Dealer of them all, as
to make the justices' age the mainspring of his attack
on the Court? He asked the question vehemently, and
the President, with the air of one explaining the mys-
teries of Realpolitik, answered that there were times
when the pressure of circumstance did not permit the
consideration of mere personalities. Then, realizing
perhaps that he was getting nowhere, the President
made the overture he had been banking on.

He did not suggest that Wheeler abandon his opposition. He was too practical for that. He took the line
that their joint first object must be to prevent faction-
alism in the Democratic party. He argued that while
there was no reason for the party to split on the court
issue, a split could hardly be avoided if Democrats like
Wheeler persisted in taking the leadership of the anti-
administration forces. Why not let the Republicans
fight in the front lines? Wheeler saw the suggestion's
purpose at once. He understood quite as well as the
President and Robinson that the Republican conspiracy
of silence was one of the opposition's essential strengths.
He turned the President down flat, and the interview
was over. The pair parted coldly, as men must when a
truce has ended and they go to fight again.

That interview between the leaders of the two sides
in the struggle rang the curtain up on the tremendous
final act of the court drama. In thus bringing the President, the hero of the piece, onto the stage at the first,
Providence or whatever other force should have credit
for the design of the play must be allowed to have

shown an admirable sense of dramatic construction. The debate began in the Senate that same afternoon, and the President had but little part in the events immediately succeeding.

Shortly after noon, while Wheeler was still with the President, Joe Robinson rose in his place in the Senate to open the debate. The grueling job of rallying the administration forces had told dreadfully on him, but his energies were not yet exhausted. The banderillas had been planted; the picadors had done their brutal work, but the aging bull of a man could still gather his strength for the last exasperated charges which, it is said, the matadors fear most. His speech was like one of those last charges of the tormented animals in the ring. Huge, red-faced and heavy-bodied, he stood in the crowded chamber, sawing the air with a violent, mechanical gesture of his right arm, bellowing his challenges and roaring his threats at the enemy. All his peculiar force, all his solidity and vitality were behind his words, so that they had a crashing impact in the confined air of the Senate. His qualities compelled respect, and those who heard him that July afternoon realized it very thoroughly.

"I am given to understand that those who oppose this bill will try to filibuster; let them try," he shouted. "I warn them now that ways will be found to meet their obstruction. It will not be tolerated."

The scene was a fascinating one. The high, wide chamber, so meaninglessly decorated with square yards of tan and gray and faded yellow Victorian baroque patterns, was colorlessly illuminated by its huge skylight. Against the undramatic, almost squalid background appeared the people. In the galleries, which run all the way round the room, like elevated bleachers at an exclusive football match, there were senators' wives, diplomats, connoisseurs of the Washington scene, hun-

dreds upon hundreds of sight-seers, and whole squads
of the Boy Scouts whose national jamboree was soon
to take place. The senators' wives and diplomats were
immensely outnumbered; the overwhelming impression
was that the plain people of America had come to see
their government in action. In the pitlike space which
the galleries enclose was the government they had
come to see, scores of rather elderly, remarkably
ordinary-looking men. Hardly a senator was absent,
and the representatives who had hurried over from the
other end of the Capitol were lined three deep along
the walls. And in the center of it all was the big, indomitable old man, trying to beat down his enemies by
sheer force of personality.

He roared his threats; he swore vengeance on the
opposition; he attacked the Court; and he defended
the President. His speech was neither concise nor elo-
quently phrased. Its arguments were simple and often
disconnected; its points repetitious and not always se-
quential; its sarcasm heavy. But it was impressive.
Oddly enough the moment which stirred the audience
most deeply, both to laughter and to excitement, was
that when Robinson forgot his vehemence and spoke
of politics in the first person, as it were. He was telling of the time which comes to men when "they have
passed the climax of their usefulness", of how often a
man will not recognize that time but keep on "running
for office and running for office until everyone gets
tired of him."

"I have often thought," he said, "that politics is not
an occupation. It is a disease, and, by the eternal, when
it gets into the blood and brain there is no cure for it."

The moment was an interruption. For the rest he
was bellicose, more bellicose than he had ever been
before, and in the past senators had rarely interrupted
Robinson in a bellicose mood. The opposition, however,

had a new kind of courage. They were in no frame of mind to sit silent under his furious denunciation, and they heckled him continually. Now Burke, now Wheeler, now O'Mahoney, now Clark—one after the other they shot their questions at him. He beat them off brutally, but they always returned to the attack. One began to have the feeling that it was unfair, that more banderillas were being placed when the bull should have been left to fight his fight in peace. As the strain increased his flush deepened; his voice grew hoarse; his gestures were more unrestrained. At last Senator Royal S. Copeland, of New York, who prides himself on being a doctor as well as a legislator, began to be really concerned. Robinson was replying to another question when Copeland left his seat near by, crossed the well of the chamber and whispered to the enraged leader:

"Joe, the cause you're fighting for isn't worth your life. For God's sake, slow down."

Robinson paused, half turned to Copeland and muttered irritably:

"I know, but those fellows make me so damned angry with their questions."

Actually Robinson could not afford to slow down, even after the hecklers had drained his last reserves, even after he had thrown up his hands and exclaimed, "That's all, good-by." During the next days the pressure of events whipped him onward, ever faster, ever more cruelly.

Each day the vital group of waverers on whom Robinson's majority depended grew more and more uneasy. They were losing what heart they had, and as their defenses weakened the opposition besieged them more tenaciously. By their efficient system of espionage the opposition senators were kept in constant touch with the waverers' states of mind. A chance remark in the cloakroom, a short talk at lunch, a minor incident on the floor—such things as these were the indicators which spurred the members of the opposition to a great extra effort to convert the waverers. If you chanced to see a waverer in the Senate corridors and cloak-rooms in those days you were certain to see one or two opposition senators pleading, persuading, exhorting or shaming the worried man into independence.

There were a score of opposition senators to share the work of leadership; on his side Robinson was alone. His troops were lukewarm; he had few lieutenants on whom he could depend to give heart to the others. Barkley, Minton, Black, Schwellenbach and La Follette gave him such help as they could, but he had assumed the sole responsibility for the command of his side; he had asked that commitments be made personally to him; he had kept all the threads of authority in his own hands. Every morning, every evening he had to work at strengthening his weak lines, pouring out his huge reservoirs of vitality until they were as dry as mud puddles in midsummer. Worst of all, he had to perform all the tasks of leadership in his off hours, for his official position added to his other duties the exhausting one of managing his side in the debate on the floor.

Hatch, of New Mexico, had followed Robinson on the first day, making an able defense of his substitute measure in his special simple, reasonable, unemphatic style. What he managed to say was only said in the intervals of a machine-gun fire of questions from the opposition, who had shrewdly planned to destroy the effectiveness of the administration speakers by heckling them until they were black in the face. Next day Senator Joseph F. Guffey, the grand panjandrum of Democratic politics in Pennsylvania, took the floor for a bitter attack on the Court. Naturally inarticulate, habituated only to command, poor Senator Guffey was no match for the hecklers. During his speech he positively refused to answer any questions at all, and when the speech was over and the questioning began he could stand it for only five minutes. After that he fled from the floor, leaving to Senator Logan the thankless task of carrying the administration standard. Logan's emphasis, conveyed with all the rich vagaries of a slightly disheveled oratory, was on loyalty to the President, and he reached his peak when he compared the Democrats who signed the report of the Judiciary Committee to a set of assassins.

"They had a right to disagree with the President," he cried; "I grant that. But when Caesar discovered that Brutus, his own friend, had turned against him, his great heart broke. He fell bleeding at the foot of the statue of Pompey."

Logan, too, was harried by the opposition, and that evening, at a conference with his lieutenants, Robinson reluctantly decided to tighten the rules of the Senate. In the absence of old John Garner, Key Pittman, of Nevada, was in the chair. Besides Robinson he was the only major member of the original Senate oligarchy to remain entirely faithful to the President. Robinson warned Pittman in advance and next morning raised a point of order at the first opposition question, arguing that a speaker need yield only for a question, and then only if he wished to do so. Pittman promptly announced that he would enforce the rule. He added that the rule limiting senators to not more than two speeches on a bill in any day would also be enforced and that the word "day" in the rule would be interpreted to mean "legislative day." A "legislative day" may last for weeks, since it is only terminated by formal adjournment of the Senate, and Robinson immediately jumped up and shouted that there would be no adjournments, nothing but recesses, until the debate was over. An extraordinary scene ensued, in which Robinson and his

followers and the leaders of the opposition were all on
their feet, all bellowing at once. Order was gone; the
fascinated galleries buzzed with excitement; and on the
floor such a scene of bitterness and hatred, fury and suspicion was enacted as the Senate had not witnessed in a
quarter century. Robinson was the butt of the opposition's attacks; his revival of the old, more stringent
rules, which had been forgotten for decades, was wildly
attacked, and by the end of the debate he was purple
and trembling.

And so the debate continued. After Logan came Minton, and then Wheeler opened for the opposition on
July 9. His speech was an infuriated denunciation of
administration's behavior in the fight, and it lost no
force from his odd habits of repetition, of hissing out
his words, of treating his enemies as though he were
the recording angel warning them that there were serious counts against them in his books. Next day Pat
McCarran took the floor, rather dramatically, for he
was ill and showed it, yet talked on vehemently and intensely for hours.

That evening Robinson left the Senate chamber perfectly exhausted. Things had been going badly and he
knew it. In the debate itself the opposition, always
vigilant for an opportunity, always able to speak with
the fervency of conviction, had had a distinct edge. In
the corridors also they had had an edge, for the waverers were wavering more seriously every day. Already
one man for whose vote Robinson had hoped, Senator
John N. Bankhead, of Alabama, had announced his
opposition to any bill involving an increase in the Court,
and there were constant rumors that others would join
him. Whereas the confident administration predictions
of an early victory had been generally accepted at the
start of the debate, now it was common talk that Robinson and the President would be forced to compro-

mise once again, and that this time the compromise would involve no increase in the Court of any kind.

McCarran spoke on a Saturday. Robinson tried to rest all Sunday. He needed rest badly. Days before he had fallen into a black mood. He was deeply hurt by the opposition's personal attacks on him, provoked by the revival of the old rules. He was greatly distressed by the spectacle of the Democratic party tearing itself to shreds on the Senate floor. And he was cut closest to the quick by the attitude of some of the young men at the White House. All through June they had harried him with messages that if he failed to get his compromise he could not have his promised place on the Supreme Court. He knew then that they had no presidential authority for their threats, and now he knew, when word came to him that they thought he was lying down on his job, that the President did not agree with them. Yet the knowledge made the wound no less painful. And if his state of mind was dark, his physical condition was worse. His heart was troubling him constantly, and after a day or so the strain of the debate upset his digestion. From July 8 on, he scarcely touched solid food and lived almost entirely on buttermilk.

The day's quiet on Sunday did him some good, and on Monday, July 13, he returned to the Senate feeling better and more cheerful. Joe Keenan, who was acting as the White House liaison man with the Senate, came up to the Hill for an early lunch with him that morning, and found him still looking dreadfully ill, but full of energy. During his speech Wheeler had quoted Keenan as having told a woman's club meeting he addressed on the court plan, that the President wanted "justices who could be trusted", whereas Keenan had really talked of "justices with open minds." Keenan suggested that a good deal might be made of this, if it were not corrected, and asked to have Minton point out Wheeler's error in a brief speech. Robinson agreed with Keenan on the advisability of a correction, thought for a moment and said:

"I'll handle it myself, Joe. It 'll be a good chance to give those fellows some of their own back."

Keenan was much distressed at this response, for he clearly saw that Robinson could not support the strain he was under. He pleaded with him not to do too much and pointed out that there were many details which he could let his lieutenants handle for him. Keenan had often complained to Robinson before that he worked too hard, and Robinson had always answered by teasing Keenan about his inveterate habit of traveling by airplane. This time Robinson threw back his head, gave his big laugh and answered:

"I'll tell you, Joe. You keep out of airplanes and I'll let someone else do my work, and we'll see who lasts the longest."

From his lunch with Keenan, Robinson went straight to the floor, where O'Mahoney began the day for the opposition with one of the most eloquent and effective speeches of the debate. O'Mahoney devoted his attention to the bill itself, describing it as a deliberate attempt to centralize the control of justice in Washington, decrying its effects on the people's liberties and warning his colleagues that if the bill should pass they would be driven from office by an "outraged" electorate. Robinson was much on his feet during the O'Mahoney speech, asking questions, replying to O'Mahoney's attack on the revival of the old Senate rules and urging on his followers in the fight. He began to tire badly, and when Senator Bailey, of North Carolina, took the floor, the leader looked haggard and deathly ill.

The Bailey speech was a fascinating phenomenon. A medium-sized, lantern-jawed man with a long sharp nose, a long upper lip and a preternaturally solemn expression, Bailey has a heavy, pedantic delivery which can be exceedingly annoying. His mannerism of hammering on his desk and shouting at every important point, as though by pure force of habit, was unfortunate, and the Senate was less ready to be stirred by Bailey because everyone knew that he had run as a fervent New Dealer and admirer of the President and had repeatedly voted in the opposite sense ever since. Nevertheless, Bailey was deeply and honestly stirred by the court fight; he had given weeks to preparing his speech; and now he delivered it with all the force of absolute conviction. The mannerisms, the bad delivery were still there. He still shouted his warnings of what would come if the independence of the judiciary were impaired, and hammered on his desk at each of the points intended to show that an impairment of the judiciary's independence was the inevitable result of the court bill. But the senators listened with complete attention. Every desk for rows around the speaker was filled—a sure sign of interest—and the chamber was perfectly still. That rare thing, a successful and convincing argument, was being made on the Senate floor, and Robinson, tired and sick as he was, sensed it at once. So disturbed was he that in midafternoon he left the chamber and telephoned to Keenan.

"Bailey's in there and he's making a great speech," he said. "He's impressing a lot of people, and I tell you I'm worried."

Keenan minimized Robinson's fears, and the leader returned wearily to his desk to wait for the end of the day. So complete was the attention which Bailey commanded that, when Robinson rose and left the chamber once more a little later, his departure was not noticed. One of the pages who was standing in the doorway as he walked out noticed that his face seemed drawn and that he was breathing hard. The boy watched Robinson make his way through the lobby and the Vice-President's Room to the Capitol portico. After a few minutes he heard Robinson call and scurried out to him. Robinson ordered him to find Sherman Minton, and he ran in and fetched him off the floor. Minton hastened to the portico and found Robinson huddled in one of the old wicker rockers which the senators like to use on fair days. It was broiling summer weather, and Robinson was purple in the face, gasping for air and beating his broad chest. Minton, very frightened, asked him what was wrong.

"I've got a terrible pain here." The words came between labored breaths. He indicated where the pain was by pressing the region over his heart. Then after an exhausted pause he went on:

"It hurts me so I can hardly stand it. Go in and tell Alben Barkley to take over for the rest of the day. I've got to go to my room."

That was the moment when the President really lost his field marshal. Next morning Robinson tried to return to his routine. He had a nine o'clock appointment with the artist, S. J. Woolf, who was to sketch and interview him. He managed to keep it, but he found he could not go on. A few minutes after Woolf left him he summoned Barkley, Minton and two or three other lieutenants, told them that he must rest and asked Barkley to act as leader until he was better. Then he returned to the ovenlike little apartment in the Methodist Building, across the plaza from the Capitol, where he had lived for many years. Mrs Robinson was away in Arkansas, and there was no one to nurse him. Always restless and irritable, he must have wandered up and down his narrow living room all day, cursing his own weakness and wondering how the fight was going without him.

Perhaps it was a kind of fate which spared him the knowledge of how the fight did go that afternoon. It was a day of portents. Early in the morning Keenan was once more on the Hill, searching for Robinson to discuss with him the reasons for his disturbance over the Bailey speech. In a corridor he ran into Henry Ashurst, more serious and less courtly than usual. Ashurst buttonholed him, warned him that things were in very poor shape and said meaningfully, "If anyone's telling the President that he can pass this court bill he's doing him a great disservice." More worried than ever, Keenan hurried off on his fruitless search for Robinson. Meanwhile Truman, of Missouri, Pat Harrison, Guffey and Ed Halsey were lunching in Halsey's commodious private office. Once more the talk was of the court bill. Halsey deplored the effect the fight was having on the Democratic party and, turning to Harrison, suggested to him that he make one of the good-tempered, joking, soothing speeches which are a specialty of his. Harrison pushed back his chair hard, slammed his fist down on the table and answered emphatically:

"By God, no, I won't do it. This thing goes deeper than you think, and I won't have any part of it."

Later in the day Hatton Sumners, the learned, stubborn chairman of the House Judiciary Committee who had done so much to checkmate the administration on that side, rose on the House floor to tell his fellow representatives that he had heard it was the scheme to jam the court bill through the Senate in any sort of shape and ask the docile House to rewrite it at the President's order. Sumners was hopping mad, and he minced no words.

"If they bring that bill into this House when we are trying to preserve the solidarity of the nation," he said, "if they bring that bill into this House for consideration, I do not believe they will have enough hide left on it to bother about."

From that point he went on to give the bill the worst lambasting it had in the whole course of the debate, and the House cheered him wildly. Yet bad as Sumners' speech and its reception looked, the event which would really have upset Robinson took place inconspicuously on the Senate floor.

Senator Copeland was speaking when two men in the freshman row, where the new Democrats were seated behind the Republicans, fell into conversation. One of them, Prentiss Brown, the serious, intelligent senator from Michigan, was on Robinson's list of fifty-one, and the other, Edward Johnson, of Colorado, was counted by Robinson as a probable marginal vote. They were both waverers. Both had been deeply moved by Bailey. Brown began the talk by revealing to Johnson that he had decided not to go along after all. He said he was ready to join the opposition in voting to recommit the court bill, unless the President should be willing to offer a substitute involving no increase of the Supreme Court. Johnson agreed with him, and they concluded together that it was their best move to go to the President, tell him of their decision, warn him that he was fighting a losing battle and plead with him to give in gracefully. To strengthen their hand, they invited two like-minded men who were sitting near them, Guy Gillette, of Iowa, and Andrews, of Florida, to join their delegation.

Gillette had already announced his adherence to the opposition, but Andrews was also on the Robinson list, so on that afternoon of July 13 the administration lost one hoped for and two definitely counted on votes. The unnoticed little conference on the Senate floor marked the moment from which the court fight moved to its tremendous climax.

THE CATASTROPHE

July 14–July 22, 1937

JULY *13* was the hundred and fifty-ninth day of the court fight. When the senators went home through the baked Washington streets that evening there was not one of them who did not wish the court fight over and done with. That evening the Sumners speech and vague reports of the Brown-Johnson-Gillette-Andrews talk persuaded the busy newspapermen to predict defeat for the President for the first time. That evening the President was still obstinately confident, but there was a smell of mischance in the air to be caught by sharp noses. That evening was a brief lull before a storm about to break. Thereafter events crowded one upon the other so pushingly that each day had its own peculiar importance.

JULY *14:* The Robinsons' maid arrived at the Methodist Building apartment very early and set to work at once preparing the senator's scanty breakfast. Joe Robinson's habits were as regular as clockwork, and by the time she had his coffee ready she expected him in the dining room. He made no sign. For a few minutes the colored girl waited, then thought the senator must be sleeping late and went to the bedroom to wake him. Her first hasty glance told her that the bed was empty

and the electric light still burning; her second that there
was no one in the bathroom and, so far as she could see,
no one in the bedroom either. Astonished, she ran out
to the hall and rang for the elevator. Had the senator
gone out? she asked the boy when the elevator came.
At his answer that he had not seen Robinson since the
day before the maid grew suddenly terrified. She refused to re-enter the apartment alone, and so it was the
elevator boy who led the way back to the bedroom.

There they found Joe Robinson lying beside his bed,
where he could not be seen from the door. He was
sprawled on the floor in his pajamas; his glasses were
on the bed, and by his right hand, from which it must
have dropped, was a copy of the *Congressional Record*
of the day before. Apparently he had been in bed studying the debate, had risen to go to the bathroom and had
been stricken by a heart attack at his first step.

The elevator boy called Kennedy Rea, secretary of
the Senate Appropriations Committee, and Chesley
Jurney, sergeant at arms of the Senate, both of whom
lived in the same building. In their turn they summoned
Leslie Biffle, secretary of the Senate majority and the
man of all others who was Robinson's closest confidant
and most relied-on subordinate. Biffle immediately telephoned the White House offices, so early that no one
was there to take his message except a minor clerk.
Presumably it was the clerk who informed President
Roosevelt of Robinson's death.

It is impossible to tell just how the President took
the news. Robinson's death meant clearly that the
President must once more take over the leadership of
the fight, and it meant, too, that the fight was lost.
Whether or no the fight would have been lost anyway
will never be decided. It must be remembered that at
the very moment when the news of Robinson's death
was sinking into the President's mind, Brown, John-

son, Andrews and Gillette were meeting to decide how
they should present their case to him and to arrange
for an appointment. Considering the four senators'
little conference on July 13, it appears by hindsight that
even Robinson could not have held his majority together, but without Robinson all hope was certainly
gone. One cannot help wondering how much of this the
President realized, how much more the word that Robinson was gone meant to him than the loss of an old
and faithful friend.

By the day's end he must have had some glimmer of
what was to come, for the most indescribable confusion
ensued on Capitol Hill. The opposition, jubilant as well
as sorrowing, saw victory suddenly close at hand. The
vision excited them to their single serious mistake:
Wheeler's demand that the President withdraw his
bill "lest he appear to be fighting against God."

As for the administration forces, they were leader-
less and without morale. The waverers' personal commitments to Robinson had been dissolved by his death,
and there was no man left among the few enthusiastic
faithful with sufficient force to beat the waverers back
into line. And the succession to Robinson's post as
majority leader suddenly began to prove horribly dis-
ruptive. The two outstanding candidates, Pat Harrison, who represented a measure of independence of the
White House, and Barkley, who stood for absolute
obedience to the President's commands, were in hot
competition. The issue between the two had already
made considerable trouble for the administration. Now,
with Robinson dead and the succession a matter that
must be settled at once, angry murmurs against White
House interference were to be heard wherever senators
foregathered. Already the factions within the Democratic party had set to quarreling on lines far broader
than the original division caused by the court fight.

JULY *15:* Brown, Johnson, Gillette and Andrews presented themselves at the White House so early in the morning that the President had not gone over to his office. The four men were determined and hopeful. Each of them had his suggestion for a substitute for the court bill. Andrews' alone involved an increase in the Court. He still favored his compromise establishing a high bench with eleven members, the ten associate justices to represent the ten federal judicial circuits and the Chief Justice to be chosen at large. All of them, Andrews as well as the others, were firm in their intention to oppose the court bill as it then stood, whether or no the President would agree to offer a substitute.

They found the President in his comfortable White House study, sitting at his desk in his shirt sleeves. He, too, was determined—determined not to let them say what they had come to say. The talk began with a mention of Robinson's death. The President seized the lead in the conversation. Robinson's death recalled to him an incident of the 1928 campaign, when Alfred E. Smith had been rude to Robinson at a meeting of Democratic leaders. He took the incident as his text and divided all Democrats into the Smiths and the Robinsons, the Tories and the believers in social progress. His listeners gathered that, in his view, every liberal Democrat must follow him as unquestioningly as Joe Robinson had done, that only men fit to address the Liberty League would oppose him. The sermon lasted half an hour before Brown found an opportunity to break in. What he said when he did get his chance was the most admirable bit of dialogue in the drama of the court fight, for it was pat to the occasion, yet it summed up one of the queerest defects in the President's conduct of his campaign.

"Mr President," said Brown, "it's the hardest thing in the world to tell you something you don't want to

hear. It's the hardest thing in the world to give you
bad news. But we're here to tell you that we can't go
along on the Hatch bill."

Although the others took up the tale, although they
pleaded and argued and did all that they could to convince him, the President remained cold. He had told
Congress what he wanted, and he expected Congress to
give it to him in some form or other, it didn't matter
what. That was his position, the position he clung to
all through the first and this second day after Robinson's death. In the end it proved an untenable position,
simply because it was based on an angry rebellion
against the plain facts of the situation.

The four senators left the White House moved and
distressed by what they saw ahead. A few hours later
Brown paid a call on Alben Barkley, partly to do another errand and partly to advise Barkley, as the acting leader of the Senate Democrats, of what he and
his friends had done. In Barkley's office he found Barkley, Minton and Schwellenbach conferring together.
They had before them a copy of a Washington afternoon paper, in which it was erroneously reported that
the President had abandoned his court plan during
Brown's and the others' morning call at the White
House. Sherman Minton brandished the paper in
Brown's face and shouted at him angrily:

"Where in hell do you stand? We've got to count
noses. The President's got to know."

In his already excited state Brown was in no mood to
give Minton less than he got.

"Damn you," he said, "you don't need to tell the
President where I stand; I've just got through telling
him myself, and I want you to know I told him I
couldn't go along."

The announcement was a bombshell to the trio of
administration leaders, and when Brown followed it

up with the news that Johnson, Andrews and Gillette were ready to take the same stand the belligerence of Minton and the two others melted away. They pleaded with Brown to change his mind, but all they could get from him was the same promise he had given the President, not to vote to recommit the court bill to the Judiciary Committee until it was clear that the White House would offer no substitute. Brown left Barkley's office after warning the trio solemnly against telling the President "this thing is in the bag."

For a few minutes Barkley, Minton and Schwellenbach discussed the implications of what Brown had told them. Then Barkley telephoned the President and talked the matter over with him. The result was the "Dear Alben" letter, hastily composed by the President during the remainder of the afternoon.

The letter had the same defiant, bitter tone as a remark of the President to a friend at this time, that "they can't use Joe Robinson's death to beat me." "I'll show them," he said to his friend, and his letter to Barkley was an effort to do just that. It accused the opposition of unseemly haste in trying to kill the court bill before Robinson was even buried. It stated that neither Robinson's death nor anything else could make the principle of the court bill less desirable. It demanded that the principle be enacted into law forthwith and it ordered Barkley to continue the struggle without asking or giving quarter. Altogether it was a splendid demonstration of the same unrealism, the same unwillingness to face the unkind facts of his situation that the President had shown in his talk with Brown and the others.

It was released for publication late in the afternoon and caused the kind of stir which might have been expected. In the Senate it cut two ways. It made the President's supporters nervous and the members of the opposition angry, and it infuriated Pat Harrison's friends by its clear indication, in the intimate, almost cozy flavor of its phrasing, that the President was backing Barkley for the leadership.

Shortly after the letter had been made public Barkley himself, with Minton, Schwellenbach and Key Pittman, of Nevada, visited the President at the White House. It may have been at this meeting that the President ceased to rebel against reality and began to move towards his second attitude, that some means, any means must be found to make it seem he was not beaten. Certainly his quartet of callers gave him a gloomy enough report. Minton brought word that besides the senators who had been to the White House with Brown three or four others were ready to desert the administration ranks, and Barkley agreed that the outlook was very dark. At the same time even the four Senate leaders had not quite grasped the full implications of the problem which confronted them. They thought they had an outside chance to cobble things up, rally their men and carry on the fight after Joe Robinson's funeral. It was with a decision to try to follow this course that the meeting came to its close.

JULY *16:* At 10 A.M. the dreary, rather makeshift ceremony of a state funeral started in the Senate chamber. The President was present, with all the other high officers of state and great figures of the Washington scene. A good many people remarked with some amusement that of all the ranks in the hierarchy only the Supreme Court was poorly represented. The other justices were on vacation, and Justice Pierce Butler sat alone in the space reserved for the judiciary.

When the last shambling prayer was spoken the President was escorted from the chamber. Before leaving for the White House he waited for a while in the President's Room, off the Senate lobby, a fantastic

apartment furnished like a very expensive Victorian
saloon bar. There the senators trooped in to speak to
him. One was Pat Harrison, whom he greeted with
something less than the subdued cordiality appropriate
to the occasion. In the interval between the publication
of the "Dear Alben" letter and the state funeral his
advisers had done some straight talking to the President on the foolishness of alienating Harrison at a
moment when every last supporter, no matter how lukewarm, counted in the court fight. And so, although his
manner was chilly, the President asked Harrison to
call on him that afternoon at his White House office.

Harrison accepted the invitation, and the interview
took place on schedule. It was a pretty stiff meeting.
Harrison told the President in no uncertain terms that
he did not like the President's interference in the leadership fight. Although his most intimate aides had been
openly lobbying for Barkley since the beginning of
June, although he himself had dropped a hint to Brown
and his friends that Barkley must succeed Robinson,
the President flatly denied that he had taken any part
in the struggle. He told Harrison that he was willing
to have his attitude made public and authorized him to
announce the neutrality of the White House to the
newspapermen waiting outside. Harrison accordingly
did so, but his statement fooled no one.

The talk with Harrison was the result of the first
of three decisions made by the President on the day of
Joe Robinson's state funeral. The second was his refusal to make the trip to Arkansas for Robinson's
burial. Where the President's pretense of neutrality in
the leadership fight was accepted as a patent fraud by
the Harrison men whom it was intended to conciliate,
his refusal to go to Arkansas irritated the friends of
Robinson, who accused the President of ingratitude.

The President's advisers, indeed, foresaw this and

pressed him to go to Little Rock. But it was as though
the President were disgusted with Congress and everything connected with it. First he said that the Far
Eastern situation made it impossible for him to leave
Washington, and then, curiously enough, considering
his fondness for breaking precedents, he maintained
that a bad precedent would be set. The President of
the United States, he argued, should not go on funeral
trips except for the Vice-President, the Speaker of the
House and the members of his Cabinet. He would not
be persuaded.

The state of mind which produced the President's
third decision was probably born at the conference with
the administration leaders of the Senate the night before, as has been remarked. The decision was simply
to accept any kind of substitute for his court bill so
long as it would allow him to tell the nation he had not
been beaten in the court fight. The problem of finding
such a substitute could, unfortunately, only be solved
by a reductio ad absurdum. To permit any appearance
of victory a bill had to be passed providing for some
additional justices on the Supreme Court. Yet since
Robinson's death there was a clear majority in the Senate against any extra justices at all.

The only way out seemed to be to accept the curious
compromise proffered by Senator Tydings, of Maryland, a day or so before Robinson's death. It was the
result of a spasm of nervousness among certain opposition leaders, particularly Wheeler, who had just com-
pleted a recheck of the Senate and found their strength
limited to the same forty-two sure votes. Worried and
unaware that the Brown-Johnson-Andrews break was
soon to come, they had thought long and hard of compromise. At length there occurred to them the notion
that passing the bill as it stood, with the single important proviso that it should not apply to the sitting

Court, would be the easiest way out. Thus the President would have his "principle", while they would avoid immediate court packing.

Wheeler put the idea up to Tydings, who liked it very little. Nevertheless, he consented to try it on with the administration, for he, too, was frightened by the opposition's failure to gain strength. He telephoned Tom Corcoran and arranged a meeting, at which he made the offer on a take-it-or-leave-it basis. Indeed, he informed Corcoran that he had been chosen to carry the message simply because it was thought he could persuade the bitter-enders, like Carter Glass and Burke, to go along, and added that even for so meaningless a measure as he offered, it would be extremely difficult to win their consent. Corcoran replied that he would take the message to the White House, and the two parted. The same afternoon Corcoran telephoned Tydings that there was nothing doing.

Now, however, the situation had changed. Exempting the sitting Court and providing for additional justices in the future looked far more attractive to the White House, where the desperate desire was to preserve, however flimsily, the "principle" of the court bill. Therefore when Joe Keenan boarded the Robinson funeral train, he was under orders to push Tydings' compromise.

JULY 17: At the White House the President conferred with his advisers and waited for news from Keenan. On the train speeding through the flat prairie country of middle America a political caucus was going on from the baggage car behind the engine to the door of the flower-banked office car carrying Robinson's body at the rear. Thirty-odd senators, assorted representatives, and Keenan and two other agents for the White House, Postmaster General James A. Farley and Undersecretary of the Interior Charles West, were traveling on that train. The opposition lobbied busily in every compartment, while Keenan bore the brunt of the work for the administration. He found the going hopelessly uphill, although he had reasons for optimism in the definiteness and urgency of the Tydings offer. The trouble was that Tydings had spoken before Joe Robinson's death destroyed the morale of the administration forces. Now Keenan was turned down flat by every member of the opposition to whom he made his proposal. By the end of the day he knew that there was nothing to gain from his substitute.

JULY *18:* The funeral train pulled into Little Rock in an already broiling dawn, and was noisily switched onto a siding before the station. Almost immediately Mrs Robinson, who had come close to breaking under the terrible shock of her husband's death and the strain of her hasty journey to Washington, was escorted off the train by Robinson's two closest friends, Bernard M. Baruch and Harvey C. Couch. The two rich and powerful men were deeply moved by the loss of their crony. They were sad as they watched Robinson's body being removed from its railroad car to a waiting hearse. The body was taken at once to the Robinson house, and Mrs Robinson, Couch and Baruch followed it together.

So began a fantastic day. Before Mrs Robinson could finish her breakfast the intimate friends and relations who had gathered at her house to welcome her home were forced to form a sort of guard around her. The local politicians of Arkansas thought of nothing but the fact that she would have something to say about the succession to her dead husband's Senate seat. Supporters of Governor Carl E. Bailey, who was then the leading candidate for the job, telephoned and called in droves, in the hope of wresting an endorsement of Bailey from Mrs Robinson before Joe's body was in its grave.

Meanwhile the senators and representatives on the funeral train were rousing themselves from an uneasy, second-night-on-the-train sleep. They breakfasted leisurely and wandered out onto the platform, where they found Vice-President Garner come to meet them. The old Texas fox had made a quick trip from Uvalde, with a purpose spurring him on. He had seen the Democratic party disintegrate in the court fight, and now he had returned to pick up the pieces. The senators greeted Garner like a long-lost father, and the whole party proceeded to the cars to be taken to the state Capitol, where Joe Robinson was lying in state. Even here the court fight and the struggle over the leadership were not forgotten. So many enmities had been sown through the clubby Senate by the two conflicts that senators quarreled over the companions they had been assigned in the waiting motors. At last all was settled, and the cortege set off for the Capitol building, with the party in every car still busily talking politics.

Politics were abandoned for a few moments in the Capitol rotunda. The senators filed solemnly past Robinson's body, where it lay amidst the massed flowers, under the eyes of an immense and quietly watchful crowd. Then the Washington party was taken to the Little Rock Country Club, high on a hill over the city. A swimming pool tempted the legislators, and for a couple of hours its tepid waters were full of them. The spectacle was a strange one. An unforgiving sun beat down from a brazen sky upon the green of the golf course, the blue of the pool's waters and the paunchy pink of the naked senatorial figures. Even thus, unclothed and in the sun, the contestants in the court fight could not forget the struggle. All around the pool they formed in little knots, talking votes for and against, discussing compromises and speculating on the President's chances of pulling his chestnuts out of the fire. Not far away, in the shade of a persimmon tree, on the eighteenth green, Joe Keenan and Sherman Minton, who had not gone swimming, had their heads together in close and worried talk. On the other side of the clubhouse, on the first tee, Senator Bulkley, of Ohio, was arguing with hometown friends of Joe Robinson's. One of them, an old county judge by the name of Burlingame, spoke the thought that was in many minds.

"Yes sir, that court bill is responsible for the funeral we're having here today," said the judge. "Joe was leading a losing fight and he knew it. It was the first fight he ever lost in the Democratic party, and that's what killed him."

The Washington delegation lunched at the country club, and politics still raged around the tables. After lunch came the service, in a simple Methodist church in the town. The hour of plain and rather moving ceremony was the longest period during which the court fight was not mentioned on the whole funeral trip. Tremendous thunderclouds were banking up on the western horizon when the funeral party left the church to go to the burial. The storm broke at last just as Robinson's body was being lowered into the grave, and the senators, most of whom were in white linen suits, were drenched to the skin. A Harrison campaign manager seized the opportunity to ingratiate himself with Senator Dieterich by trying to shield him from the wet, and by the time the party was back on the funeral train once more, ready to return to Washington, Dieterich was a converted Harrisonite. And so the day ended, with Jack Garner on the train, starting his task of picking up the pieces.

JULY *19:* Soon after breakfast Garner began a series of conferences with representatives of both sides in the fight. The office car which had taken Robinson's body to Arkansas had been kept on the train for Garner's use, and so Garner saw the senators in the same apartment which had contained the coffin a short twenty-four hours before. The scent of the flowers must almost have lingered in the upholstery, but there was nothing funereal in the genial realism with which Garner assessed the situation. By the day's end he was convinced that the jig was up for the administration.

By evening the opposition had ample reasons to be jubilant. Although Wheeler and his colleagues did not know of it, Keenan had returned to Washington by night plane and reported to the President. His report was that even such a flimsy pretext of a bill as had been hoped for was impracticable. Then, during the day on the train, Prentiss Brown, Andrews, of Florida, and Overton, of Louisiana, had decided to hold a meeting of uncommitted senators as soon as they arrived in Washington. That augured badly for the administration. And in the afternoon, at Parkersburg, W. Va., news reached the train of a letter from Governor Herbert H. Lehman, of New York, to Senator Robert F. Wagner, attacking the court plan and asking Senator Wagner, as New York's representative, to vote against it. When the train pulled into the capital shortly before midnight the members of the opposition went home in cheerful mood indeed.

JULY 20: Jack Garner marched up the White House steps before the morning coolness had left the air. The President received him at once and greeted him with a great show of cordiality. Garner told him that he had come to talk about the court fight, and the President nodded acquiescently.

"Do you want it with the bark on or the bark off?" Garner asked.

The President replied that he didn't understand the country phrase, and Garner explained that in his part

of Texas people asked for it "with the bark off" if they
wanted the naked truth, whereas if they desired their
feelings to be spared they asked to have it "with the
bark on." The President threw back his head and
laughed his hearty laugh. He would have it "with the
bark off" then, he said.

He got it. Garner informed him bluntly that he was
licked, that he had best fold his tents and steal away
from the court issue as rapidly as possible. The President shrugged his shoulders. He was ready to accept
Garner's appraisal of the situation. His rebellion
against the facts of his situation was a thing of the past.
He had failed in his desperate effort to seem, at least, to
win. Once more he had changed his attitude towards
the state of affairs that followed Robinson's death. Now
he was prepared for defeat. He knew that there was
no way out of an immediate humiliation, but he had
made up his mind that if he had to suffer the men in
Congress whom he held responsible would suffer
doubly later on. He was convinced that the voters were
still overwhelmingly on his side. In spite of the absence
of evidence of popular enthusiasm for the court plan
he still repeated, "The people are with me. I know it."
He expected the voters to see him as a sort of martyr
to the willfulness of an obstinate and disloyal Senate,
and he counted on them taking their feelings out on the
appropriate senators. Therefore he made no objection
when Garner turned the conversation to the best method
of liquidating the problem at once. After some talk it
was decided that Garner should spend the day on the
Hill feeling out how things stood and return late in the
afternoon with Alben Barkley, Pat Harrison and Key
Pittman to plan out the next step.

A couple of hours after Garner left the President
the uncommitted senators gathered in Prentiss Brown's
suite in the Senate Office Building. Bulow, of South

Dakota, Andrews, Herring, of Iowa, Johnson, of Colorado, Overton, Russell, of Georgia, Adams, of Colorado, and Brown made up the group. Various suggestions, such as a joint motion to recommit the court bill to the Judiciary Committee, with instructions to the committee to prepare a constitutional amendment reorganizing the judiciary, were talked back and forth. At length it was obvious that in any case everyone there, except Russell, of Georgia, was ready to vote to recommit. And their readiness to vote to recommit meant, of course, that they were ready to kill the bill, for recommittal is a sort of legislative death. Bulow, the acute old countryman, interrupted the discussion.

"Jack Garner's office is right across the hall," he said. "He told the President this morning he thought he was out on a limb and he's going down again to see him this afternoon. How about going over and talking to him?"

Brown telephoned Garner to see if he was free, and five minutes later the whole group, still with the exception of Russell, trooped into the Texan's lair. Garner greeted them like long-lost brothers—so warmly, in fact, that some of the senators suspected him of wondering whether he had oversold the President on his defeat, and being delighted to have his warning so quickly confirmed. He listened eagerly while they told him they were in no hurry but that if, within a reasonable time, the President did not offer a substitute bill involving no additional justices on the Supreme Court, they would all vote for recommittal.

It was about five o'clock when Garner carried the news to the President. He and Harrison, Barkley and Pittman found a surprisingly realistic Franklin Roosevelt. Once more Garner was allowed to dominate the discussion. It was taken for granted that the Supreme Court was out of the picture. Different face-saving expedients were canvassed, and Harrison proposed that a sort of arbitration committee, made up of five administration and five opposition senators, might be delegated to work out a substitute bill dealing with the lower courts. The President liked the Harrison proposal, but the leadership contest was still pending and had to be decided. A final settlement of the fate of the court bill was put off until after the vote on the majority leadership next morning. The President said good night to his callers pleasantly enough. Garner left the White House so coolly in command of himself and the situation that he remembered to telephone Senator Wagner immediately, to warn him not to answer the Lehman letter.

JULY 21: The Democratic members of the Senate met for the vote on the leadership at 10 A.M. in the white marble Caucus Room of the Senate Office Building. That strange chamber, which looks as if it had been decorated by an expert in the architecture of wedding cakes, contained a deal of bitterness by the time the assembly was complete. The President's pretended neutrality in the leadership contest had not lasted long. At the morning meeting the Harrison supporters were saying the President had "double-crossed Pat", and their anger only increased the factional fury of the enemies in the court fight.

The Harrison men remembered the early White House pressure for Barkley and the White House announcement of neutrality. They knew that, the announcement notwithstanding, the Long junta in Louisiana had been put to work for Barkley with Senator Overton, and had succeeded. They had been told by Senator Dieterich, once active in their councils, that White House pressure was too strong for him. They knew, too, of the zero-hour administration effort to make Senator Harry Truman, of Missouri, a Barkley voter. They were laughing, more than maliciously, at the story of how a telegram ostentatiously sent to Truman by the Pendergasts' Kansas City organization had been preceded by a telephone call telling him to pay no attention, to stick to Harrison.

The voting was by secret ballot, and the votes were counted one by one. With only the last ballot still unopened the count stood: Harrison, 37, Barkley, 37. Barkley bit through his pipe stem while the teller was fumbling with the slip of paper's folds. Finally the teller tore the ballot open. It was for Barkley.

Jack Garner had been waiting eagerly for news. Word of Barkley's election was carried to him at once, and he acted without hesitating an instant. He went straight to the office of Senator Wheeler, where he was received with open arms.

"Burt, you can write your own ticket," were his first words.

Wheeler's suspicious caution did not desert him. Such a triumphant delight filled him that he had to hold onto himself to keep from war-whooping. Yet he told Garner cautiously that he would have to talk to the other senators of the opposition and see what they had to suggest. Garner bustled off, and Wheeler hurried over to the Capitol to gather a war council. Having just learned that he had won the greatest fight of his career, he was wildly nervous and excited. It was lunchtime, and the Senate was not in session. He ran through the deserted corridors, searching for a friendly face, until he came to the senator's poky little private dining room. There Senator Bailey was eating his midday meal at the big common table. Wheeler saw him and dashed up to him. Bailey, noticing Wheeler's flushed color and his taut expression, was not surprised when Wheeler said tensely:

"Joe, I've got to see you as soon as possible. Something very important to us has just happened."

Bailey offered to leave his food unfinished and go with him at once. Wheeler demurred, told him to finish his lunch and asked him to come over to the Senate Office Building as soon as he had done lunching. Bailey agreed. Wheeler charged out of the dining room again, and Bailey wolfed his meal as rapidly as he could. Within ten minutes he was in the Senate Office Building, on his way to Wheeler's office. In the corridor he ran into Wheeler, who had been so worked up he could not wait for Bailey and had set out to look for him. They went into Bailey's office, and Wheeler related to Bailey what Garner had said. Bailey promptly asked Wheeler precisely what Garner meant by his general statement, and Wheeler could not answer him. Bailey suggested that it would be best to find out Garner's exact meaning, and accordingly the two set off to see Garner again and get him to come down to cases. They found the old fox in his Senate Office Building lair, just after lunch. The two senators put their question to him.

"I meant, God damn it, that you'd have to be reasonable," said Garner. "Why not pass the bill and have it relate to the future—say to 1941 and thereafter?"

Garner knew perfectly well that this was the compromise on which Keenan had been turned down, but he wanted to do the best he could for the President. Wheeler and Bailey disappointed him. Wheeler said that he had heard that one before, and Bailey pointed out cannily that such a bill would put the opposition in the position of not trusting the President and preferring to give great powers to his unknown successor. Garner peered quizzically out at them under his bushy eyebrows, grinned and quickly agreed.

Since his first suggestion didn't suit, he said, he had

another. Why not appoint a peace commission of ten members, five administration men and five oppositionists? It was the Harrison plan. At first Wheeler and Bailey were inclined to it. But Bailey is a fast thinker, and it occurred to him that such an arrangement would take the court fight out of the hands of the Judiciary Committee and leave the men who had signed the caustic majority report sitting on a limb. Wheeler took up the argument with considerable firmness, telling Garner that the opposition had enough votes to do as it pleased. Once more Garner grinned and agreed. Then Wheeler and Bailey put their question the second time. Just what had Garner meant? Garner, aware that he had done everything possible for the White House, replied simply:

"I meant just what I said. Go ahead and write your own ticket, but for God's sake and the sake of the party, be reasonable."

The talk veered to the problem of a substitute bill, and Wheeler and Bailey made it plain to Garner that no measure could be passed which affected the Supreme Court in any way. Their terms were that the Supreme Court sections, the section providing for roving judges in the lower courts and the provision for a proctor to be attached to the high bench should be expunged from the substitute. The terms were hardly new to Garner, who had already told the President that he might as well give up all hope of doing anything about the Supreme Court.

Wheeler and Bailey said, and Garner agreed, that such vital alterations in the pending bill could not be accomplished without the measure's recommittal to the Judiciary Committee. Garner seized the opportunity to warn the two senators against an immediate move to recommit and suggested that before anything further was decided it would be best to call Henry Ashurst into

consultation. Ashurst was thereupon summoned. It did
not take long to locate him, and in a few minutes he
appeared in the door of Garner's office. For once his
smile and his courtliness were gone. He was dead serious, marching solemnly into the room and sitting down
with the air of a man with a purpose. As soon as he was
seated he went to the heart of the problem.

"I'm tired of all this foolishness," he said. "I think
the best thing to do is to throw this damn discredited
thing out the first window we come to."

Garner's queer, high nasal voice broke in. He told
Ashurst that the bill was already dead.

"All we want you to do, Henry," he said, "is act as
undertaker."

Ashurst was all smiles again in a second. He giggled
and bowed and bowed and giggled, then answered in
his best senatorial manner:

"Gentlemen, if there is some ceremony you want me
to perform, of course, gentlemen, I am at your service."

Discussion of the best way to handle the recommittal
was resumed. Ashurst interrupted it to suggest that
Barkley should be allowed to have his say in the matter,
and the others approved his proposal. A call was sent
out for the new majority leader, and he was located by
Garner's secretary in a Senate Office Building corridor,
searching for Wheeler. As it happened he was on his
way back from the White House. He and Harrison
had been asked to lunch with the President after the
vote on the leadership, ostensibly to smoke the pipe of
peace, actually to try to get Harrison's help in the coming debacle. Harrison had preferred his own cigar to
the peace pipe. He had sat back, puffing and listening
and making it quite clear that he did not feel obliged
to strain himself to save the President's face. Therefore it was Barkley who had proposed that he be

allowed to work something out with Wheeler. The
President had approved and only asked that the court
bill should remain on the Senate calendar. Therefore
when he arrived at the Capitol, Barkley regarded no
immediate disposal of the court bill as the sine qua non.

Bailey let him know that he would have to do without his sine qua non the moment he walked in the door
of Garner's office. Barkley tried to bluster, but Wheeler
told him that if he continued to object the opposition
would go into the Senate chamber the next morning
with a motion for immediate recommittal.

"We've got the votes, make no mistake about that,"
said Wheeler. "We're so sure of it we'll take the chance
of a vote any time."

That ended Barkley's protest, although he still refused to agree to the recommittal demand. The others
said there was no use arguing, and it was proposed that
details of the court bill's funeral be left to be settled at
the meeting of a judiciary committee the next morning.
Ashurst was instructed to call the meeting and promised
to do so. He also invited Garner, Wheeler and Barkley
to attend, and the meeting time was set. After that the
gathering in Garner's office broke up, and Wheeler and
Bailey went off to talk over what had happened in
Wheeler's suite of rooms. They chatted animatedly on
the way, but when they reached the threshold of
Wheeler's office their conversation was cut short by
pure astonishment.

After his first visit from Garner, Wheeler had mentioned the new development to one or two friends. The
news had spread like wildfire. Opposition senators to
whom the word was passed had made for Wheeler's
office without delay, and, once there, they began telephoning their colleagues. By the time Wheeler and
Bailey arrived the small, dark, bleak room was positively seething with members of the opposition. Alto-

gether twenty-seven senators had gathered to hear the news. Some of them were arguing loudly in corners; others were sprawled on the chairs, irritably chewing cigar stubs and wondering what the next move ought to be. The moment Wheeler and Bailey appeared all twenty-seven rushed at them to find out what had happened. While Wheeler and Bailey were recounting the happenings at the meeting in Garner's office, old Senator King, of Utah, was marching up and down the room with his hands joined behind his back, twiddling his fingers, twitching his eyebrows and chewing gum at a tremendous rate. When Wheeler was done he spoke up.

"I think this thing's gone far enough," he said. "I move that our leader, the senator from Montana, Mr Wheeler, be instructed to move when the Senate convenes tomorrow to recommit the so-called court bill to the Committee on the Judiciary."

Wheeler sensed that King's words had the opinion of the assembly behind them. He put King's motion and heard it carried with some relief, for it ended the uncertainty in his mind. The other senators left his office at once. When he and Bailey were alone again they immediately concluded that Barkley should be informed of the vote of the meeting. For the last time they set off together. They found Barkley in his room and gave him the news. After five minutes Wheeler, whose nerves had been badly jangled by the long, hectic negotiations, departed to rest, but Bailey, who has a leathery constitution, stayed behind to gossip for another half-hour. Although he and Barkley talked freely of the day's strange happenings he could not persuade Barkley to consent to recommittal. And so the day ended.

JULY 22: The Judiciary Committee assembled at ten o'clock, with Garner, Wheeler and Barkley also present. Every leading figure in the court fight, except the President, Joe Robinson and the plan's original author,

Attorney General Homer S. Cummings, was there around the table. Garner opened the proceedings with a stump speech to the Democrats, calling upon them to bury the court bill and their animosities together as quickly as they could, "for the good of the country and the Democratic party."

"I think that's very important, too," said the Republican Borah, who was worried by the fight's effect on the national temper.

There was a brief laugh. Garner turned to Wheeler and reminded him of the terms that had been arrived at with Bailey the day before. The others in the committee room listened intently while Garner, at Wheeler's prompting, outlined the settlement. "The Supreme Court out of it, no roving judges, no Supreme Court proctor." Joe O'Mahoney hastily noted down the provisions on a scratch pad, and they were generally approved. Discussion of how to make the terms effective began at once. Barkley interrupted it, trying to assert his new leadership with a vehement renewal of his demand that the court bill stay on the calendar until a substitute should be ready to be acted on. An extraordinary scene ensued. The senators of the opposition, and especially the Democrats, turned furiously on Barkley and shouted him down. They were joined in milder fashion by the faithful administration men, who were aching with anxiety to end the struggle in which they had been fruitlessly engaged for so long. Even Garner showed some irritation. Barkley, baffled and somewhat humiliated, reddened noticeably, but there was nothing for him to do but be silent.

A time of many voices followed. Several of the senators had their own notions about the best course to pursue, and everyone talked at once. It was clear that the meeting was getting nowhere, and the more impatient men present began to drum on the table with annoyance. Finally Burke acted to bring things to a head. He offered a motion that the Judiciary Committee formally request the Senate to recommit to it the court bill, for revision along the agreed-on lines. Barkley could not stand that. He protested loudly, and this time he was joined by other administration supporters. Ashurst, the old master of inconsistency, spoke up soothingly.

"Senators, Senators, let the Chair state that we did not meet here today to take any action," he said.

The natural reply was that the Judiciary Committee was in full session and could do as it pleased. It came loudly, from half-a-dozen mouths. The Arizonan rose, grinning as usual, and made a low bow to the men around the table.

"Quite right, gentlemen," he said. "Ashurst, to Ashurst . . ."

Burke's motion was put to the meeting forthwith and passed by an acclaiming vote. Someone suggested that Barkley might like to propose the recommittal on the floor, and it was pointed out that this would be an evidence of good feeling all around. But Barkley, horribly disturbed by the proceedings, wanted nothing to do with their results. He hastily refused, in his rather solemn way. Another administration man had to be found, therefore, to offer the recommittal motion, and Logan, of Kentucky, was deputed to do it. O'Mahoney turned his notes over to Logan, and Logan set to work scribbling a draft of the motion on one of the scratch pads on the committee table.

The elated senators were in a happy mood, and it was desired to do everything possible to spare the President, now that he had been so thoroughly beaten. For that reason it was agreed that the necessary action on the floor should be got through as quickly as possible and that the words "Supreme Court" would not be mentioned by Logan or anyone else. The meeting broke up on a note of peace and general relief. To the departing senators Garner promised that there would be no political reprisals against Democratic members of the opposition, and Barkley echoed him, significantly adding, however, "so far as I personally am concerned."

The Judiciary Committee meeting was over just before noon. A few minutes later the Senate convened. Logan could not bring his motion onto the floor at once, since another motion, to override the President's veto of the measure continuing low interest rates on federal farm mortgages, already had the preferred place. It was with this that the Senate occupied itself distraughtly for the next couple of hours. The result was a foregone conclusion. The veto would be overridden because the senators could not bear to increase the interest payments of their agricultural constituents. But the fact that the President was to be flouted in this minor fashion, before the major disappointment of the recommittal of the court bill, charged the air in the Senate chamber with an extra tenseness. Senators clustered in little groups, gossiping fervently. Representatives came over in hordes from the House end of the Capitol and established themselves on the couches around the chamber walls. Friendly senators joined them to tell them all the news. The galleries filled until no seat was left, for the Washington crowd has a vulturine faculty of being in at important deaths.

Everyone waited anxiously for the inevitable vote on the issue of the veto and for the moment when old Logan would rise in his place and speak the all-important word on the court bill. There was a roll call on the farm mortgage veto, and the President was overwhelmingly voted down. For a few moments Senator Elmer Thomas, the logorrheic soft-money man from Oklahoma, talked about an interstate compact to conserve oil and gas. The big crowd in the chamber bit its fingers with impatience. Finally Logan got slowly to his feet. He was recognized at once by Vice-President Garner, who was in the chair.

"Mr President," he said in his harsh, elderly voice, "I rise to ask unanimous consent to make a motion to recommit to the Committee on the Judiciary Senate Bill 1392, to reorganize the judicial branch of the government, with all amendments thereto. I might say by way of explanation that after a very full and free hearing this morning the Committee on the Judiciary directed me to make this request with the understanding that it would be instructed to report a bill for the reform of the judiciary within ten days if the motion should prevail. I ask unanimous consent that I may be authorized to make the motion at this time."

Garner's falsetto, "Is there objection?" cracked out, and Barkley nervously asked a technical question in regard to the motion proposed by Logan. There was one of those brief, meticulous procedural disputes which are a specialty in the Senate. McNary joined it in his drawling, cynical way, but after a few seconds Logan received permission to make his motion in due course. Not content, he requested that he be allowed to insert in the *Record* a long speech for the court bill which he had prepared some days before. There was no objection, and the aborted oration was handed to one of the Senate stenographers. Thereupon Garner put the question on the Logan motion for recommittal. Austin, of Vermont, always suspicious of the Democrats in small things and big, rose to ask:

"Should not the agreement be stated somewhat differently from the way it has been stated, namely, that the report hereafter to be made is not to be a report on a bill to reform the judiciary but a bill for reform of judicial procedure?"

As a member of the Judiciary Committee, Austin well knew the agreement that had been made at the morning meeting, and his question was calculated to come as close as possible to a statement that the Supreme Court would not be affected without a mention of the Court's name. Logan saw perfectly the tendency of Austin's question. He answered rather irritably that he had shown his motion to Senator Burke and had obtained his approval. The crowd in the galleries, growing ever more tense with unsatisfied anticipation, sighed audibly when Austin signified his willingness to accept Logan's explanation. Then for a split second the whole chamber was deathly silent while the aged and ailing Hiram Johnson, of California, struggled heavily to his feet. More than any other member of the Senate, perhaps, he had been stirred to his depths by the court fight. He was not one to allow paltry agreements in the Judiciary Committee to stand in his way. He would drain the cup of victory to its last drop, and let no one forbid him.

"Mr President," he said stridently, "I desire to know what the judicial reform refers to. Does it refer to the Supreme Court or to the inferior courts?"

The spell had been broken. The words had been mentioned. Logan bumbled out another account of the Judiciary Committee's morning meeting; then saw that he would have to take his medicine and stated that the terms accepted by both sides "did not refer to the Supreme Court." When he blurted the thing out there was a rustle through the galleries like the rustle of wind in a wheat field. He added that the Court was "not to be considered at all." But Johnson was implacable. Once again his cracked voice shattered the silence.

"The Supreme Court is out of the way?"

"The Supreme Court is out of the way," replied Logan solemnly.

"Glory be to God!" exclaimed Johnson and sat down.

The triumphant words were heard from one end of the Senate chamber to the other, although Johnson spoke them half to himself. They sounded a little ludicrous, a little melodramatic, but the crowd had no time to think of such things. There was a twentieth of a second's utter quiet and then a wild clapping, a rude spate of sound. Garner let the crowd clap its fill. At last there was a lull. He seized his chance, shouting:

"The question is on agreeing to the motion of the senator from Kentucky."

McNary asked for the ayes and nays, and the clerk began the repetitious business of calling the roll. Everyone listened intently as the senators answered their names. Jim Ham Lewis could not resist the opening for one of his little displays of florid senatorial technique and announced the absence of Senator John H. Bankhead, of Alabama, "because of illness in his family." One or two other senators also announced absences. When the roll call was over the clerk roared out a recapitulation of the vote. The ayes were seventy. The nays, a little band of die-hards and curriers of administration favor, were twenty. Five senators did not vote. The recapitulation was handed up to the rostrum, and Garner snapped out the numerical result. The motion had carried. The court bill was dead, and Ashurst appropriately took the floor to promise, in his usual baroque manner, that his committee would work "with zeal and fidelity" to report an emasculated and meaningless substitute within ten days.

Next week Ashurst fulfilled his promise. The substitute was duly presented to the Senate, and Garner jammed it through to passage, while the galleries grinned, in just fifty-seven minutes.

Epilogue

With the court bill out of the way the most conspicuous remaining object on the Washington stage was the cast-off judicial robe of Justice Van Devanter. The ultimate disposal of the right to wear that handsome garment of black faille silk was the fitting postlude to the drama of the court fight.

The fight had conferred a strange, almost a lurid importance on the President's choice for the Supreme Court vacancy. Yet the President was ill prepared for the difficult task of filling it. Defeat had left him sore and vengeful. His judgment was as badly distorted now by the bitter aftertaste of failure as it had once been by the intoxication of success. From the moment Van Devanter left the bench and cheerfully began currying his mules on his Maryland farm the President had expected to replace him with Joe Robinson. Now Robinson was suddenly and tragically dead, and the President had no substitute candidate ready. Yet he knew he must choose carefully, for the Senate had to confirm his nominee, and the Senate had relapsed into a mood of seething irritability from which another great rebellion could easily flare up.

The problem of finding a successor for Van Devanter became acute the moment the court bill was killed, on July 22. By that time Washington was a sweltering, half-dead city, from which the Congress and the President desired to get away as soon as possible. With this in mind, and perhaps with some hope of annoying his senatorial enemies by keeping them waiting, the President's first decision was to delay the court choice until after the session ended. There was some doubt as to the constitutionality of an interim appointment. The President went through the usual ritual of consulting Homer Cummings, and the obedient Justice Department, whose constitutional interpretations rarely deviate from the President's own, assured the White House that all would be well. Unfortunately the Senate's constitutionalists were less sympathetic than the Justice Department's.

The ever-suspicious senators of the opposition foresaw that the President might use the recess of Congress to make a fait accompli of a supremely disagreeable appointment. They feared that they would be forced to vote for or against the confirmation of a hated justice after he had taken part in the Court's deliberations. Senator Vandenberg made a speech. Senator Wheeler murmured a threat, and Senator Burke opined that no man with a respect for constitutional processes could take his seat on the bench before being confirmed by the Senate. The storm blew up so rapidly and so darkly that the President soon realized delay would only keep alive the angers of the just-ended struggle. He gave in to the senators.

Once more—but under circumstances how immensely different from those in that post-election November— he summoned Homer Cummings to the White House. Once more he requested Cummings to prepare him a list of alternatives, but of candidates for the high

bench, not of bills to curb it. And once more Cummings
hurried back to his office to do a big job.

Within a day or so Cummings had a list of sixty
names ready prepared. Federal judges, eminent law
professors, leading liberals, faithful Democrats—he
included every man among the crowding candidates for
the great office whose abilities or connections were in
the least impressive. He took his list to the President,
and they set to work together culling it over.

Their first move was to lay down their specifications
for the ideal appointee. First he must be a thumping,
evangelical New Deal liberal. Second he must be con-
firmable by the Senate. Third, after so much emphasis
on the unwisdoms of old age, he must be reasonably
young. And fourth he must come from one of the sections of the country not already well represented on the
Court. Once again Cummings, always susceptible where
statistics were concerned, grew excited by them. To insure fulfillment of the fourth specification he had rather
elaborate figures prepared on the population, congressional representation and national political significance
of each of the unrepresented judicial circuits. These led
to the decision that the appointee must be either a
Westerner or a Southerner.

Except for Cummings' statistics the President did
not trouble himself with much research material. It had
not been the Justice Department's past practice to examine the records of candidates for the Supreme Bench,
and the President and Cummings concluded that they
would not be likely to choose a man so little known
as to need investigation. They contented themselves
with applying their four specifications and, where they
were in doubt as to how to apply them, telephoning
knowledgeable senators and congressmen to inquire into
a candidate's qualifications. By this method the work
of paring the list went very quickly. Almost daily Cum-

mings quietly called on the President at the White House. Almost daily the two men cut three or four or five names from their list. Soon after August 1 they succeeded in reducing it to a mere seven names.

The remaining candidates were Circuit Court Judge Samuel H. Sibley, of Georgia; Circuit Court Judge Joseph C. Hutcheson, of Texas; Circuit Court Judge Sam G. Bratton, of New Mexico; Chief Justice W. P. Stacy, of the North Carolina Supreme Court; Solicitor General Stanley Reed, who was a Kentuckian; Senator Sherman Minton, of Indiana; and Senator Hugo Lafayette Black, of Alabama.

At this point the President succumbed to a brief indecision. For a while he found it hard to make up his mind among the seven on the list. Party potentates pressed the claims of one candidate or another, and especially those of the four judges. The Senate exhibited a mounting impatience, and the heat grew worse by the hour. But the President's indecision did not last long. After a day or so he concluded that the liberalism of the four judges was insufficiently intense—altogether too judicial in fact. The judges' chances of promotion were ended, and the list was cut to three.

Of the three men whose claims the President and Cummings pondered so endlessly in those broiling, early August days, Stanley Reed was the least colorful. He was kindly, urbane, well learned in the law. He had performed with some distinction his thankless duty of defending the government before the Supreme Court. The Senate liked him, and his subordinates in the Justice Department were devoted to him. Yet there was no getting away from it: he had no fire. Even his politics had not been overly fiery. He had been a Democrat for all his fifty-two years, but it was the old Hoover Farm Board which brought him to Washington, from a Kentucky law practice, to be its general counsel. In the first years of the New Deal he served in the general counsel's office of the Reconstruction Finance Corporation, and then in 1935, when the Justice Department was bracing itself for the great legal battles before the high bench, he was made Solicitor General. Then, as now, he had had the strong backing of Tom Corcoran, whose close friend and ex-boss he was. He had been a faithful subordinate of the President's, and his age, his origin, his opinions, his legal scholarship and his general personableness all made him a wholly acceptable candidate for the high bench. General acceptability to all groups was his best asset. Unfortunately the President wanted a candidate who would combine certain confirmability by the Senate with the maximum degree of unacceptability to the groups which had offended him. He longed to give the Senate a bitter pill to swallow, yet make the rebellious legislators gulp it down.

Equally certain of confirmation by the Senate, but far more disagreeable than Reed to the members of the court bill opposition were the two senators, Minton and Black. The ancient rule of senatorial courtesy put their confirmation beyond question, but the things they had said about, and some things they had done to, their enemies in the court fight were furiously remembered against them.

Of the pair Minton was younger. At forty-seven he was one of the really promising Democratic politicians in Washington, the only threat to his future being the control of the state machine back home in Indiana by the Rotarianized political drill sergeant, former Governor Paul V. McNutt, and McNutt's successor, Governor M. Clifford Townsend. Minton had made the law, in which he was expert enough to hold a master's degree from Yale, his avenue to politics. In politics he had been fortunate in espousing the cause of the De-

mocrary in its poor times. The great Democratic land-
slide which started the New Deal opened the door of
the state counselor's office to him, and thence, in 1934,
he went to the Senate. As a freshman senator he made
his name remarkably rapidly. A big, burly, rather obviously handsome man, he possessed agreeable, straightforward manners, an excellent ability to deal with his
fellows and a good, shrewd head. His political thinking, while it seldom transcended the partisan, was honestly liberal and deeply felt. He was one of those
rare politicians who really mean most of what they say
about "the common man." Altogether he commanded
the respect of those with whom he worked, and his
qualities were rewarded when the administration leadership chose him out as their leading lieutenant among
the younger men. It has already been seen how forceful
and energetic a part he took in the court fight.

Hugo Black was an older man and a more complex
character than his friend Minton. At fifty-one he had
come a long way from his beginning as a poor country
shopkeeper's son in Clay County, Alabama. Born to be
an inhabitant of Tobacco Road, he had escaped from
his origins by a long process of self-education. He was
a slight man, younger looking than his years, with a
soft, Southern voice and unusually pleasing manners.
In politics he was an absolute anomaly—an intellectual
leftist liberal from below the Mason and Dixon line.
If Southern politicians pretend to leftism at all, the
brand they boast is a sort of poor-white populism. The
Southern legislator who travels the country districts
in overalls, telling the share-croppers that Wall Street
is a den of thieves, and then hurries to Washington to
collect whatever is collectible from Wall Street or elsewhere, is a fairly familiar figure. Hugo Black was a cat
of a different color.

In the first place he had made himself a learned man.

Although he was entirely self-educated, he had acquired a remarkable intellectual background in economics and history. From Polybius to Karl Marx, and back by way of Adam Smith and Jefferson, he had read the historians, economists and theoreticians of government who have influenced intelligent modern political thought. Out of his reading and his own thinking he had forged his own left liberalism. The revolutionary Jefferson and Justice Brandeis on the curse of bigness were the particular sources of his inspiration, although his study of Marx had taken him rather further to the left than either Brandeis or Jefferson could have. He was, in fact, probably the most radical man in the Senate. The best test of his radicalism's honesty and sincerity is the fact that for political convenience in his own state he would have done much better to howl for higher cotton prices and keep silent on other matters.

In the Senate he was a rather lonely figure. Although he was a practical politician—his fight on the antilynching bill proved that—his leftism made the Southern oligarchs deeply suspicious of him. He was intensely partisan and an unforgiving fighter, not one to stand up and lay about him with a bludgeon, but a cruel strategist with a biting tongue in debate. Men who had crossed swords with him rarely forgot or forgave the experience, and his friends on the floor were few. His many enemies accused him of meanness and small-spiritedness, and even his friends regretted the excesses —such as some incidents of his lobbying investigation —into which his partisanship sometimes led him.

To be understood at all he had to be viewed in the light of his past. No man can come up whole and unscathed, by his own efforts only, from the prejudiced backwardness of the rural South to the position Black had come to occupy. The long struggle had left its marks on him.

It has already been said that he was entirely self-
educated, and this is literally true, although by great
shifts and self-denials he managed to get a law degree
from the University of Alabama. He was a brilliant
student and consumingly ambitious. After a false start
in his own poverty-stricken home country he settled
down to practice law in Birmingham without a dollar
of capital or a single important connection. He specialized in what lawyers call "the anticorporative field",
and he was soon successful. Within a few years he was
the principal trades union attorney in the city. From
such a position it was natural for him to edge over
into politics. He did so, and although he began here as
elsewhere as an outsider, he attracted a dependable
following. In 1926 Alabama sent him to the Senate.

The circumstances of that election were later to
arouse a violent excitement. They were simple enough.
The year 1926 was the year of the Ku Klux Klan's
peak power in the South. The immense majority of the
people of Alabama—businessmen, unionized workers
in Birmingham, farmers in the back country, Main
Streeters, teachers in the schools, men of all kinds and
classes—belonged to the Klan. A few such stiff-necked
men as Oscar W. Underwood held aloof, but Black
was no Underwood. He had not left Alabama, and he
had not escaped from its ways of thought. He was
young, unbacked, unbefriended, and he had an over-
mastering desire to get ahead in the world. His self-
education had not progressed to the point where he
saw much shame in the Klan. He joined it, and after
some political legerdemain he became the Klan candidate in the Senate race. At the time it was universally
known that Klan backing had given him the victory.

Now, in the hot and troubled summer of 1937, the
events of that Alabama primary of eleven years ago
were all but forgotten. Black himself, to whom a larger

experience had brought quite different values, had done his best to drive the memory of the primary from his mind. The minds of a few experts in the Washington scene retained the fact that Black had been a Klan candidate, but none was certain he had been an actual member. The President was unaware of Black's Klan connection, although if he had chosen to make the least inquiry he would have run on it. Charlie Michelson, his own publicity expert, had written a series of articles about Black and the Klan for the old New York *World* when Black was elected. But once again the President was working things out in seclusion with Cummings and wanted no advice.

Such were the three men, Reed, Minton and Black, to whom the President's field of choice was reduced by the end of the first week in August. Of the three men Minton might have seemed to have the best chance, for he was closest to Cummings, the President's sole adviser in the matter. But Minton did not want the office. Minton's reasons exhibited a delicacy of feeling singular in a politician and job holder. During the court fight he had attacked the justices of the high bench with an intemperate fury, accusing them of insincerity, political-mindedness and calculating Toryism. Where Black, who was also an administration leader in the struggle, had spoken in more general terms, Minton had made the justices the chief victims of his oratory. He believed in the first place that it would be extremely embarrassing for him to become a member of a court on which he had expressed himself in such unbridled fashion. In the second, he suspected that the justices might take his appointment as a personal insult and be all the more inclined to give the President his comeuppance in the future.

He expressed these feelings first to Joe Keenan, and a day or so later, at a quiet dinner at Cummings' Washington house, to Cummings himself. Whether or no it was these doubts of Minton's which caused his name to be stricken from the list at last, it was so stricken about August 9. Cummings' statistics on unrepresented judicial circuits, which were in Black's favor, probably had something to do with the matter. Other considerations may have been Minton's possible future usefulness to the Democratic party—greater than Black's, since Black was too much a political anomaly in the South; the fact that Minton would have been replaced by the highly undesirable and exceedingly pushing McNutt; and Minton's excellent and needed work as an administration lieutenant in the Senate.

Minton's quiet dinner with Cummings was on the evening of Sunday, August 8. There was a discussion of the whole situation regarding the court appointment, in which Minton strongly urged the claims of his friend Black. Cummings suddenly asked Minton, in his genial, foxy way, to sound out Black's feelings in the matter. Minton agreed and went home puzzled about the probable outcome.

Next morning he visited Black in the musty, paper-littered little hideaway on the Senate Office Building first floor, where the Alabaman used to escape to write his speeches and read his economists. Minton found his friend working in the dreary, uncomfortable room. After the usual exchange of pleasantries he broke the ice very frankly. He told Black that someone, no matter who, but someone of importance, had asked how Black would feel about taking the court appointment. He said he had no authority to state who would get it, but he pointed out that the fact that the information about Black was desired must mean something.

Black replied with an equal frankness. So far as he personally was concerned, he said, he had no desire to leave the Senate. Owing to the exertions of Alabama

conservatives, he had a hard primary fight on his hands
in 1938, but he was quite confident that he would win.
And he preferred the rough-and-tumble and the opportunity for real policy-making of a senator's place to
the important but secluded eminence of the high bench.
At the same time, he added, there were other considerations. Mrs Black, a charming and intelligent Alabama
woman from a place in life far higher than Black's own,
hated the dust and dirt of politics. For some years she
had been after him to leave the Senate and return to his
Birmingham law practice. Moreover, his eldest son, a
brilliant child and the apple of his eye, was not well.
He wanted more time to see something of the boy.
Therefore, he told Minton, he would have to think the
matter over and defer giving a definite answer until he
could talk to Mrs Black.

That evening he hurried to his quiet, unpretentious
suburban house to put his problem in his wife's lap. Her
persuasions succeeded. Next morning Black informed
Minton that he had decided to accept the court place
if it should be offered him. That day Minton was very
busy and failed to give Cummings the news.

The next day was Wednesday, August 11. In the
morning Cummings went to see the President, as he
had been doing daily since the beginning of the month.
For the last time the two men talked over the qualifications of their proposed nominees to the high bench.
Now there were only two, Reed and Black, but that
made the problem no easier. Reed had much in his
favor, Black much in his. Especially favorable to Black
were the intensity of his New Dealishness, the fervor
with which he had fought the administration's battles
and his sectional origin. Not only was the circuit which
included Alabama one of the two largest unrepresented
on the Court; it was the circuit whence came several of
the most conspicuous conservative Democratic rebels

against the New Deal. To give the rebels' part of the
country so important an appointment, yet give it to one
of the two or three left-wingers in the Senate was a neat
and cruel irony irresistible to the rather vengeful President. Nevertheless, the President was still undecided,
and when Cummings left the White House he had no
notion whether Black or Reed would be the final choice.

About midday Minton got in touch with Cummings,
passed him the word for Black and once more pressed
his friend's claims. Cummings informed the White
House of what he had heard but did not return to see
the President and hear his decision.

The President reached his decision that afternoon.
The factors in Black's favor were too appealing to him.
With his mind made up he gave his orders, and one of
his secretaries telephoned Black on the Hill. Would
the senator drop in to see the President the same evening after dinner? The question was put, as it were,
blankly, for the President had kept his own counsel,
and no one around him knew what he had decided.
Black replied rather nervously that he would be delighted. He called at the White House accordingly at
the appointed hour.

He was received by the President in the comfortable,
cluttered upstairs study where the court bill message
had been so endlessly criticized by Cummings, Reed,
Richberg and Rosenman. The President greeted him
genially, and Black, who has a gift for self-contain-
ment, returned the greeting easily enough. The recollection of his talk with Minton was in his mind, but
there was nothing to indicate that he had not been summoned to discuss the wage-hour bill, sponsored in the
Senate by himself and now blocked in the House by the
Southern conservatives of the Rules Committee. There
was a moment's talk.

And then the President drew a paper from the litter

on his desk and showed it to Black. It was one of the commissions which must be filled in when a presidential nomination goes to the Senate. The space reserved for the office concerned had "Associate Justice of the Supreme Court of the United States" written into it in the President's own hand. The space for the nominee's name was blank. The President pointed smilingly to the blank space and said to Black:

"Hugo, I'd like to write your name here."

Black gave the expected answer, and the President scrawled "Hugo L. Black, of Alabama" across the space in his handsome, readable hand, signed his name and put the filled-in commission in an envelope. Black thanked him warmly and, after some more talk, took his departure. Throughout the interview the question of Black's record and qualifications for the high post was never once raised by the President. Black, who had half forgotten the Klan days, who knew himself for a man so changed from that time, quite naturally failed to recall his past.

On Thursday morning Cummings had another appointment with the President. It was then that he learned of the happenings of the night before and the decision which preceded them. The President showed him the sealed envelope containing the commission and laughed with him at the joke they were playing on all Washington. Besides themselves, Black and Mrs Black, who had been told by her husband on his return from the White House, no one in the city knew what was to come. Nor was anyone to be told until the great surprise could be sprung on the whole world. The President's old friend and first political adviser, Postmaster General James A. Farley, dropped into the White House offices at eleven o'clock and had a long talk with the President. The President did not mention Black. He said nothing of Black to his secretarial staff, and

shortly after Farley left the White House Steve Early
predicted to newspapermen that the court appointment
would be delayed for a couple of weeks. He said nothing to anyone until noon, when a White House messenger was summoned, handed the sealed envelope and
sent off to the Senate.

At the Senate chamber, where the messenger arrived
a few minutes later, the old and formal procedure was
gone through. The messenger bowed at the door, and
one of the Senate staff announced his presence. The
messenger then turned over the envelope, which was
taken down the aisle to the rostrum and presented to
Vice-President John N. Garner. Perhaps because he had
been warned of the interest of its contents, the Vice-
President tore it open at once and read off the commission in a high, astonished voice.

Black was in his seat, pale with nerves. At the reading of the message he half flinched, as men will at such
moments, when an enormous anticipation becomes a
fact. Among his colleagues the commission's contents
produced the effect of an explosive shell. Among those
whom it offended, and they were many, the first reaction was incredulity, which was slowly replaced with
a dark and fruitless irritation. Black's friends, the
liberals, rose and went to his seat to congratulate him
—among them Bob La Follette, who shook his hand
energetically and seemed to try to make up for the lack
of warmth of the many senators who took Black's
nomination as a sort of personal outrage. It was a
queer scene, for those who were pleased by the event
were so completely pleased, and those who were not
were so publicly angry.

Henry Ashurst, courtly as ever, broke the tension
after a few seconds. Rising with his accustomed
baroque grace, he congratulated Black and asked for
immediate confirmation, in accordance with the old

custom of senatorial courtesy. Hiram Johnson, dogged
as ever, caring as little for senatorial courtesy as for
private senatorial agreements, promptly objected. The
nomination was therefore referred to the Judiciary
Committee for consideration. Black left the floor
hurriedly to give the photographers their chance at
him and, when they were done, took a lonely lunch at
the Senate restaurant. The Senate abandoned itself to
discussion of the amazing news.

There ensued a very singular five days. At the White
House the President was utterly delighted with his
stroke, for the fact that he had found the sort of man
he wanted to sit on the Court pleased him almost less
than the open discomfiture of his senatorial enemies.
In the Senate there was a deal of murmuring but no
preparation to make the murmurs effective. Once the
nomination arrived at Capitol Hill, all the memories of
the Klan episode in Black's career were furbished up.
It was the chief topic of senatorial gossip, and there
were some who hoped that it would be investigated by
the subcommittee of the Judiciary Committee named by
Henry Ashurst to examine into Black's qualifications.
The subcommittee, however, was headed by the hectoring Neely, who refused angrily to make the examination
more than a mere formality. The subcommittee reported favorably; the Judiciary Committee itself
hurriedly followed suit, and debate promptly began on
the floor.

In the debate the whole matter of the Klan was
handled in gingerly fashion. Copeland, the senator-
doctor from New York, who was conducting a New
York City mayoralty campaign from the Senate
chamber, raised it most positively in his pious, orotund
fashion. Burke, of Nebraska, stated that he could bring
before the Senate two men who were willing to testify
that Black had been a Klan member, and one or two

Republicans orated briefly on the subject. Borah's stand
was, perhaps, the strangest of all. Although he had
personally arranged for Justice Van Devanter's retirement he took the position that the retirement meant
nothing. By a quirk of constitutional interpretation he
maintained that Van Devanter's retention of judicial
status in order to safeguard his salary implied a retention of his seat on the Supreme Bench. Thus he opposed
confirmation for Black, since he declared that Black's
confirmation would mean an increase in the size of the
Court.

At the same time he warmly defended Black the man,
as distinguished from Black the nominee. He spoke
highly of his character and qualities, praised his learning and his liberalism and stated that he would be
altogether delighted to vote his confirmation if it were
not for his singular constitutional doubts.

Like Borah, the other sincere Senate liberals had
considerable liking and admiration for Black. They followed Borah to his defense. La Follette spoke admirably for him on the floor, and old George Norris, who
was away, telegraphed a long and moving tribute to
Black, which La Follette read into the record.

While the debate was in progress Black himself remained off the Senate floor. When the Klan issue was
raised several of his friends went to him and asked
him to make a statement on the subject. They found
him in the same little private office where Minton had
found him on the Monday before the nomination. They
presented the problem to him brusquely but sym-
pathetically. He thought awhile before he gave his
answer.

The thoughts which raced through his mind on that
occasion may well be imagined. A buried episode of his
past had risen up to haunt him. It brought back a time
which was infinitely distant from him not only in days

and hours, but even more in experience and mode of thought. Since then all his values, all his beliefs had enlarged and deepened and altered. And yet he did not say, "Yes, I joined the Klan, but that was long ago, when I was not the man I am today." He could not say it without bringing the house down about his ears and the President's as well. He knew that it would not only be harmful to himself to admit Klan membership; he perfectly understood that it would be desperately damaging to the President. With these considerations, selfish and all human, in his mind, he chose to avoid the open admission.

He replied to his friends that he would make no statement on the Klan question; that he would say nothing of it even to them except that he was not now a Klansman. But he added that if any of his friends was concerned lest he might have been a Klansman in the past, he would ask that man to vote against his confirmation. It was on the basis of Black's reply to his friends that Borah told the Senate that there "was not a scintilla of evidence" that Black was a Klansman. Unfortunately Borah worded his remark rather ambiguously, and for a time it was thought Borah had said Black never had been. Later Borah was to clear this question up in a public statement, exculpating Black of ever attempting to deceive him.

But at the time all the controversy was in the future. The debate trailed wearily along after the week end, until the motion to confirm was put on the afternoon of August 17. There was a brief flurry of excitement as the galleries watched how the opponents of the court bill lined up on the roll call. And then the clerk announced the result, 63 votes for confirmation and 16 against. Within a day or so thereafter the new justice quietly took his oath in the office of one of the clerks of the Senate. A little later he sailed for abroad.

For a while Black was forgotten. And then, in mid-September, appeared the first of a series of newspaper articles offering proof that he had been a member of the Klan. The proof was incontrovertible and positive. It could not be ignored.

The President's reaction was, perhaps, the oddest of all the extremely violent ones which the proofs of Black's Klan membership provoked. He allowed his subordinates to give it out that he had been deceived by Black, although he had asked Black no question remotely suggesting any interest in his past and had not troubled to make the slightest outside inquiry, which would certainly have revealed Black's Klan connections if not his membership. He reinforced the impression created by his subordinates with an "It's up to the justice to do the explaining" sort of statement and then departed for the West.

As for Black himself, he wished at first to keep silent. He soon found he could not hope to. Reporters watched for him on his doorstep, jumped out at his wife from hotel corridors, bribed their way into his rooms and took apartments opposite his own to watch his comings and goings. He gave in, and sailed for the United States. Once here, he announced he would make his answer to the Klan charges on the radio. Still harried by the press, he took refuge with his wife's sister and brother-in-law, Mr and Mrs Clifford J. Durr, in their modest, pleasantly countrified house in Alexandria, across the river from Washington. For two days he worked on his radio speech. Finally, on the evening of October 1, it was delivered.

In a strained, solemn voice he admitted his membership in the Klan. He exposed his own present beliefs. He denied that the prejudices usually attributed to the Klan could be attributed to him. And so he ended, and so the court fight ended, on a curious note of irony.